Robe...
Aug...
Salem, OR

r 1 August, 1993 , Jan. 1994

THE
MAGICIAN
WITHIN

"Magus" Margaret Ayers-Hemphill, 1992

"Come," said Gandalf. "We are needed. There is much that you can yet do."

THE
MAGICIAN
WITHIN

ACCESSING
THE SHAMAN IN THE
MALE PSYCHE

Robert Moore
and
Douglas Gillette

WILLIAM MORROW AND COMPANY, INC.
NEW YORK

Grateful acknowledgment is made for permission to use material from the following:

Chapter 4: *Black Elk Speaks,* by John G. Neihardt, reprinted by permission of the University of Nebraska Press. Copyright 1932, 1959, 1972 by John G. Neihardt. Copyright © by the John G. Neihardt Trust.

Chapter 5: *The Seasons of a Man's Life,* by Daniel J. Levinson, et al. Copyright © 1978 by Daniel J. Levinson. Reprinted by permission of Alfred A. Knopf, Inc.

Chapter 6: *Duino Elegies* by Rainer Maria Rilke, translated by J. B. Leishman and S. Spender. Reprinted by permission of W. W. Norton & Company.

Black-and-white illustrations: Frontispiece painting by Margaret Hemphill. Reprinted by permission of Margaret Hemphill.

Photograph of Nyanga tribesman wearing mask, first printed in *Man and His Symbols* by Carl Jung. Reprinted by permission of Paul Popper.

Photograph of Stonehenge with superimposed diagram as it appears in *Mysteries of the Past* by J. Thorndike. Copyright © 1977 by American Heritage. Reprinted by permission of Rapho/Photo Researchers.

Illustration of Merlin and Arthur at Stonehenge by Trevor Stubley, taken from from T. H. White, *The Book of Merlin.* Copyright © 1977. Reprinted by permission of The University of Texas Press.

Photograph of Australian Aborigine circumcision rite by Fritz Goro from *The Power of Myth* by Joseph Campbell with Bill Moyers. Reprinted by permission of Life Picture Sales, a department of The Time, Inc., Magazine Company.

Two paintings, "Moses Before the Children of Isreal in Egypt" and "Jacob Tricks Esau," by Feodor Royankovsky from *The Golden Bible* by Werner. Copyright 1946. Reprinted by permission of Simon & Schuster.

Photograph of Carl Jung in 1959 by Hugo Charteris from Jung, *Word and Image.* Reprinted by permission of Princeton University Press and Hugo Chateris.

Color plates: Cro-Magnon magician from *The Epic of Man.* Copyright © 1961 by Time-Life. Reprinted by permission of Life Pictures Sales, a department of The Time, Inc., Magazine Company.

Photograph of man being scarred, by Fritz Goro from *The Epic of Man.* Copyright © 1961 by Time-Life. Reprinted by permission of Life Picture Sales, a department of The Time, Inc., Magazine Company.

Painting by Standing Bear, "Black Elk Before the Six Grandfathers," from *Black Elk Speaks.* Copyright © 1972. Reprinted by permission of The Western Historical Manuscripts Collection.

It is the policy of William Morrow and Company, Inc., and its imprints and affiliates, recognizing the importance of preserving what has been written, to print the books we publish on acid-free paper, and we exert our best efforts to that end.

Library of Congress Cataloging-in-Publication Data

Moore, Robert L.
   The magician within : accessing the shaman in the male psyche / Robert Moore and Douglas Gillette.
     p. cm.
   Includes bibliographical references and index.
   ISBN 0-688-09594-1
   1. Men—Psychology. 2. Masculinity (Psychology) 3. Archetype (Psychology) 4. Magicians—Miscellanea. I. Gillette, Douglas. II. Title.
BF175.5.M37M68   1993
155.3'32—dc20   92-23557
                                          CIP

Printed in the United States of America

First Edition

1 2 3 4 5 6 7 8 9 10

BOOK DESIGN BY RICHARD ORIOLO

For Imhotep, Quetzalcoatl, Socrates, Lao-tzu, Giordano Bruno, Paul Tillich, Alfred North Whitehead, Orville and Wilbur Wright, Albert Einstein, Jonas Salk, Victor Turner, Louis B. Leakey, and all the male shamans, prophets, healers, scientists, gurus, thinkers, inventors, and pioneers of unseen worlds who have devoted their lives to the transformation of humankind through knowledge, enlightenment, and tireless devotion to the cause of wholeness.

PREFACE

THE MAGICIAN
IN THE MASCULINE
SOUL

D EEP IN THE WOMB OF MOTHER EARTH, IN THE
Magdalenian caves of central France, a painted image
prefigures the future of a remarkable species. The image, in a
crypt at the end of the labyrinthine passageways of the Lascaux cave, is of a man wearing a bird mask. To his right lies
a bison, disemboweled and dying from a hunter's spear. To his
left a rhinoceros flees the scene. The birdman's engorged penis
points aggressively and erotically at the dying bison. His
wand, which lies at his right hand, is topped with an image of
a bird.

This birdman is almost certainly a Magician. He is the

cf
Maria
Gimbutas
on
The Bird
Goddess

The Birdman:
Shamanic Figure from
the Crypt of the
Temple Cave at
Lascaux
(Dordogne, France,
circa 20,000 to
18,000 B.C.E.)

master of his culture's power, imagination, and technology. His powers give him the ability to remake the things of his world. Through inner vision, this man has even managed to refashion himself. He has become a bird, a soaring being of pure spirit. The energy he has drawn upon to fuel this transformation still serves the generations that have descended from the birdman. Artists, theologians, academics, and physicists, all will draw on the same archetype of the Magician in their own ecstasies of mind and spirit. And their visions will transform the world, too, as they bring their ecstatic dreams into concrete form.

Moving from the Old Stone Age to the second century A.D., leaving one historic cave for another, we find in a catacomb carved by human hands another striking image of the Magician. Under the ancient city of Rome, Christ's early worshipers painted him in a magician's robe, wand in hand, before the linen-bound body of his friend Lazarus. By touching his friend with his magic staff, Christ turns death into life!

Like all magicians, he understands the technology of power—the primal energies of the psyche which lend our human enterprises substance and meaning. This is the energy that rescues lost souls, those who are bewildered and locked away in the "death" of a neurosis, a complex, or an obsession. This energy is available to us all, because there is a Magician within every one of us. Historically there have been a number

10

of masters of this energy who guide us in our efforts to use it ourselves. Christ was so much a master that after his own resurrection he was able to take wing—as the ancient birdman had before him—and ascend into the light-filled heavens.

Those readers who are new to this series will find in Chapters 1 and 2 a basic grounding in the Jungian concepts we have extended in this work. In the three appendices we expand, for the interested reader, on some intriguing structural aspects of the psyche that lend support to our work. These two chapters and the three appendices are common to all four books in this series. The new reader can find all the basic information he needs in any single book. The reader who is familiar with another book in the series may choose to turn straight to Chapter 3.

Taken together, the four books of this series are a "male quartet" which, when held together as a whole, offers a balanced vision of responsible stewardship of the four masculine "horses of power." *If we, like knights of old, learn to ride such spirited steeds, perhaps the "four horsemen of the apocalypse" will take on a new, more hopeful, meaning.*

ACKNOWLEDGMENTS

THE AUTHORS WISH TO THANK GRACIELA INFANTE for her careful reading of the manuscript. Doug especially wishes to express his appreciation for her ongoing support, encouragement, and many helpful suggestions during the long times of intensive work on the manuscript.

Robert wants to express especial appreciation to Margaret Shanahan for her inspiration and encouragement since the days when many of these ideas were being formulated initially as lectures. Since 1985 her ongoing companionship and support have not only stimulated his work but deeply enriched his life and his understanding of the four powers of the psyche.

Both authors wish to thank Patrick Nugent and Angela Smith for their transcriptions of Robert Moore's lecture tapes, Noel Kaufmann for his location of research sources, Max Havlick for his work on permissions and bibliography, and Rudy Vetter for his excellent photography.

Especial thanks go to Maria Guarnaschelli (vice-president and senior editor at William Morrow) for her innovative vision for this series and for her intensive and superlative editorial work. Katharina Buck has been tireless in her ongoing liaison work and in her commitment to effective coordination and getting all the details together for preparation of the manuscript. Kurt Aldeg has given his insights into how best to communicate the ideas in this book to the widest audience. These and the other outstanding Morrow staff have made the success of this book possible.

In addition, the authors wish to acknowledge the many men, inside and outside the men's movement, who have reflected on their personal experience as men and helped refine the understanding of the four powers and four masculine initiations presented in this series of books. With their continuing help, perhaps these masculine powers can be accessed in more helpful and generative ways.

CONTENTS

CONTENTS

PART 3
THE UNINITIATED MAGICIAN: MALFUNCTIONS AND SHADOW FORMS

PART 4
BECOMING A SHAMAN: THE CHALLENGE OF MASCULINE MAGICIAN INITIATION

APPENDICES

"Know Thyself!"
—From an inscription dedicated to the Seven
Sages on the Temple of Apollo at Delphi

PART 1

HARD WIRING: THE MASCULINE SOUL

"real differences" in
biology are always
socially interpreted
& encoded — how much
those differences are
emphasized + how they
are valued is the
issue

I have trouble when
"average differences" are
applied to individuals
as a strait jacket
— I have no difficulty
knowing I am a man
with some different
biology, but w/o narrow
confines

1

GENDER IDENTITY, GENDER ASYMMETRY, AND THE SEXUAL IMBALANCE OF POWER

INCREASINGLY TODAY, MEN AND WOMEN ARE STRUG-
gling to live in a twilight world of gender confusion. Anx-
iously they wonder what, if anything, constitutes their own
unique sexual identity. Women don business suits and
become bankers and lawyers. Men clean house and learn to
change diapers. These shifts in traditional work roles may be
all to the good. But are there any real differences between men
and women? If not, what joy is left us in sexual union? Have
we become interchangeable parts, androgynous to the core?

Some teach us to feel ashamed of our sex-specific differences. Supporters of radical androgyny go so far as to discour-

[handwritten left margin top: another example of complimentary]

age research into the dissimilarities in brain structure, or in the chemical, hormonal, or instinctual configurations that may influence some culturally exaggerated scripts.[1]

Some theorists offer stereotyped ideals of "feminine" psychological characteristics, now alone deemed fully human.[2] Boys are said to be developmentally inferior to girls. Men are held to be biologically and emotionally inferior to women. Some radical feminists assert women would be better off without men entirely—or that male children should be genetically or socially engineered to eliminate "masculine aggressiveness." *[handwritten: that most violence is perpetrated by males is certainly a major issue for Theorists] [handwritten: not all]*

This is not to say that all feminist criticism is invalid. The feminist critique of patriarchal societies makes a great deal of sense. Patriarchy *does* tend to institutionalize a particular kind of masculinity, prone to exploiting and oppressing other human beings, other species, and the environment. But oppressive, "macho" societies deny *men* their mature masculinity as certainly as they degrade women and feminine attributes. Typically a small minority of underdeveloped *[handwritten left margin: yes tho]* males at the top of the social pyramid will control power and wealth to the exclusion of all others, male and female. They rank these others in a descending order of usefulness to themselves and defend against them with all the force of their inflated self-regard. Patriarchy is therefore a manifestation of the infantile grandiosity suffered by its leaders. *[handwritten left margin: minimizing?]*

Patriarchy is set up and run not for men as a gender or for masculinity in its fullness or in its mature expressions but rather by men who are fundamentally *immature*. It is really the rule of boys, often cruel and abusive boys. For the most part, we believe human societies have always consisted of boys and girls more or less unconsciously acting out their immature and grandiose fantasies. Our planetary home more often than not has resembled the island world in William Golding's *Lord of the Flies*. Thus our societies have, on the whole, opposed *[handwritten left margin: of Schmookler]*

22

I'd generally agree with this, but still have some problem with the radical distinction of masculine & feminine psyches. compare the complementarity of the two in eastern thought

the realization and expression of *both* mature feminine and masculine psyches. + in both sexes

Brutalized children—and for most children in most times and places brutality is a commonplace—become brutal adults. But they are not really adults. They can only pretend to be adults while they still operate on a level of childish self-aggrandizement. The developmental crippling that generates patriarchy is not, however, the sole responsibility of childish males. Immature males *and* females are unconscious partners in the socially sanctioned repression of children. A child's sense of self is distorted by a mother who fails to confront her own emotional issues, and her own unresolved needs for power and adulation. The therapist Alice Miller has written a pioneering series of books that addresses poisonous pedagogy,[3] as she calls this problem. Childish men and women never outgrow being self-interested and self-involved, and they pass their own wounds on to their children. Mature men and women find ways to be selfless in their regard for others, even as they are manifestly self-caring.

In sum, we feel it is wrong to view patriarchy as the expression of mature masculinity or of masculinity in its essence. Patriarchal societies are out of balance partly because at their helm are unbalanced men. And while we abhor the often horrific abuses of patriarchal systems, we also remember that males helped generate, from earlier urban neolithic cultures, all the higher civilizations we know from recorded history.[4] The efforts of dynamic, life-engendering men have left an astounding record of discovery and achievement. Clearly the energies of men, in partnership with women and their feminine energies, have fueled (and will continue to fuel) the significant advances of imagination and social organization that characterize our species. Men of the past, in every tribe and nation, have struggled to learn how to use their power to bless the human community. We continue to struggle today.

yes
yes

cf Gerder Lerner the creation of Patriarchy

cf On Caring

that begs a lot of questions!

to say that early kingships were life engendering is quite problematic cf Gimbutas Schmookler esp! Hers

Lost in Childhood:

Failed Initiation (Egyptian figure of mourning)

Defining masculine and feminine characteristics has led to much discussion. After years of research, depth psychologists and others argue that each sex carries both the psychological and physical traits of the other.[5] No man is purely masculine, just as there is no purely feminine woman.[6] Jungian psychologists call the feminine characteristics of the male psyche the Anima; the female psyche's masculine characteristics they call the Animus.

Both the Animus and the Anima develop in complex fashion as the personality grows to maturity. Neither men nor women can reach psychological maturity without integrating their respective contra-sexual other. A man's female elements enhance his manhood, just as a woman's male aspects enhance her womanhood. Typically masculine characteristics are dominant in a man, as are feminine characteristics in a woman. Of course there are exceptions, but this is usually the case. Central to all these discussions is the question of whether masculinity is in its *essence* more coercive, more abusive of power, more compulsively dominance-seeking than feminity. Many have implied or argued that biological gender differences *necessitate* rigid sex-role differentiation and make masculine dominance *inevitable*.

For example, the changing history of male and female roles within the Israeli kibbutzim are presented as evidence of innate masculine and feminine characteristics. The kibbutzim were founded as farming communities in the late nineteenth century under the influence of Marxist ideals. Men and women were viewed not only as equal, but as inherently the same. In the fields, women worked the same long hours as the men. In the kitchens, nurseries, and children's dormitories men worked the same long hours as the women.

As the years passed, however, an unexpected development occurred. Slowly the women left the fields, the traditional areas of men's work. More and more they specialized in the work of the kitchens, nurseries, and dormitories. Gradually, the men specialized in the field work. Against the enormous pressure of kibbutz ideology most men and women sorted themselves into "traditional" gender-specific roles. Was this the result of biology or immature manipulation of masculine power? According to sociobiology, primate ethology, and brain-structure/hormonal research, there *may* be instinctual biological roots for such tendencies in social behavior.[8] In addition, the anthropologist David Gilmore, in his *Manhood in the Making*—the first extensively documented cross-cultural examination of the "cult of manhood"—strongly indicates a widespread societal support for a division of social and work roles among men and women.[9]

Even if it could be proved, however, that some traditionally masculine or feminine *tendencies* may be inherited this would not be a basis for justifying the usual caricatures of these traits. Above all, it does not justify the assumption that men are inherently violent, inordinately aggressive, insensitive, and uninterested in intimate relationships, nor that women have a monopoly on gentle, nurturing, emotional, and intuitive behaviors. Probably the most accurate argument is that men are more "hard-wired" for some psychological tendencies and women for others. Unfortunately, historical cultures nearly always have amplified rather than helped us compensate for these tendencies.

Important as all these considerations may be, in this book our purpose is not to focus on gender difference. We intend rather to advance understanding of the deep masculine and the challenge of stewarding masculine power. *For whatever the source of masculine abuse of power, it is our responsibility as contemporary men to understand it and to develop the emotional and spiritual resources to end it.* We want to help men express what psychoanalyst Erik Erikson termed the "generative man" within themselves.[10] We will do this by exploring how masculinity is anchored in the place where body, instinct, mind, and soul arise in men.

Contrary to those thinkers who, with Reinhold Niebuhr, regard power itself as inevitably leading to evil,[11] we believe it is possible to steward power responsibly. The drive toward attaining personal and corporate empowerment is as much a part of our instinctual makeup as eating, sleeping, and pro-creating. We cannot wish away what psychologist Alfred Adler called the "will to power,"[12] the desire to overcome. "We shall overcome" is not just a civil-rights rallying cry—it is a human instinct to achieve efficacy and competence in adaptation. We cannot and should not raise our children to eschew this primal and ultimately life-enhancing instinct.[13] The issue should never be how to get rid of the urge for power, masculine or feminine. The real issue is how to steward it, and how to channel our other instincts along with it into life-giving and world-building activities.

are those equivalent to power

or perhaps to make a real distinction between 1 + 2 below

I question whether [proper for] 1) will to power + 2) urge to achieve efficacy + competence are the same

cf Maslow Mayeroff

THE PROBLEM OF THE MODERN ATTACK ON
MYTH AND RITUAL

The creative use of instinctual male energies, like the good use of any energy source, requires maturity. Human maturity has probably always been a rare commodity. But we believe it was, at least in some respects, more available in the past than it is today. It was more available even in patriarchal states, with all of their drawbacks, than it is in our modern societies. In the past there were powerful rites of initiation presided over by ritual elders to help boys and girls remake themselves into men and women capable of assuming their social responsibili-ties.[14] The scope of these premodern initiation rituals was

When ??

? ? ? ?

cf Schmookler

even when those were defined in manifestly immature terms — you can't really have it both ways either: patriarchy is immature masculinity but initiation into roles of it is good

27

often limited by inflexible cultural norms. But they did provide boys and girls with workable blueprints for achieving gender-specific maturity and were based on mythic visions of the tribe's view of the best in human nature—their normative vision of the possible human.

An apprentice electrician must be initiated by an experienced master into the mysteries of electricity's sources, methods of generation, and technologies of distribution. Whatever the apprentice does not take care to understand is a danger to him, because electricity carries force enough to kill him. In similar fashion all human beings need to be initiated into the wise and life-enhancing uses of human psychological resources. Where misunderstood, the energies of our psyches can wreak havoc upon our lives. Despite the elaborate training our modern society provides an individual mastering a trade, we do not think to offer anything similar to the man who wishes to master his own psyche. But our lack of teachers doesn't change our need to learn how to access the powerful energies of our deep souls.

Essentially, the process of initiation removes our Ego from the center of the universe. When a society abandons initiation rituals, individual Egos lose an appropriate means of learning this valuable lesson. Life circumstances will urge the same lesson upon the Ego eventually, but perhaps in a very painful, inopportune manner. But by far the most serious consequence of ceasing initiatory practices is the loss of a periodic social forum for considering the nature of maturity. A society has to know what maturity is before it can pass the knowledge on. It's as if we no longer have a map to get us to maturity. If you don't know where something is, and you don't have a map, how do you get there? A few will stumble across the destination. But most of us end up getting hopelessly lost. When people bemoan our culture's loss of values, in part they are missing the old transformative rituals—for

conflicts with pp 22-23 where you talk about the immaturity of males in patriarchal societies

of paths Beyond Ego?

rituals provide a structure within which social values can be recalled and reconsidered.

In many tribal societies initiation ceremonies are still given the prominence they deserve. Through ritual training and the special imparting of carefully stewarded wisdom, the Ego is displaced into an "orbital" position around a Transpersonal Other. The Ego may experience this Transpersonal Other as any kind of group or task to which the individual pledges his or her loyalties, best efforts, even his or her life. In premodern societies, such group tasks and loyalties are always themselves ultimately subordinate to and given meaning by a greater Transpersonal Other, which religions of the world call "God."

As a complete cultural system, modernity has largely turned its back on God, on effective processes of initiation, on ritual elders, and even on family, tribe, and nation. Consequently, an individual Ego can no longer reach the sober but joyous realization of its *non*central position in the psyche and in the wider universe. Nature fills the vacuum modernity has created with our modern Egos, which expand terrifically to fill the empty space. Where a powerful Transpersonal Other is missing, God is replaced by unconscious pretensions to godhood.

An individual psyche, bloated by dangerously distorted assessments of self, and others around it—family, friends, lovers, company, nation, and perhaps the entire globe—must pay the price for its infantilism. Corrupt politicians, money-hungry yuppies, drug dealers, wife (and husband) abusers, and new racists are but a few examples of infantilism run amok. Petty dictators, self-styled fundamentalist "messiahs" and their terrorist henchmen, Khmer Rouge genocidal murderers, Chinese Communist-party bullies, and irresponsible international oil company executives, among many others, cause the social and environmental devastation that always

[handwritten margin notes:]
cf Colin Turnbull The Human Cycle
?
cf Schmookler
cf Disappearing Through the Skylight (sic?)

[handwritten bottom note:]
but cf Schmookler for the historical problem of this even in societies w/ god, initiation elders etc

accompanies the Ego inflation of the human psyche un-
checked by a sense of limits grounded in a Transpersonal
Other. These would-be men and women have failed to grasp a
sufficiently wide and deep vision of the archetypal realities
upon which our psyche is founded. It is time we look again to
these deep structures and draw from them the psychic support
our modern era so desperately needs.

the distinction you want to be making may more accurately be between Tribal societies (small scale ones) and the advent of civilization rather than between modernity & prior societies!

of Naess; turnbull deep ecologists Schmookler Gimbytas & others

how can we *embed*, nest the structures, the support for maturity of small, human scale tribal societies within civilizations, let alone the world wide culture of modernity??

of traditional chinese culture

how can we *balance* the need for structure / support with the complementary advantages of freedom & individualism

DECODING THE MALE PSYCHE

C ARL GUSTAV JUNG FOUNDED THE SCHOOL OF ANA-
lytical or "depth" psychology that provides the overall
framework of our work.[1] We rely heavily also on insights from
theorists of other schools such as Sigmund Freud, Erik Erikson, D. W. Winnicott, Heinz Kohut, and Alice Miller. But we
believe Jung's approach is the only one to provide a truly
transcultural understanding of our human psyche. His is also
the only approach to adequately bridge the gap between modern science and the mythological and spiritual traditions of
our species.

Jungian depth psychology values the mysteries of the

*but
cf
Paths
Beyond
Ego*

*he may fundamentally
misperceive the importance
of the perennial
philosophy!*

human soul. Dreams, visions, symbols, images, and cultural achievements arise from those mysterious depths that the world's religions understand as the "spiritual dimension." Depth psychology embraces all human experience as authentic to the psyche. Consequently, phenomena such as the "soul," "demonic possession," "revelation," "prayer," or "god" are completely compatible with scientific truth. Because all experiences are psychological, all are real, no matter how strange.[2] Above all, *any* human experience is both *based on* and *perceived by* the deep psychological structures within us.[3]

Before we explore the deep structures of the male psyche, it will be helpful to define a few Jungian terms.

MYTH: For depth psychologists myth does not imply a naïve, untrue, prescientific tale about the origins of the world or humankind. Myths are true stories that describe the ways of the psyche and the means by which our psychological energies interact.[4] Myths project our inner dynamics onto the outer world and allow us to experience it through the filter of how we think and feel.[5]

Since in a real sense we *are* the universe and the universe is us, myths often accurately describe the workings of the larger universe by using anthropomorphic images. That is to say, we are products of the universe in the same way that galaxies, oceans, and trees are. It would be a very strange thing indeed if our psyche did not mirror the structures found outside in the cosmos. An immediate and intimate correspondence between *inner* and *outer* is fundamental to our nature as beings. If no such link existed, we would be unable to acquire any realistic or workable knowledge of the world. We would be unable to survive. Ultimately, it is possible that *inner* and *outer* are purely subjective, pragmatic distinctions made by our consciousness in order to navigate within a mystery it cannot fully fathom.

Creation myths illustrate this beautifully. In the Bible, the Hebrew God Yahweh creates the material world by speaking. He says, "Let there be such and such!" and there is such and such. Behind this concept of creation stands the idea that naming something brings it into existence. Of course, modern science maintains the world did not come into being through a divine uttering of words or the naming of material objects. The biblical account does not convey a scientific truth about the world's origin. The truth it speaks is psychological.

Human consciousness at its height is developed largely by the mastering of words. Arising from language, at the same time it gives rise *to* language, consciousness creates our experience as it defines creation. The words we use for things allow us to distinguish *this* from *that*. They also profoundly color how we think and feel about those things. What we cannot name is therefore not fully real or fully experienced for us. As far as our psyche is concerned, an unnamed thing is "uncreated."[6] Thus the biblical image of Yahweh creating the world by naming it is true to human psychological processes. At the same time, if we assume there is an intelligence behind the created world, it might be true that that intelligence manifested the universe through some process analogous to the human use of language. If this were so, the biblical story would be working both as a psychological parable and as a visionary expression of a process that really *is* occurring in the universe as a whole.

EGO: When Jungian psychoanalysts talk about the Ego, they usually mean the "I" we normally think of as ourselves. The Ego is who we believe ourselves to be, the part of our psyche we identify with our name. When we say, "*I* feel this way about something," or "*I* think I'll do that," the Ego is probably speaking. Jungian theorists sometimes define the Ego as a *complex*. By this they mean a structural element of the total psyche that exhibits certain specific features. The Ego oper-

33

The Sacred King Making Words and His Magician Scribe
(King Barrakab of Sam'al with his scribe)

ates in what we imagine to be our capacity to think rationally, in our feelings, in our ability to will actions, remember the past, and create the future, and in our encounter with consciousness.

In reality, however, the question of the Ego is more complicated. Often "I" am not the one who is thinking, feeling, acting, willing, or deciding. Rather some *autonomous complex* other than the Ego may temporarily "possess" it and make it operate out of the complex's perspective. Since the Ego is largely unaware of these other complexes, it is tricked into the illusory feeling of holding a solitary place in the psyche, and into an accompanying illusion of its "free will." According to Jung, the other complexes operate largely from the personal unconscious, but may also be anchored in a transpersonal unconscious which exerts a deeper influence on the psyche.

CONSCIOUSNESS: Consciousness is not confined to the Ego. The *sub*conscious or *un*conscious is itself conscious. It is only unconscious—invisible and indistinct—from the *Ego*'s perspective.[8] Personal complexes other than the Ego, and the deeper transpersonal psychological structures of the unconscious, can be conscious of each other and of the Ego, and they operate out of their own agendas. The case of multiple-personality disorder demonstrates this clearly. Here highly activated complexes usurp the place of the Ego in the daily affairs of the afflicted person, causing him or her to behave in ways the Ego neither wishes nor sometimes even remembers afterward.

What is true for people who suffer multiple-personality disorder is true, though to a lesser extent, for all of us. We all at times act in ways contrary to how our Ego wills us to behave, perhaps through deep mood swings and emotionally violent outbursts of fear and rage. When we return to a state of Ego consciousness, we say such things as "I went out of my head" or "I don't know what came over me." What came over us, like a wave of energy that shifted our whole mode of perceiving, feeling, and acting, was an autonomous complex, another consciousness from within the total psychic system that is our Self.

Autonomous complexes are usually (though not always) organized around traumatic childhood experiences.[9] During early traumas, our emerging Egos split off and repressed aspects of the psyche that parents, siblings, or society found unacceptable. These split-off aspects could be thoughts, feelings, images, or associations. Often they are valuable and worth recall. They may carry hidden talents, intuitions, abilities, or accurate feelings that would make our personalities wiser and more complete if we could reintegrate them. Until reintegration can occur, our psyches are like the pieces of a broken mirror, which hold in fragments what was once a complete reflection. Through all our complexes, including the Ego, and the vast territory of the unconscious, consciousness pervades our psyche.

ARCHETYPES: Archetypes operate at a level of the psyche deeper than that of the personal unconscious with its autonomous complexes. They are [the hard-wired components] of our genetically transmitted psychic machine.[10] They are the bedrock structures that define the human psyche's own nature, and make it the same, regardless of the culture in which an individual lives. In this sense archetypes represent transpersonal human psychological characteristics. They are dynamic, energic elements in all of us. They well up and fall deep within our unconscious like tidal pulls. Our daily life is influenced by these energies in ways we can never fully understand.

trans personal or universal + trans cultural

Jung declared that the archetypes are equivalent to the instincts of other animals. He located them in what he called the *collective unconscious.*[11] The existence of an unconscious, or what many called the subconscious, had been noted for some time. But Freud was the first to make it the focus of major psychological investigation. Before him, even where psychologists acknowledged the subconscious mind's existence, they usually dismissed it as an inert repository of forgotten or repressed experiences.

Freud's interest in the mind's possibilities had been aroused during his medical studies with the great Parisian hypnotist, Jean Martin Charcot. Charcot dismissed the results of his own experimental demonstrations as stemming from patient hysteria. Whatever their source, the hypnotic manifestations witnessed by the young Freud convinced him he'd found a rich field for further study.

Common to all of us, Freud's life work implied, was a subconscious deeper than a particular personal one. He called this instinctually based subconscious the *Id* (the Latin word for "it").[12] This wild, primitive Id was responsible for all kinds of enormously powerful and irrational impulses, especially [aggressive] sexuality.

Classic Freudians have tended to regard the subconscious as more or less unstructured. But a number of neo-Freudians maintain that the deep psyche, far from being chaotic, is

characterized by structure. Erik Erikson talks about "instinctive structures" and "preformed action patterns," which,
under appropriate circumstances, call up "drive energy for
instantaneous, vigorous, and skillful release."[13] He proposes
the existence of "a general psychic energy (instinctual force)
which can be put to use by a variety of preformed and relatively autonomous instinctive patterns."[14] He also says, "the
action patterns—the modes and modalities—are all present in
the ground plan from the beginning, yet they have their special time of ascending."[15] His thoughts come remarkably close
to the Jungian conception of time-and-circumstance-released
archetypal "action patterns" from the collective unconscious.

   Jung pushed the exploration of the collective unconscious structures a step further. Stored within them, he
claimed, are both the human psyche's archetypal building
blocks and the accumulated collective memory of the entire
human race. He reached this conclusion because he discovered
that symbols, images, myths, and Gods from different cultures
and epochs bore striking resemblances to one another and also
to the images that appeared in his patients' dreams. According
to his conception, the collective unconscious is the source and
the limitless reservoir of all the images recorded in human art,
mythology, and religion. From it leap both the poet's song and
the scientist's insight. From it flow the signal dreams which
have implication often for an entire society as much as for
their dreamer.

   The psyche's archetypal structures serve as conduits for
great charges of primal psychological energy. Because of their
own dynamic configuration, they mold this energy, imparting
to it their particular patterns. Psychologists call this life-force
in psychic form the *Libido*.[16] Freud believed that Libido is
fundamentally sexual. Any expression of the Libido redirected
into pursuits other than sexual ones he called "sublimations."
Jung, on the other hand, believed that the Libido is a general-

37

ized life-force that expresses itself through imaginal and spiritual impulses, as well as through sexuality.

For any individual the archetypes may be creative and life-enhancing or destructive and death-dealing. The result depends in part on how the Ego is able to relate to them based on its own developmental history. Properly accessing and using the Libido available to the psyche amount to a sort of psychological technology. If we learn the technology and use it properly, we can use the energy to make generative men and women of ourselves. But if we fail to learn how to use these vast energy resources, or misuse them, we will be courting our own destruction, and we may take others with us. If we try to ignore the archetypes, they exert their mighty influence upon us nonetheless. They bend us to their nonhuman, sometimes *in*human wills. We must therefore face the evidence depth psychology and other studies have provided us. We are not as free of instinct or unconscious content as we have been encouraged to believe. Genuine freedom for the Ego results from acknowledging and properly accessing the chemical fires that burn hot in our unconscious minds.

Some Jungian analysts romanticize the archetypes.[17] They encourage their patients to find and claim the particular archetype or myth that has organized their lives. Life then becomes a process of affirming and living out this myth. In our opinion our goal should not be to identify with an archetypal pattern, or to allow a mythic expression of it to make of our lives what it will. We believe that when we romantically *identify* with any archetype we cease to be viable human beings moving toward wholeness. If we are drawn to an archetype by its seductive power, its promise that we can shirk our individual responsibilities and the pain involved in being a person with a personal Ego, we will be crushed by the sheer weight of unconscious compulsive impulses.

On the other hand, our goal is not to become *ordinary* in

our quest for psychic health. We must not lose the vital connection with the libidinal energy the archetypes supply us so that we can live our lives fully, energetically, and creatively. Our goal is to learn how to *differentiate* ourselves from the archetypes without completely *disassociating* ourselves from them. If we learn to access them successfully, they become resources of energy both for our personal lives and for healing our planet—we become more radiant in every area of our lives. *individuation — is it complementary to the path beyond ego? of esp zen*

More precisely stated, our objective is to develop mature Ego structures strong enough to channel useful libidinal energy into our daily lives. We can begin by making ourselves conscious of how archetypal energies already possess us. Only then can we begin to access them creatively, through a process that provides us with a greater sense of free will in the choices of our lives. The effort to achieve liberation for ourselves will in turn motivate us to help others do the same. Our renewed energies benefit ourselves and others on all the levels of our psychic organization: the personal, the familial, the communal, national, and global.

SHADOW: Jung himself occasionally identified the Shadow with the totality of the unconscious. But most depth psychologists view the Shadow as a more or less defined and delineated, although multifaceted, contra-Ego, of the same sex as the Ego.[18] If the Ego is a photograph, the Shadow is its negative. Standing in direct opposition to the Ego, the Shadow is an autonomous complex, which holds opinions, expresses feelings, and generally wills an agenda radically different from the Ego's.

Like most autonomous complexes, the Shadow results from childhood trauma. Those qualities of a person's total psyche that are diametrically opposed to the emerging Ego, and that the Ego rejects because of the pressures of the childhood environment, coalesce in the unconscious. There they form a distinct, conscious, willing entity. Unless reintegrated later in life, they forever seek to sabotage the Ego's plans and behaviors.

We have all had the experience of willing one scenario and living quite another. For example, we intend to remain friendly while visiting our in-laws, but then find ourselves drawn irresistibly into arguments and confrontation. Our Egos want to maintain an image of family harmony. Our Shadows, unable to tolerate such hypocrisy, and feeling real animosity toward our in-laws, compel us to behave in a more honest, if more destructive, way.

The animosity we feel is ultimately toward ourselves, but it often takes a lot of work before we can realize this. The Shadow endorses this work because it longs for reintegration. It is the Shadow's method to lead us into holding our impossibly defensive, illogical positions—in order to confront us with whatever psychic complexes we would rather forget. Our "real world" hatreds are most usually against these inner complexes, and our Shadow works by *repetition compulsion* to call our attention to them.

Rather than face any rejected qualities, either positive or negative, within ourselves, we frequently deal with our Shadow by projecting those qualities onto others.[19] As an Ego, we don't project them. But our Shadow does so in order to focus our interest on its feelings, wishes, and agendas. Our Shadow induces us to see other people we disapprove of or dislike in colors that are perhaps only marginally like their "true" colors but which *are* colors that the Shadow itself possesses.

Jung believed withdrawing a projection of the Shadow and owning it as a part of ourselves requires enormous moral courage. He also believed that what we will not face within our psyche we will be forced to confront in the outer world. So, if we can claim our Shadow's qualities, and learn from them, we defuse much of the interpersonal conflict we would otherwise encounter. People who have served as the screens for our Shadow's projections become less odious, and more human. At the same time, we experience ourselves as richer, more complex, and more powerful individuals.

how fits w Paths Beyond Ego

THE TRIANGULAR STRUCTURE
OF THE ARCHETYPES

In this book our definition of the Shadow includes this traditional Jungian understanding, but introduces another archetypal, transpersonal aspect to it as well. We believe masculine and feminine archetypes possess their own Shadows. The King, the Warrior, the Magician, and the Lover are the masculine archetypal structures we have undertaken to study in this series. In one sense these archetypes are operating at more primitive levels than the Ego accessing them, and each has its own Shadow.

In our extended definition, a Shadow always manifests where there is an immature, fragmentary psyche, because splitting is always a symptom of unintegrated development.[20] In the traditional Jungian view of maturity, wholeness is achieved largely to the degree that the split between the Ego and the Shadow is overcome. In large part, psychological maturity is a measure of how thoroughly the Ego is able to integrate the Shadow into its consciousness.

We maintain that the Ego/Shadow split represents a Shadow system in itself. The split actually involves the Ego in the *bipolar* Shadow of one or more archetypes. In this situation our Ego usually identifies with one pole of the archetypal Shadow and disassociates from the other. In our view, then, the Shadow can still be regarded in the traditional way as the psychic area from which the Ego is divided but, more fully, as a bipolar *system* characterized by splitting, repression, and projection *within* the energy field of an archetype.

For a long time psychologists associated "bipolar disorder" almost exclusively with the manic-depressive personality.[21] Then, in his *Modern Psychopathology*, Theodore Millon extended the idea of bipolarity to include passive and active dimensions in all the major disorders of personality.[22] In a similar fashion, some Jungians have described a bipolar relationship between certain archetypes (though they are not in themselves personality disorders) that gave rise to such archetypal pairs as the senex-puer (old man–eternal boy), the domina-puella (old woman–eternal girl) and others.[23]

In the case of the Warrior archetype, for example, neither the Sadist nor the Masochist (the two poles of the Warrior's Shadow) represents personal growth or fulfillment. The full embodiment of the Warrior is to be found in a third transcending option that integrates the two poles into a creative psychological structure. Since they define psychic wholeness, archetypes always reconcile opposing forces in this way. Both of the opposing poles in the archetypal Shadow systems contain qualities essential for psychological health. But if left in their state of chronic tension, they will condemn the Ego to a fragmented and immature existence. Guided by the archetypes in their transcending fullness, a mature personality integrates these important qualities by reconciling the divisions in the archetypal Shadow.

Our refined understanding of how the archetypes work suggests interesting analogies with other schools of thought. The psychologist Alfred Adler, a contemporary of Freud and Jung, believed personality disorders appear both in active and passive modes in a way similar to our view of how archetypal

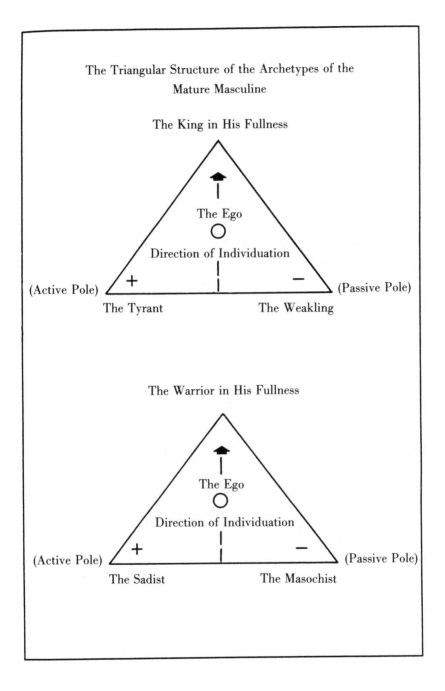

The Triangular Structure of the Archetypes of the
Mature Masculine

The King in His Fullness

The Ego

Direction of Individuation

(Active Pole)   (Passive Pole)

The Tyrant   The Weakling

The Warrior in His Fullness

The Ego

Direction of Individuation

(Active Pole)   (Passive Pole)

The Sadist   The Masochist

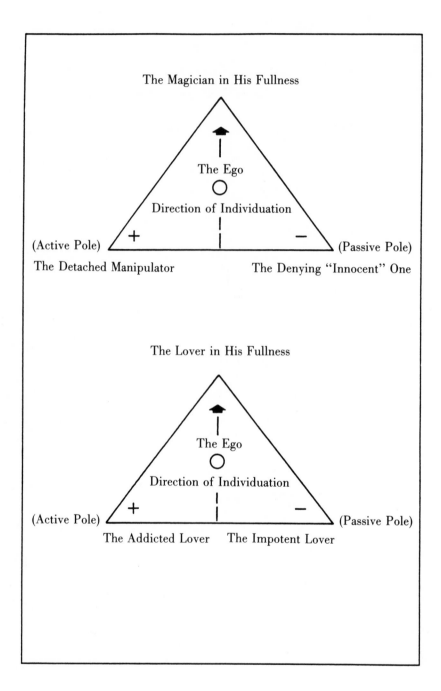

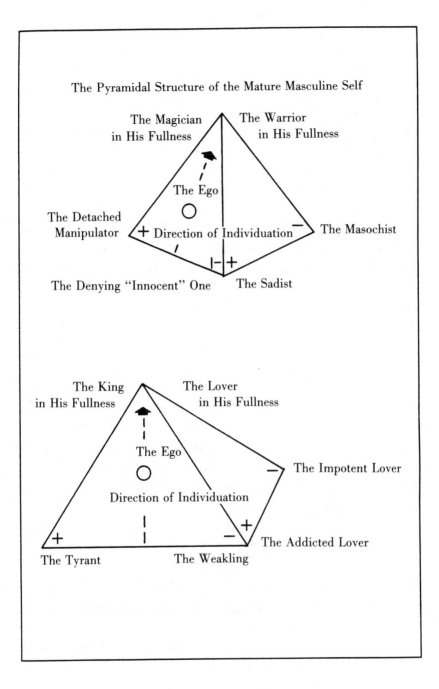

The Pyramidal Structure of the Mature Masculine Self

Shadow systems work. The Christian theologian Paul Tillich grounded his thought with a belief in what he called the "ambiguities" of space and time in the created world. He believed that these ambiguities find their resolution in a third, higher reality "above" history.[24] The impulse to achieve this comes from the "Spirit." The German philosopher Hegel saw the forward movement of the universe as occurring through a "thesis, antithesis, synthesis" process in which each synthesis became a new thesis, and so on in a continual upward program of evolutionary complexity and integration.[25] Alfred North Whitehead, the great twentieth-century American philosopher, sees the whole "adventure of ideas," ideas that *create* the world, as a process by which God lures the created world forward in tiny increments, which he calls "occasions."[26] These occasions are like Hegel's theses, and God is the ever-changing antithesis. Whitehead calls this unceasing process "creative advance."

Similarly, Jung drew from his alchemical studies the idea of the *coniunctio oppositorum* ("union of opposites")[27] impelled by a "transcendent function"—the conceptual equivalent to Tillich's "Spirit" and Whitehead's "lure." Jung believed it is essential for the Ego to balance opposing images, feelings, and points of view without allowing either of the opposing sides to disappear into the unconscious. Eventually, when this struggle is consciously experienced with all the suffering it demands, our psyche can follow a transcendent third possibility into greater wholeness.

Jung's followers have largely neglected the Ego's vital role in determining how the archetypes will shape our everyday lives. With our model of the triangular structure of the archetypes, an individual can take care to see that the archetypes will manifest in their fullest form rather than in their Shadow structures. An Ego that does not properly *access* an archetype

46

will be *possessed* by that archetype's Shadow, and left oscillating between the Shadow's two poles. At one the Ego will suffer
positive inflation (explosion) and at the other *negative inflation* (implosion). Separated, the Shadow's two poles express a
pathological darkness, which is only "enlightened" by polar
integration into the transcendent third of the archetype. Their
pathology is transformed by the Ego into a creative advance.

The action of the Ego is the key to this transformative
experience. The Ego and the elements of the archetype exercise a kind of gravitational pull on each other. To allow transformation, the Ego must position itself "above" time and
space, in the domain of the Spirit, or the collective unconscious. The Ego will serve ultimately as an occasion for the
archetype's expression in time and space. Unless the Ego can
work above the spatiotemporal dimension, the archetype will
appear largely in its fragmented polar aspects, and the Ego will
attract these to itself. In the Spirit's domain, the Ego can
instead keep its proper fix on the lodestar the archetype's
transcendent third represents.

cf
Paths
Beyond
Ego

The archetype's bipolar arrangement in time and space is
portrayed in the mythic image of the Symplegades, the Clashing Rocks the Ego must pass between in pursuit of the archetype's transcendent third.[28] The Ego needs to be *lured* by this
full expression of the archetype to experience creative advance
on its own and in the world. And the archetype needs the Ego
in order to experience itself in space and time, and to recover
its lost Shadow fragments. The act of recovery empowers the
archetype's ongoing creative action in the world.

According to our theory, there are four foundational archetypes of the mature masculine (as well as of the immature
masculine). Each of these triangles—King, Warrior, Magician, and Lover—since they are interdependent aspects of the
single masculine Self, fit together into a pyramidal form. The
pyramid as it has appeared throughout the ages can be inter-

preted as a symbol for the masculine Self. Pyramids from Egypt to Mesoamerica, from Mesopotamia to Hawaii, are representations of the universe in miniature and often display a layered or stepped form. The layers of the pyramids nearly always stand for the layers of the universe, the different cosmic levels of reality. By ascending the pyramid, an individual climbed from the profane dimension to the sacred, from the less divine to the fullest manifestation of divinity.

This idea parallels ours about the "upward" direction of the Ego's individuation from a less integrated (profane) state to a fully integrated (sacred or "divine") state. A man's Ego must ascend the four faces of the stepped pyramid of the masculine Self, thereby overcoming the bipolar Shadow split at the base of each of the faces. The Ego must keep its eye on the capstone of the pyramid, which represents the fullest expression in an individual life of the four archetypes in perfect unity. This ascent of Ego-consciousness, according to Jung, is always a matter of reconciling opposites and of integrating split psychic materials. As a man's Ego ascends through each of the triangular structures of the archetypes, he becomes more integrated and whole. And he is better and better able to access the archetypes in their fullness at the top of the pyramid. On the King side, he integrates the Tyrant and the Weakling. On the Warrior face, he integrates the Sadist and the Masochist. On the Magician surface, he integrates the Detached Manipulator and the Denying "Innocent" One. And on the Lover side, he integrates the Addicted Lover with the Impotent Lover. Each of the poles of the split Shadows of the four major archetypes possesses insights and strengths that, when the Ego integrates them, contribute to a consolidated sense of Self. Each of the bipolar opposites, when united, reveals the "transcendent third" of the archetype in its fullness. By overcoming the splitness in the bipolar archetypal Shadows, a man comes to feel inwardly empowered. And, in

48

The "Mountain of God" at the Center of the Urban Complex
(The Temple Tower Esagila at Babylon: a reconstruction)

From Xibalba to the Skies
The Levels of Reality in the Maya Pyramid (Tikal)

Teotihuacán:
Raising the King-Energy and Generating a World

Stairway to the Sky:
Khmer Temple-Mountain of Koh Ker (tenth century A.D.)

Pyramid Power:
Great Morai Pappara, Otaheite (Tahiti)

The Masculine Self on a Monumental Scale:
The Pyramid of Khufu (Giza)

a sense, while he is *building* internal masculine structure he is also *discovering* the pyramid of the masculine Self, which has always been within him, at his core.

THE ARCHETYPES AND BRAIN STRUCTURE

Startling resonances are being discovered between the fields of brain research and depth psychology. In his book *Archetypes: A Natural History of the Self*, the psychologist Anthony Stevens has extended the exploration of areas of the brain that may be the loci of archetypal forms.[29] He tries to explain Jung's theory of personality types in terms of brain structures. Jung's intuitive types, he speculates, might be using predominantly their Right Brains, and those who favor their Left Brains would correspond to Jung's thinking types.

Briefly, the Right Brain (the right hemisphere of the cerebral cortex) "thinks" in images and symbols, grasps situations and patterns as wholes, and is the primary center for the generation of dreams, visions, and fantasies. The Left Brain (the corresponding left hemisphere) thinks sequentially, analyzes situations and patterns logically, and uses language in its cognitive processes. Many locate the Ego entirely in the Left Brain. In contrast, Stevens proposes that while the Ego may function most of the time in the Left Brain, it also draws on the Right Brain. Consciousness, he says, is a pervasive function of the whole brain, though Right- and Left-Brain modes of consciousness are quite distinct. The personal unconscious and its various complexes seem to manifest in the Right Brain. By dreaming, the Right Brain communicates with the still primarily Left Brain-identified Ego.

Rather than locating the archetypes in the Right Brain, Stevens proposes that they arise in deeper, older layers of the brain, layers that, according to brain researcher Paul Mac-

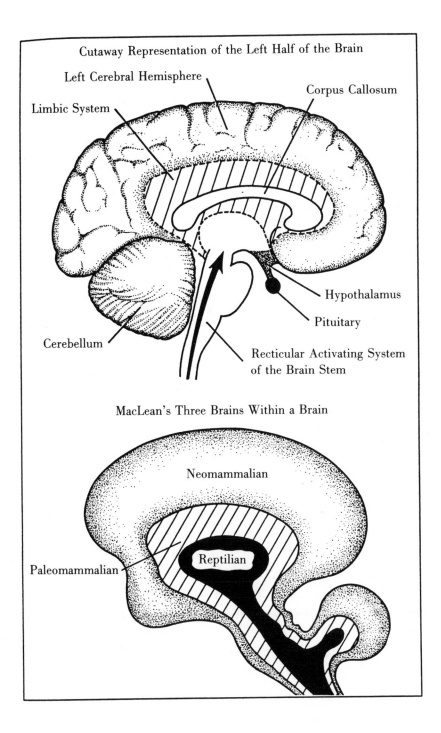

Cutaway Representation of the Left Half of the Brain

Left Cerebral Hemisphere

Corpus Callosum

Limbic System

Hypothalamus

Pituitary

Cerebellum

Recticular Activating System of the Brain Stem

MacLean's Three Brains Within a Brain

Neomammalian

Reptilian

Paleomammalian

Lean, have remained largely unchanged for millions of years of animal evolution.[30] The dihemispheric cerebral cortex we think of as the human brain is only the most recently evolved element of three distinct neurological regions. Before it, in ascending order of antiquity, come the neocortex, or neomammalian brain, apparently responsible for cognition and sophisticated perception; the midbrain, or paleomammalian brain (limbic system), which seems to generate the basic emotions of fear and anger, affiliation, and maternity as well as species-characteristic individual and social behaviors; and the upward growth of the spinal cord, the reptilian brain, or R-complex, responsible for basic life activities, also probably the seat of our most basic instincts and our routine-driven behavior patterns. These three brains within a brain function relatively autonomously. Our process of psychological integration is, in part, an attempt to unify and synchronize these three regions of the brain.

If archetypes arise, as Jung believed, at a fundamentally instinctual level, then it could be that they originate in our most primitive region, the reptilian brain. Elaborated as they pass upward through the paleomammalian and neomammalian brains, the imagistic, intuitive structures of the archetypes would rise primarily into our Right Brains. But since our Ego's experience of the archetypes will also be mediated via the Left Brain, they will also be influenced by the linguistic and logical modes of thinking centered there. Archetypes hold a sense of otherness[31] perhaps because they originate in levels of the brain so much deeper than the source of Ego-consciousness, and then must be translated into terms that make sense especially to the Left Brain. Archetypes in their fullness involve *both* Left- and Right-Brain functions. This is clearly the case with the four foundational archetypes of the mature masculine, which we are outlining in this series. Certainly the rational, strategic, and emotionally detached modes of the

Magician and the Warrior are characteristic of Left-Brain processes, although they seem to draw secondarily on Right-Brain functions, and the visually oriented, aesthetic, intuitive modes of the Lover are characteristic of Right-Brain functions, although the Lover also seems to draw on Left-Brain processes. We attempt a more thorough discussion of the origin of the four archetypes of mature masculinity and the brain's limbic system (paleomammalian brain) in Appendix B. This field of inquiry is wide open to exciting future research.

COVERGENCE OF THE MATURE
MASCULINE ARCHETYPES

Depth psychologists often merge the mature masculine archetypes. Because only the most perfectly realized Ego apprehends an archetype's full expression, for most of us they retain a degree of mystery. The very images and symbols archetypes use to communicate to us refer beyond themselves to other images and symbols in an almost infinitely complex way. For example, the phallus, the cross, the tree, the *axis mundi*, the spine, the sacred mountain, and the pyramid can each be read symbolically as aspects of one another.[32] There are dangers, however, involved with overinterpretations. An individual can easily lose himself, as Yeats was warned in the course of his occult researches, along the Path of the Chameleon, a labyrinthine trail of correspondences. Besides this, the four basic archetypes that influence a mature man, the King, the Warrior, the Magician, and the Lover, are the fragments of a primevally whole Self, and complement each other to such a degree that no one of them receives its fullest expression without incorporating the others.

These archetypes have historically merged and diverged

again in a bewildering variety of configurations. Rain magicians, for example, give rise to rain kings, who appoint priests to elect warrior kings, who commission other warriors to serve magicians who themselves become kings. A mortal king, to the extent that he fully expresses the archetypal King, is a warrior who enforces order within his kingdom and who may take military action to extend his kingdom. He is also a high-priest magician who mediates between the spiritual dimension and his people.[33] He is also a lover, of his people, and in a special sense of his sacred queen, since he cannot rule legitimately or effectively unless their union is fruitful.[34] Despite these uncertain boundaries, it is useful to distinguish masculine archetypes in order to enhance the Ego's capacity to access these psychic structures in all their richness and complexity. In this book we will be focusing on the magician sector of the empowered masculine self.

THE ALPHA MALE AND HIS WARRIORS:
PRIMATE PREFIGURATIONS

Chimpanzees are our closest living animal relatives.[35] Their genetic profile is over 98 percent identical to ours.[36] Primate ethology research suggests close correspondences between their social structures and interpersonal behaviors and ours. It seems likely that similar psychological processes are at work.[37]

While of course we cannot *know* fully what other animals feel and think, in many ways we cannot be sure we *know* what another *human* feels or thinks. In either case we make judgments based on observable behaviors. Our great advantage in observing humans obviously is spoken language, but we still have the subjective task of interpreting linguistic signs. Chimpanzees, while they cannot speak, *can* communicate with us in sign language and through other quasi-verbal methods de-

King, Warrior, Magician, Lover:
The Alpha Male "Displaying" (Figan as Alpha Male at Gombe)

signed by researchers.[38] In addition, their complex range of body signals bears a striking resemblance to our own body language. It seems reasonably safe to assume that when chimpanzees *appear* to be fearful, wrathful, submissive, loving, or awed, they are in fact experiencing these emotions. Probably their emotional experience is less self-conscious and complicated than ours, but still it offers clues into primate psychology, including our own.

The hierarchical power blocs and coalitions of chimpan-

Yeroen, the Old Fox (Arnhem Zoo)

zee society center around a dominant adult male ethologists call the *Alpha Male*.[39] Successful Alpha Males are usually mature and physically powerful. They display foresight, courage, and what can only be called "character." Alpha Males exhibit many behaviors common to the sacred king, the specific archetypally inspired figure we explored in *The King Within*.

Alpha Males surround themselves with male "knights" to help protect and defend their "realms." These warrior males exhibit characteristics of what David Gilmore calls the "cult of manhood" in human males. Like their human counterparts, chimpanzee males are protectors and providers for the females and the young of their societies.[40]

Alpha Males in chimpanzee and other primate societies often show characteristics of the Magician function of the human psyche. They frequently make decisions that call for cognitive discernment—for example, when to move the troop or the tribe in order to avoid predators, where best to "camp" for the night, when it's time to change feeding sites, and so forth. In addition, the Magician power, both as a function of modulating mechanisms in the primate brain that serve to balance and control aggressive and sexual impulses, and as a function of higher thinking processes, is part of the psychological equipment of every chimpanzee—male and female—and is a hallmark of the primates in general. This creative, strategizing, reflective archetype enables chimpanzees in particular to make and use a wide range of tools—from clubs and stones to termite sticks and even "toilet paper"—strong evidence of incipient technology, one of the gifts of the Magician.

We offer this book and the series as a whole to the man who is looking for an operator's manual to the psyche, and to the woman who wants a guide to the hard wiring of men, and to her own inner masculine as well. Just as no jet pilot would try to fly a 747 without knowing its capabilities and instruments inside and out, the only way to "fly" successfully an immensely complicated male psyche is to know it inside and out, with a clear understanding of how to access its archetypal energy systems. The mindful use of this energy will bring a man safely into his mature manhood.

PART 2

IMAGES OF THE MASCULINE MAGICIAN

THE SHAMANIC
TRADITION:
THE BIRDMAN'S
DESCENDANTS

T HE MAGICIAN IS THE ARCHETYPE BEHIND A MULTI-
tude of human professions and "callings." The Magician
urges us on into the unseen. He is the mediator and communi-
cator of hidden knowledge, the healer, technologist, teacher,
and contemplative—he is behind our insatiable human curios-
ity. He keeps his inner eye fixed on the blueprint for the
self—"image of God" or "Diamond Body" we each have
within us and he seeks to initiate us into a wiser, fuller way of
being human.

Whenever a person manipulates hidden forces in his profession, whether those be psychological or physical, he is ac-

A Priest of Attis (bas-relief from Ostia)

cessing the Magician. Many professions operate under his aegis. Scientists, technicians, mathematicians, cosmologists, lawyers, physicians, psychiatrists, psychologists, philosophers, teachers, researchers, economists, sociologists, politicians, priests, prophets, shamans, psychics, artists—all these professions and more express and utilize the energies of the Magician.

Those professions which emphasize mental discipline and technical proficiency are also heavily influenced by the Warrior, the archetype of self-discipline and perseverance. A few Magician professions rely more on the feeling and relating qualities typical of the Lover. Artists are especially under the Magician and the Lover's combined sway; with the Lover to guide them they key into the underlying, libidinal unity of all things, and the Magician provides a deep connection with the unconscious. The Lover's intuition of the unity of time and space, in which past, present, and future are experienced as a single moment, and all points in the universe as ultimately coincidental, is also expressed in the Magician's manifestation as prophet, seer, or psychic.

The medicine men and the rainmakers of traditional cultures work equally in the dimension of introverted self-discipline and extroverted, caring commitment to a greater community. Other holy men, yogis, for example, follow rigorous, ascetic disciplines that impel them into a relationship centered in a transcendental reality. Analogous contemporary professions are those of the teacher, psychologist, psychiatrist, and physician.

Politicians and salesmen also draw on the Magician's skills at manipulating appearances. Both can make things appear to be what they are not, but hopefully they have enough contact with the King to remember the greater good of the community.

The priesthoods of every religion traditionally have been

concerned with mediating, to their flocks, the power of the spirit world (what we would call the collective unconscious). Many priests, of course, draw on the Warrior as well as the Magician. Think of the Jesuits—an order founded explicitly as "soldiers of Christ." The main requirement for the priesthood has always been proficiency in the evocation, containment, and distribution of Magician power, but not necessarily direct experience of it. In contrast prophets, seers, psychics, and religious poets are *directly* acquainted with that power, and live their lives in deep communion with the archetype. The priest is more concerned with structure—established ceremony—where these other spiritual individuals look for ecstatic communion and engage in transformative rituals. Such ecstatic communion is almost always in tension with structure. Hence the conflicts, throughout history, between prophets and priests.

Technically oriented professionals work with knowledge that is generally unknown outside of a given profession. Technology is the Magician's specialty, and the application and drive required to master a highly technological profession is supplied by the Warrior. The Lover has little influence over such a profession. Though many individuals in these walks of life may be intensely relational in their personal lives, their work tends to be removed from the dimension of human feeling. Responsibility is as limited as the focus is narrow in these kinds of jobs. The work is seldom directly concerned with serving others. Of course, there are exceptions—the researcher who tries to come up with a cure for AIDS, or the public defender who labors to establish a useful precedent—but most usually the concerns of these professions are limited in scope. The Lover energy only gives to these men their sudden insights and unexpected solutions to difficult problems.

The Magician energy is the most introverted energy of

the four foundational archetypes of the masculine psyche. It can be the most difficult energy to understand, since it requires more patience and subtlety of mind than the Lover, Warrior, or King energy. One of the reasons practitioners tend to mystify the archetypal Magician is to counteract our short attention spans. They try to impress us with their mystifications so that we won't lose interest in what it is the Magician actually does.

E. M. Butler was one scholar who didn't fall into the trap of trying to make his subject mysterious. In his book *The Myth of the Magus,* he set out ten elements common to the stories of all the great historical magicians. From Jesus to the anonymous shamans we will soon examine, the myths of a magician's life remain remarkably consistent.

First, a magician's origin is supernatural or mysterious. He may be a divine or a demonic infant, but he is never ordinary. Second, there are portents at his birth to indicate his mysterious origins, and his supernatural powers. For example, when Mohammed was born the story is that all the idols of the world fell down. In a more familiar tradition, think of the star that led the three magi to the baby Jesus.

The third common element is that the baby magus is imperiled in his infancy. Evil wishes, or simply the power of evil, try to do the magus in at birth. A fourth element is some kind of initiation. Austerities and temptations occur which are either preceded or followed by a fifth stage, of distant wanderings. The magus wanders either to seek for wisdom, or to spread wisdom he has already acquired. The journeys may be supernatural. They may involve a descent into the underworld, or an ascent into heaven.

Again it is easy to locate Jesus in this tradition. Allegedly he went into the underworld. The esoteric traditions of the Gnostics tell of a Jesus who journeyed to India to study with the sages there. Other stories tell that Jesus went to the Hima-

67

layas, and was initiated there. The place for initiation in the Himalayas would be, of course, the legendary secret chamber that opens onto Shangri-la.

In his sixth stage a magus faces a magical contest. Butler maintains that this is a constant feature in the lives of all Magicians, both legendary and real. He offers, for example, the biblical contest between Elijah and the prophets of Ba'al. The seventh stage almost always holds a trial or a persecution. Eighth, there is a last scene, which often includes a solemn and prophetic farewell. The Last Supper clearly fits into this eighth stage.

In the ninth stage there is often a violent or a mysterious death, and in the tenth, a resurrection or an ascension. These last stages throw a very interesting light on human nature. Why a trial or a persecution? Because human beings are virtuosos of denial. People work very carefully to be unaware of any problem when awareness might require taking an active part in finding a solution. The trial comes because the Magician knows too many uncomfortable truths and calls for action.

An individual becomes a community scapegoat when he reveals his community's Shadow. If we consider the story of Jesus in this respect, we see a man who knows a lot, reveals a lot, and is killed for his efforts. But interestingly the myth's tenth stage suggests how hard it is to kill the truth. There is a vindication at the story's end, because the magus comes back, transcending his torturers. And it is his truth that ultimately is remembered.

THE MAGICIAN AS SHAMAN

There is no archetype of the shaman, as some would argue; he is only one of the Magician's many faces, along with the medi-

Yeibichai Navajo Shaman from the Night Chant Ceremony

cine man, the warlock, the wizard, therapist, or physicist. But the shaman's calling is, of all human professions, the fullest expression of the Magician archetype.

The shaman was first studied by anthropologists among the indigenous tribes of central and northern Asia. (The term is taken from the language of a Siberian tribe.) Subsequently shamans have been identified in traditional cultures from Australia and the Cape of Africa to the Yucatán. Many scholars now theorize that shamanism is the psychospiritual phenomenon underlying the emergence of history's great spiritual traditions. Science, ancient and modern, also owes a debt to the intuitive insights of the shaman.

The shaman was the guardian of esoteric knowledge and the technician of sacred power. His secret wisdom was of natural laws and psychological dynamics. The shaman knew, and could interpret, the cycles of nature, the workings of the heavens—the phases of the moon, the progress of the sun— and, perhaps most important, the movements of the herds upon which the lives of his people depended. It was the shaman who was called upon to locate, consecrate, and steward the sacred places and times which periodically would erupt into ordinary time and space.

The shaman understood that the human psyche is made up of energy flows and dynamic structures which can be brought into harmonious integration with one another. He called the structures he encountered demons, angels, or spirits. Today we would call the same things neuroses, complexes, and archetypes. He conducted his research into the hidden worlds of nature and the psyche by altering his consciousness, often by rhythmic drumming, and less often by the use of hallucinogenic drugs. His inward questing forced him to integrate his own fragmented psyche and confront his own complexes.

In fact, it was often a childhood nervous illness that

marked a boy as a possible heir to an elder shaman. Butler's first and second mythic stages can be located in a boy's psychic illness—in its mysterious origin, and its portents of gathering supernatural powers. Instead of curing the illness, the elder shaman would encourage it to run its course, thus giving his pupil a practical lesson in the healing dynamics of the human psyche.

But a shaman's primary objective was helping his fellow tribe members. He communicated his ecstatic visions, and his diagnoses of the illnesses afflicting his fellows and their world, through poetry and song. Thus he was healer, artist, and technician—the magician par excellence. By virtue of his spiritual power, he also became economic advisor, designer, architect, and politician—in fact he was consulted in every matter of importance to the community as a whole.

Many times the Magician is expressed through individuals who would rather study a problem than solve one. *The shaman is the most developed embodiment of the Magician because of the problems he is willing to take on. He has the capacity to care, which comes from the King; to fight, which comes from the Warrior; and to value someone enough to fight for them, which last is a gift from the Lover.*

CONFLATION OF THE ARCHETYPES

As we have noted, scholars have shown a tendency to conflate the four foundational archetypes of mature masculinity, and this is one of Butler's failings. While he does an admirable job discerning the stages of the life of a magus, he tends to collapse the King and the Warrior archetypes into the Magician. He correctly recognizes that there is very little Lover energy in most magicians. The Magician is the most disembodied archetype of the four.

Given the tangled web of interaction between the four, it is easy to see how they can be confused. The Magician combines with the Warrior, and only occasionally the Lover, in influencing many human professions. But the closest relationship is between the Magician and the King.

The institution of sacred kingship seems to have arisen, at least in Africa and Central Asia, from the office of rainmaker or shaman. In other areas of the world, the most difficult struggles were between tribes rather than against the weather, and kings there came from the warrior class. But in all sacred kingships, the king was believed to mystically embody the vital center of the created world. Through him the various dimensions of reality came together, working harmoniously for the good of all things.

All of the king's offices thus grew out of the shaman's responsibilities. Before the king it had been the shaman's office to bridge the gaps between the underworld, the earthly plane, and the heavens. It was the shaman who had first imposed order upon chaos, through the force of a powerful will, and by intuited directive from the Self. Thus it had been the shaman once who constellated the *axis mundi*—the center of the world—for his tribe to build their lives around.

There is much room for scholarly disagreement over when exactly these shamanic duties were taken over by the king, and also why this happened. And because of their similar tasks, it can be difficult to make a clear distinction between shaman and king.

What scholars find difficulty unraveling, the popular culture has confused even further. Sacred kings were always believed to embody magical powers, including the power to heal their subjects and kingdoms, and the power equally to strike them down. Certain magicians have likewise been popularly vested with kingly attributes. Jesus the Magician was believed by the earliest Christians to be the true King of Israel.

Later worshipers dubbed him Christ Pantocrator, the cosmic King. The three magi who came to worship the infant Jesus— the three astrologer magicians, probably from Persia, borrowed by the Gospel's author from an ancient account of Zoroaster's birth—are often called kings. In Mexico they are "the three magician kings," and we hear this association clearly in an English carol, "We three kings of orient are."

Yet it is worth discriminating between the Magician and the King, in order to identify which energies are operative in different situations. The King's realm includes a political sphere, which the Magician rarely enters into, except for the shaman in the limited context of a traditional society. The King is fundamentally concerned with creative ordering and structure, where the Magician is more concerned with the liminal areas outside of structures. The King is the most inclusive of the archetypes—in a mature personality structure, he reigns over the other archetypes, and brings order to the whole Self. But since the Magician's focus is inward, he is an introverted and withdrawn archetype.

Perhaps the clearest distinction can be made between the two in the context of sexual relations. The King is always in an intimate, erotic relationship with the Queen. The Magician, unlike the King, is rarely fully related to any feminine energy. The Magician archetype has its own contra-sexual component (see Appendix C), but a man who is possessed by the archetype rarely has a deep sexual involvement with a woman, and most usually is asexual. His androgyny offers him complete autonomy.[1] Some few shamans are and were gay. While this doesn't preclude a relationship with the Anima, homosexuality clearly renders a full relationship with a woman impossible. And of course, it precludes any offspring.

The Magician is split off, in the very essence of his structure, from full sexual expression. The man whose dominant archetype is the Magician experiences ecstasy primarily in his

73

mind and heart. He may also feel it in his body, contained and channeled through dance, song, or artistic expression. But he will not be able to experience sexual ecstasy. He will have his muse, as Dante had his Beatrice—but just as Dante never enjoyed her carnally, he will never experience full embodiment with a flesh and blood woman.

THE MAGICIAN'S BIPOLAR SHADOW

The Precocious Child demonstrates a young form of Magician energy.[2] The unusually gifted child may be either a socially outgoing overachiever, or extremely withdrawn and painfully shy. In traditional societies, gifted children are closely watched for signs of developing shamanistic capabilities.

The fully expressed archetype, even in a child, integrates and transcends its bipolar Shadow. Most often, however, we encounter its Shadow forms. The bipolar Shadow of the immature Magician manifests as the Trickster, on the one hand, and the Innocent on the other. These immature Shadow forms are often carried forward into the adult years. A man caught in the bipolar Shadow demonstrates internal psychological splitting, inordinate self-involvement, and dysfunctional behaviors. Maturity always involves the integration of psychic opposites and the transcendence of inner divisions.

The system of the bipolar Shadow we have delineated is analogous to the Adlerian realization that personality disorders appear in both passive and active modes. Our model also fits well with Hegelian thought, in which the universe moves forward through a process of thesis, antithesis, and synthesis. Alfred North Whitehead sees an "adventure of ideas" luring the created world forward in tiny increments he calls "occasions." These occasions interact with God (or an archetype, from a psychological perspective), resulting in a "creative advance." The Whitehead model of forward movement, like the Hegelian, is directly parallel to the action of the Ego, when it is able to integrate the warring opposites of the bipolar Shadow, and so transcend the Shadow system.

Most significantly our theory is in accord with Jung's conception of the *coniunctio oppositorum,* in which opposites are reconciled through the "transcendent function." Jung believed the Ego's essential task was to hold opposite points of view, opposite impulses, emotions, and imaginal realms, in tension, not allowing either pole of the dialectic to disappear into the unconscious. Eventually this titanic struggle, if held in consciousness and suffered and endured, would produce a transcendent third option that had not been felt or imagined before.

Our theory emphasizes—in a way that Jungian psychology since Jung has not—the vital importance of the Ego in relation to the dynamic archetypal structures. If the Ego is not properly accessing the archetype as a whole (including the bipolar Shadow, integrated into the archetype as a transcendent third), then the Ego will be possessed by the Shadow, and left oscillating between the Shadow's two poles. One pole will lead to "positive inflation," or the explosion of the Ego, and the other pole will cause the implosion of the Ego, or "negative inflation."

When the two poles are integrated into a transcendent third they lose their pathological impact. In their resulting fusion, their pathology is transformed into a creative advance—reminiscent of Saint Paul's Christ, whose death is "swallowed up in victory."

The key to this transformative experience is the action of the Ego. It must position itself for the maximum apprehension of the intimation of the archetype "above space and time," in the world of the "spirit," or the collective unconscious. The Ego acts like an attractive body, as do the three elements of the archetype, each exercising a kind of gravitational pull on the others.

In the collective unconscious the archetype is whole, with the Shadow fully integrated into it. The Ego functions properly as an occasion for the archetype's embodiment in space and time. In the fragmenting dimension of space and time, the archetype appears to the Ego largely in its bipolar Shadow form, communicating only intimations of its wholeness. The Ego must perceive the wholeness sufficiently well to keep it from mistaking the fragments of the Shadow for the archetype as a whole.

The bipolar Shadow is akin to the Symplegades—the Clashing Rocks between which the Ego must steer a middle course, guided by its intuition of the archetype, lest it be destroyed. If the middle course is managed, the Ego fashions the vital Ego-archetypal axis by which energy exchange is made possible. The Ego needs the lure of the archetype in order to experience creative advance. And the archetype needs the Ego in order to become augmented and enriched for future creative action in the world.

By the Ego's action the opposites of the bipolar Shadow can be reintegrated into the archetype as a whole. The Ego's methods for achieving this include analytical techniques such as dream interpretation and active imagination.

With the assistance of the Magician, intuitions and whole patterns arise in the Right Brain, and are translated into logical Left Brain arguments.[3] The Magician uses the Left Brain's technological and rational processes; from the Right Brain he marshals imaginative, intuitive, and inspirational energies.

None of the archetypes can be located in any one part of the brain. The Magician is manifested most fully in the shaman, who manages a balanced access of both hemispheres of the brain. As we've mentioned, research into modes of thought indicates that women tend to access the Right and

Left Brain more holistically than men do. The shaman too uses the modes of perception and thought equally—in some ways his *modus operandi* is more a woman's than a man's. Perhaps this accounts for his asexual, or occasionally homosexual, orientation.

THE SHAMAN AND SCHIZOID PHENOMENA

Some scholars have noted the similarity between the shaman's altered state of consciousness and schizophrenia. Others have noted the similarities, but pointed out crucial differences. It is true that the shaman's otherworldly journeys involve alien entities, both hostile and friendly. In psychological terms we would describe these aliens as entities "within" the unconscious, both collective and personal.

Perhaps the shaman's Ego consciousness resides in his Left Brain, and its forays are into the Right Brain. The entities would then be images produced by the Right Brain for the benefit of the voyaging Ego. The corpus callosum, the neuronal bridge between the Left and Right Brain, would become exceptionally activated, facilitating a flood of impulses between the two hemispheres.

Schizophrenics demonstrate just such a lowering of the natural inhibitions against left and right hemispheric communication. There is evidence that something similar may occur in those suffering multiple personality disorders. In *The Origins of Consciousness in the Breakdown of the Bicameral Mind*, controversial author Julian Jaynes links the mental processes of modern schizophrenics with the processes of our human ancestors before the development of Ego consciousness. He believes modern Ego consciousness began sometime in the ninth century B.C. Before this time he argues that all people, and particularly seers and prophets, experienced the

The Schizoid Magician: A Nyanga Tribesman of the Congo Wearing
the Mask of the Hornbill—His Bush Soul

nearly continuous eruption of Right Brain images and voices into Left Brain processes. In the absence of Ego consciousness, people lived their lives heeding directives from the voices of the Right Brain.

Those serving shamanic functions—the Oracle at Delphi, for example—were especially sensitive to these voices. They heard the "gods" in much the same way that modern schizophrenics hear their voices. Although aspects of Jaynes's theory are doubtful, it may well be that intuition and poetic inspiration are related to schizophrenic phenomena. We believe the dysfunctional Magician is definitely schizoid. He displays characteristics that, if pushed to an extreme, seem to invite schizophrenic traits.

Those who argue against an identification of schizophrenic and shamanic states of consciousness point out, with justification, that a schizophrenic's voices are almost always persecuting and hostile, whereas a shaman's visions are often positive and self-affirming. There is little question that a budding shaman undergoes severe psychological disruption, in which he often experiences himself as being dismembered and eaten by various gods or demons. He dies to his old mode of Ego consciousness and is reconstituted with the aid of "inner helpers." After this ferocious initiation he finds a more integrated method of being human. Unlike the schizophrenic, he retains his Ego; he becomes "the master of the spirits" rather than their passive victim.

It may be that any major life crisis involves a sudden and wrenching opening of communication between Left and Right Brain. If so, the altered state of consciousness that results is always marginally related to schizophrenic states of consciousness. But even so, the Magician archetype in its fullness actually frees the Ego from possession by the "gods," reconstituting Ego structures with the aid of "inner helpers," "power animals," and "spirit guides." Thereby the Ego grows stronger, with an enhanced sense of integrity and capability.

THE CONSTELLATION OF THE MAGICIAN

When the Magician is constellated in a man, several things happen. First of all, the man becomes a quester. He starts looking for a magus to guide him.

In *Close Encounters of the Third Kind*, Richard Dreyfuss plays the part of an ordinary man. He has his kids, his wife, and his pickup, and he's going along quite contentedly with his life, until he has an encounter with what Jung called the numinous—in his case a UFO that almost lands on his

79

truck. After that point his life is never the same again. He becomes a quester.

When you start on a quest, you may not have the slightest idea of what you are looking for. You are looking for the Magician. Some people travel through twenty or thirty cults looking for the real Magician. But the goal being sought isn't out there in the world, it is deep inside. And one of the purposes of an initiation is to teach that simple truth.

An initiatory sacred geography is the second phenomenon to unfold once the archetype of the Magician is constellated. Your whole life becomes structured according to the archetype of initiation. Once you become a quester, you embark on a pilgrimage in sacred geography, and you will remain on it until you have run the course.

The third thing to happen is the search for a transformative space. This transformative space is the place where an initiation can be completed, and a quester can be discharged from his quest. When people speak of a power spot, they are referring to a place in the sacred geography that is transformative. These places are special and rare, and this is why the shaman's role in locating, consecrating, and stewarding the energy of a transformative space was so vital to his people.

Under the guidance of the Magician energy, appropriately accessed, we can brave the perils of our inner worlds. Our "deaths" are preludes to our "rebirths" as we become more wholly human. In chapters to come we will explore the nature of the quester, his initiation, and the sacred spaces he is looking to discover.

IMAGES OF
THE MAGICIAN IN
MYTH AND HISTORY

I T USED TO BE THAT WE POINTED TO OUR CULTURAL heritage as being one of the things that made us unique among animals. Other animals were unable, we argued, to create and transmit a culture—their habits were solely attributable to instinct. But this criterion has fallen in recent years, along with so many of our other measures of our own niqeness.

Contemporary Japanese monkeys have achieved what can only be described as a cultural breakthrough.[1] Careful observers noted a number of years ago a single female making a major advance in food preparation. She came up with the

Haunting Presence: Adolescent Footprints in the Cave at Niaux
(Ariège, France, 10,000-plus B.C.)

idea of washing her food in the ocean before eating. After her discovery, she was seen instructing other members of the tribe in this new technique. Soon monkeys on other Japanese islands were doing the same thing.

Far to the west, African chimpanzees have been seen to strip the leaves from stems, then dip the stems into termite mounds in order to extract the insects.[2] The termites are a chimpanzee delicacy. The young eagerly watch their mothers' technique, and soon begin to experiment themselves. Some ancestral chimp obviously thought of using the stem tool, and implemented the new technology—and his tasty cultural innovation was then passed on to succeeding generations.

Language use and transmission has been argued to be another gift unique to humans. But chimpanzees, although they lack the biological equipment necessary to use verbal language, have been taught by humans to use sign language.[3] Some of these chimps have been seen teaching this form of communication to their young. They even have the ability to create language. One chimp, on seeing ducks on a pond for the first time, excitedly signed "water" and "bird," thus creating the word "waterbird," a description that was exactly correct.

If the Magician is the archetype of the knower and the technologist of power, his energy is demonstrably present in at least some of the other primates. He probably arose in the psyche of our species in a very remote, prehuman past.

The Lascaux caves of southern France offer the earliest known tangible evidence of human psychospirituality. They are filled with lush, vibrant representations of the animals that filled the imaginations of the Paleolithic hunters. The care with which these magnificent beasts are rendered gives us some hint of the psychological and spiritual relationship our distant ancestors felt they had with them.

Many scholars have interpreted the caves as sanctuaries dedicated to masculine rites of initiation. Certainly the majority of the painted figures illustrate masculine concerns, and the few human beings represented are almost always men. Some are the shamanistic birdmen we described in the Introduction.

However, as Riane Eisler rightly points out in her book *The Chalice and the Blade,* figurines of what appears to be a Mother Goddess also abound in these caves. She raises the question of just how exclusively these caves were devoted to male interests. But she minimizes unnecessarily the clear evidence that the caves were used by a male hunting culture headed by a male shaman.

If we add to the evidence the caves offer us the circumstantial evidence that the primary deity is male in most primitive cultures even to this day—from the Australian aborigines to most African tribes—then we will not make the mistake of undervaluing the role of a masculine God in the Old Stone Age religion.[4] It seems perfectly plausible to imagine that Paleolithic peoples understood that both masculine and feminine principles were essential for the realization of abundance and fertility in the human and natural worlds.[5]

We may suppose a remote, invisible sky father played an important role in the early religion, beside a visible, tangible earth mother. She was represented in concrete form because her earthly realm was also palpable. He was represented only by hints and signs, because of the dangers inherent in rendering the ineffable. And perhaps the clay figures of the Mother Goddess were used to teach the boys the secrets of sexuality. It would be no surprise to see an Earth Mother present in ceremonies held by the ancient hunters. An ancient shamanic consciousness might understand the cave sanctuaries as the womb and birth canal of Mother Earth, and use them as sanctuaries for the initiation of boys into manhood—a process by which the boys are essentially "reborn" from the earth's womb.[6]

When we turn to primitive societies that have survived

into the modern era, we see abundant evidence of Magician energy. From the African savannas to the rain forests of Brazil, from northern snow-blanketed Asia to Australia's deserts— everywhere we look, we see shamans, magicians, rainmakers, and medicine men.[7] Their functions are more or less the same, though one culture's emphasis may be on engineering fertility, and another's on helping dead spirits move confidently into the afterlife. What is remarkable is the universality of sha- manic phenomena, as an expression of the Magician arche- type. In one way or another, the Magician has everywhere inspired our species to journey within, reflect, conserve, and create. He has taught us to guide and steward our precious psychic energy in order to ensure harmony within ourselves, and without, in nature.

HISTORIC MAGICIANS

The first historical example we have of the embodied Magician is that of the ancient Egyptian vizier, Imhotep (circa 2800 B.C.).[8] Chief counsel to Djoser, a Second Dynasty pharaoh, Imhotep was a powerful healer and physician. His medical innovations were so staggering to ancient peoples that he even- tually was deified. The Greeks knew him as the god Asklepios.

Imhotep was, besides being the greatest healer of his era, the architect of sacred space and time. He designed King Djoser's magnificent "city of the dead" at Saqqara on the Nile's west bank, and oversaw the building. Here was built a miniature city, complete with storehouses, houselike tombs, a racecourse, and paved streets, all centered around the first fully developed pyramid tomb of the ancient world. This as- tounding achievement in monumental architecture was com- pletely covered in gleaming white limestone, and surrounded by a beautifully appointed wall.

The Saqqara complex was sacred as a microcosmic repre-

Imhotep as a Boy Scribe

sentation of the universe. Within its precincts, death was returned to life. King Djoser ran here his periodic *heb sed* race to demonstrate his continuing vigor, and thus his fitness to continue his kingship. He was reinvigorated at the same time by accompanying magical rituals. After his death, Djoser was laid to rest in the pyramid—a limestone representation of the rays of the sun, the Egyptian "stairway to heaven." At the sacred time of renewal, Imhotep affirmed his power to transform the pharaoh's mummy into spirit.

Imhotep was not alone in working the feats of magic that created civilization. Every ancient civilization had its wizards and sorcerers, its astrologers, astronomers, philosophers, and theologians, its metallurgists, architects, chemists, and physicists. Egyptian literature abounds with short stories that celebrate the exploits of famed magicians. Babylonian wizards were known far and wide. The Persian magi later completely transformed the cultures and religions of the entire Near East. Their impact on the worlds of Greece and Rome was profound, and through that channel they have influenced all subsequent flowering of Western civilization.[9]

The Bible's Samuel, Elijah, and Elisha are all shamanic figures. After their miraculous births, they hear an inner voice they identify as Yahweh or Elohim. They perform great feats of magic—calling fire down from an empty sky, for example, or raising the dead—and their deaths are occasions of great mystery. In Elijah's case, he was lifted bodily into the heavens in a fiery chariot. The biblical prophets were likewise inspired by Magician energy, which offered remarkable insight into human nature, the contemporary world situation, and perhaps even the future. Like others in the shamanic tradition, they recorded much of their oracular material in metered verse.

Jesus is the greatest biblical magician of all. Though not part of the canonical tradition, there are stories of the boy Jesus making clay birds and transforming them into real birds, which flew off praising their creator. As an adult he multiplied loaves and fishes, turned water into wine, healed the sick, calmed storms, walked on water, drove demons out of people, and even raised the dead to life. He passed on a reinterpreted mythological heritage of his people, as shamans often do. And his parables, while not poetry by conventional standards, were certainly lyrical in composition and content. In the end he performed the greatest disappearing act in history, leaving his tomb empty for the generations to ponder. Like many shamans, he took the illnesses of his people upon himself, and was killed because of his self-sacrificial efforts. And then, like many magicians before him, he was deified.

In the Greek mystery religions, the Magician-guided

Dionysian Mysteries: The Drama of Initiation from the Villa of the
Mysteries (outside Pompeii)

initiatory process became the central theme. Men and women
of all ages were brought face to face with the deep mysteries
of life and death in secret rites honoring Demeter, the earth
Goddess. Forced to face their own mortality, initiates achieved
a wiser, more profound maturity. They were sobered and
enlivened through exposure to the mechanisms of the human
psyche.

Though the initiated were sworn to secrecy, Plutarch left
a limited account of the proceedings behind him. Without
knowing the specifics of the ceremony, we do know this much:

> . . . the candidates were made to roam through winding
> subterranean passages. It was a peregrination through the
> dark, a journey to an invisible end, which put to the test
> all one's presence of mind. And then, at the moment of
> decision, the initiates were subjected to terrors. They
> experienced shudders and trembling, they sweated with
> fear and were paralyzed with terror, until light was gradu-
> ally admitted, and the day restored. With sacred chants
> and dancing choruses a magnificent place opened before
> them . . . The initiated was crowned with garlands, and

by the side of pure and holy men he enjoyed the festival of rebirth.[10]

We find here again the use of an underground journey as a symbol for rebirth out of the earth's womb. Caves are used so often in initiation practices throughout the world it would seem the metaphor of cave as womb is an archetypal one. Initiation is a matter of dying to an outmoded Ego structure, so that a wiser one can be formed; luckily for the Greeks their mystery rites were stewarded by ritual elders who worked carefully to pass their wisdom on.

The Magician is on intimate terms with death. He is the guide of souls; as the shaman he is the rescuer of lost souls. He also knows the deep secret—hidden at the wellspring of all things—that out of death comes life, renewed, transformed, and triumphant.

Beginning at the time of Christ, and continuing for the next several centuries, a Christian movement known as Gnosticism developed from earlier Hermetic traditions.[11] Hermes had been a Greek God, the "conductor of souls." Signposts along a road were once known as "herms." Gnostic texts rest on the conviction that matter is evil, and emancipation is attainable only through knowledge, or *gnosis*. In their reliance on a purely mental means of salvation, Gnostics show themselves powerfully influenced by the Magician. Their sacred texts rely upon a deep introversion, a profound self-reflection, and a conviction that enlightenment lies within. Jung thought of the Gnostics as forerunners of modern depth psychology.

The Catholic Church persecuted adherents of the Gnostic faith until their traditions disappeared. However, their ideas resurfaced from time to time in the "heresies" of the European Middle Ages. Some scholars argue for an unbroken Gnostic tradition, kept alive through the efforts of individuals passing books and practices down through the centuries; peri-

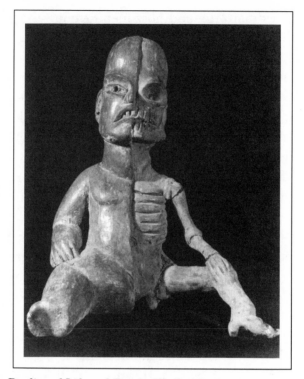

The Duality of Life and Death: Tlatilco Sculpture from Ancient
Mexico

odically, these scholars argue, the teachings reached a larger
audience and full-scale movements (such as the Albigensian
heresy) developed out of them. Others note the similarities
between various heretical outbreaks, but argue that they occurred in isolation from one another—what was similar was
the archetypal forces behind the heresies, and not the heresies
themselves. Regardless of which history is true, the Magician
energy was clearly an important part of these underground
movements.

The Magician also played an important part in the occult
traditions, which continued to be secretly practiced throughout European history. Eventually the Magician publicly di-

rected the Church's emerging Scholastic movement, and privately continued to influence the beliefs of the alchemists.

The stories of Merlin, the legendary British wizard, offer a glimpse into the way the Magician was venerated by the folk but abhorred by the Church in medieval Europe. The Merlin stories present a composite figure drawn from accounts of various Druidic shamans. The Druids were the priests of the Celtic pre-Christian religion, who survived more or less publicly for a time into the Christian era. They were the knowers of the mysterious powers of nature, the keepers of astronomical and astrological lore—Stonehenge was one of their shrines, built to mark and celebrate the seasons and the solstices—and the guardians of the forests and peoples of Britain and Gaul.[12]

Stonehenge was said to have been Merlin's project. A huge boundary of megaliths surrounds a sacred space, in whose center stands a stone altar. Another stone is situated in the perimeter so that, at dawn on the solstice, the sun's rays pass up along this stone and finally break over the top of it to illuminate the central altar. We can only imagine what kind of sacrifice or ceremony was performed on the altar at that powerful moment. Merlin was given credit for the conception of the shrine, and for engineering the cutting, transportation, and erection of the stones.

The enormous, impossibly heavy stones were quarried at a site far removed from Stonehenge, and had to be transported across England on the ground, since there was no river between the two locations. Many different possible schemes have been proposed to account for the transportation of the stones. Legend has it, of course, that Merlin transported them magically.

In the Arthurian legends Merlin is credited as the genius behind Camelot, the English paradigm for paradise on earth. It was Merlin who brought design to the seasons, and who inspired Arthur to bring law and order to his anarchic land,

Stonehenge

and introduce to his court the civilized customs of chivalry. Most tales of Camelot show a deep reverence for Merlin.

Some versions of the story, though, give a harsher, Christian, and depreciating portrait of the old magician. In some he appears to be an ineffectual, bumbling old fool, and in others he seems little better than a shadow magician, whose diabolical schemes devastate the kingdom. In T. H. White's beautiful, melancholy retellings of the Arthurian legends, Merlin appears alternately as a well-intentioned but absentminded buffoon and an irritable, bitter old man. But Merlin still works his magic on our imaginations today. And the sacred perfection of Camelot still draws us to a vision of a sublime way of being human, inspired and guided by the powers of the Magician.

Merlin and Arthur at Stonehenge

The alchemists relied very heavily on the Magician's powers. While initially their interest was in finding a way to turn
baser stuffs into gold, they very soon determined to effect also
an inner integration. Their thinking was that they would be
unable to successfully transform and purify metals until they
had first transformed and purified themselves. They engaged
in esoteric ceremonies learned from the Gnostics and the occultists, whose ultimate purpose was more focused on the
integration of the various psychic entities encountered in the
imaginal realm than on the furtherance of chemical science.
They encountered the energy levels at the deepest layers of the
psyche—where the "power animals" and "spirits" of the shamanic traditions reside, or the archetypes and complexes of

93

modern psychology—and attempted to bring about the "chymical wedding," a marriage of inner and outer opposites. Through this wedding, material gold emerges just as surely as the gold of the soul, or Self.

One of the real chemical discoveries of the alchemists was due to this research into opposites. Some believed that potential gold would be found only in a materially opposite substance, and so Brandt, a burgher of Hamburg (d. 1692),[13] made concerted efforts to investigate, separate, and distill the components of urine—discovering phosphorus in the process.

The Jews of medieval Europe also took strength from the Magician.[14] The same energy that had once influenced their developing laws, customs, and theologies inspired them to continue the sciences of the Greek philosophers, which eventually led to the practices of the Kabbalah. As the Jewish Talmud was compiled—remarkable interpretive texts which were in themselves an outpouring of Magician energy—there also arose an intricate and profound study of the human psyche. The Kabbalah, as this study became known, paralleled and surpassed the work of the Gnostics, the occultists, and the alchemists.

In common with the Gnostics, the Kabbalists believed there to be tremendous inherent power in certain words and incantations. They believed the Old Testament was a symbolic text behind whose parables lay revelatory knowledge. Nothing was taken at face value; everything referred to something beyond itself. This tradition probably grew from a cultural background of magical incantations—words that were believed to be so powerful in certain contexts that they could make things happen.

Every passage in the Old Testament was believed to hold a code, which a subtle enough mind could detect. For the Kabbalists salvation lay in tremendous intellectual effort. As had happened with alchemy, the Kabbalah led its adherents to an exploration of the hidden layers of the psyche. Whether or not their original foundation was a solid one, in their delineation and invocation of the ten "aspects" of God, the kabbalists were investigating for themselves the archetypes in the collective unconscious.

Though ardently suppressed by the rationalizing rabbis of the eighteenth and nineteenth centuries, the kabbalistic tradition persisted in Eastern Europe until the early days of the twentieth century. For an excellent popular representation of this Jewish shamanic tradition as it had become at the turn of the century, see the Isaac Bashevis Singer story "The Magician," or the movie of the same name.

Yoshi (who bears the same name as Jesus—Yeshua in Hebrew) is a stage magician at the opening of the movie. He yearns like the kabbalists to know from God, as he says, "how you do it." He wants to experience the divine magic of creation, of real transformation and re-creation. Yoshi is also a would-be inventor. As we've seen, an interest in technology is another of the aspects of the Magician. Yoshi spends his free time and his extra money trying to build and fly primitive airplanes.

After a series of personal and professional disasters Yoshi becomes an ascetic, bricking himself up in a hut from which there is no exit. He builds the stone hut around himself, leaving only a small window in one wall. Through this he receives his meager meals, and offers counsel and insight to those who come seeking his wisdom and healing.

In the final, gripping scene, a woman and her son visit Yoshi. Believing themselves to have been wronged by him, they rain accusations down upon him. They incite some of the villagers to riot. The mob goes to work against Yoshi's hut. Block by block it comes crashing down. Yoshi's wife and his friends try to intervene, but they are pushed out of the way. When the last wall of the hut is destroyed, amid the rubble, the mob finds—no one!

Yoshi has performed the greatest trick of all, one that

harks back to the paintings in the Paleolithic caves. As the crowd stands in the ruins of his cell, a flock of wild geese flies overhead. One goose calls loudly, and Yoshi's wife looks heavenward, her face registering anguish and amazement. Like all good shamans, Yoshi has ascended into the heavens. He has become a birdman! He has realized his dream of flying through the spiritual technology of the soul.

Native American cultures were replete with shamans. We are fortunate to have a record of one of the last great shamans of the Oglala Sioux, the now famous Black Elk. Black Elk felt he must find an interpreter to record and "save his Great Vision for men," and he found him in John G. Neihardt.[15] Neihardt presents a series of interviews with this great shaman, in which Black Elk tells of the course of his life, and of the unfolding of the shamanic calling and consciousness within him.

Black Elk relates his early illnesses and revelatory visions, which culminated in his "Great Vision." In this vision he saw revealed to him, among other things, the structure of the universe and the nature of divine beings. Through voices and visual hallucinations he was commissioned as a shaman. The cosmic grandfathers, as Neihardt records, handed Black Elk a wooden cup:

> . . . and it was full of water and in the water was the sky. "Take this," the Grandfather said. "It is the power to make live, and it is yours."
> Now he had a bow in his hands. "Take this," he said. "It is the power to destroy, and it is yours."[16]

Black Elk, like every shaman (and every mystic), came to see the most closely guarded secret of all.

> I saw more than I can tell and I understood more than I saw; for I was seeing in a sacred manner the shapes of all

Black Elk

things in the spirit, and the shape of all shapes as they must live together like one being. And I saw that the sacred hoop of my people was one of many hoops that made one circle, wide as daylight and as starlight, and in the center grew one mighty flowering tree to shelter all the children of one mother and father. And I saw that it was holy.[17]

Within a few years of Black Elk's Great Vision, in a wholly different cultural context, the Magician energy surfaced in two new sciences that managed between them to completely overturn European assumptions about reality. Just as society finally absorbed the teachings of the materialistic scientists, which proclaimed that all there was to reality was contained in a three-dimensional spatiotemporal universe, work by the pioneers of depth psychology and subatomic physics demonstrated the opposite to be true. Their message was an ancient one, one every shaman, medicine man, and parlor magician has always known: "Things are not at all what they seem!"

The new discoveries of subatomic physics revealed that the apparently solid material world is really a grand illusion, made up of energy fields and time-space warps in which wave/particles and quanta of energy manifest transiently and for undiscoverable reasons.[18] Einstein—perhaps the greatest magician in this magic show—demonstrated that time and space are aspects of the same phenomenon, and that both are defined by movement. He proved time/space to be a flexible, malleable thing. His work led to colleagues' mathematically determined discoveries of the possibilities of other dimensions, worm holes, and black holes; and of other universes, perhaps millions of them, which flourish in expanding bubbles in a time/space very different from our own.

Soon the magicians were put to work at Los Alamos,

En-lighten-ment?: The Power of the Magician

running the cosmic clock backward billions of years in an effort to re-create the processes at work deep in the interior of stars. Robert Oppenheimer, their leader, was profoundly shaken as he witnessed the first atomic bomb detonated in the desert darkness. In that supernal flash of unthinkable light and heat, Oppenheimer recalled the lines of a shaman-poet, one who had foreseen such an event in the depths of his inner wanderings—the shaman who had written the *Bhagavad-Gita*, "The Song of God."

> Time I am, the destroyer of the worlds, and I have come to engage all people . . .

During the same era, Sigmund Freud's researches into the inner world of the human psyche confirmed that not everything was as simple as it appeared to be. Freud was the first to

Freud

pursue a systematic probing of the unconscious. The general public soon was fascinated to learn that motives are often not what they are claimed to be, and that the "I" once thought of as a whole personality is no more than the tip of an iceberg that extends far down into layers of a soul as deep, dark, and mysterious as the ocean.

Consciously or not, Freud took what was formerly an occult preserve—dream interpretation—and extended its means and its precision. He also "divined" the hidden meanings of the accidental things we say (accidents we now know as "Freudian slips"). As Freud explored the mysterious and regenerative world within, he became an adventurer, like the shaman, into the unseen dimensions of reality. He was the steward, in his analytic practice, of the sacred space and time of the subconscious. He became a kind of "soul guide," like the ritual elder of a traditional society, one helping to initiate immature and fragmented human beings into adulthood. This modern magician, significantly, kept a statuette of the Egyptian Imhotep on his desk, to whom, it is said, he often talked. Perhaps it was from Imhotep that Freud heard the oracles that often inspired him.

Freud's younger colleague, Carl Jung, took the exploration of inner space and time much further than had his mentor. Jung discovered complex structures in the unconscious, which he called archetypes. These corresponded to the "demons" and "angels" of another age. Jung's intelligence was inclusive and inquisitive, and his interests in the supernatural, in paranormal psychic experience, world mythology, Eastern spirituality, dreams, and world social and political events were all embraced by his comprehensive and deeply spiritual exegesis of the human psyche. He ended up providing, through his psychology, a bridge between the humanities and the sciences. Also connected and related in his work are the spiritual traditions of our species, our biology, and our traditions of gnostic and occultic practice. Through his discoveries of the basic structures and dynamics of the psyche—which finally went far beyond Freud's—the Magician energy that inspired this "wise old man" enabled us to understand ourselves in our modern context. For the first time in the modern age of scientific faith we were able to reclaim the powers of the observing Ego, to detach ourselves from our possessing complexes, to develop insulation for ourselves against the numinosity of the archetypes while finding creative ways to access them.

Several independent innovators, and a host of schools of psychology, have followed the lead of these two modern magicians. Among the most insightful and helpful psychological thinkers are Alice Miller, Heinz Kohut and D. W. Winnicott, all psychoanalytic self-psychologists, and psychoanalyst Erik Erikson, who left to us his conception of the "generative man."[19]

A renewed popular interest in the occult has accompanied the discoveries of these psychological thinkers. Beginning in the mid-nineteenth century, and accelerating up to the present moment, a general interest has been demonstrated in everything from astral projections to séances, tarot cards to Zen. Many ordinary Westerners have begun to journey inward. Bankers, stockbrokers, insurance salespeople, and politicians have joined the Theosophists, the Neo-Pagans, the Scientologists, or other groups; a plethora of new religions have sprung up, along with "support groups" for every conceivable movement and circle.

One of the hallmarks of these alternative psychoreligious organizations is an interest in and an appreciation—though practiced with differing levels of wisdom and sophistication—for sacred space and time, ritual elders, and the initiatory process. Mircea Eliade, a great scholar of comparative religion and mythology, pointed to initiation as the underlying dynamic of human life, the process that lends life meaning and dignity. Eliade believed there to be an absence of sacred space in modern life, and he attributed our modern malaise to this. We think he was wrong, that there is sacred space available to us, because it is a part of our archetypal wiring; our problem is more in knowing what to do with it than in not having it at all.

Although the leaders of many of these alternative groups and religions may have more in common with the sorcerer's apprentice than the sorcerer, still these groups show some connection to the deep psychospiritual processes of the soul. This is a connection most establishment churches and synagogues have long since lost. In their attempts to come to terms with the prevalent worship of science and rationalism of the modern era, most establishment religions have lost their essential spirituality and purpose. This is why so many people have turned away from established religion, and often toward occult movements.

Modernity has left its acculturated citizens cut off from their psychological depths. Because of this they are denied the wellspring of creative life. Modernity collapses all experience into one space/time dimension, ignores anything that cannot be apprehended by the five senses—or the scientific instruments that extend them—and will not come to grips, despite all of the evidence amassed over the past ninety years, with the reality of the collective unconscious behind the Ego.

Modernity has reduced sacred space and time to a two-week Caribbean cruise. Bar and bas mitzvahs and confirmation classes are the only remaining relics of our ancestral sacred rites of initiation. Dreams have been reduced to the electrochemical discharges of the "sleep centers" in the brain. With nothing but a material world to live in, modernity has made religions of consumerism and materialism. While our modern era is possessed by the Magician as knower and technologist, his knowledge and his technologies are limited to material forms and material energies.

As we'll see, the Magician may always have a tendency to become schizoid, and split himself off from the realm of deep feeling. We have seen modernity carry this tendency to its logical extreme, and we see the Shadow Magician's energy running wild. The threats of nuclear destruction, ecological devastation, and the mass extinctions of other species hang heavily over our heads. The "power shadow" of the Magician in his negative, manipulative, and destructive aspect has unleashed forces he is unable to control.

But we are moment by moment moving into a postmodern world. Heralded by the rise of depth psychology, subatomic physics, and occultic practices, there has begun a revaluing of the unseen world, a reappropriation of sacred time and space, a reconnection to the power of images and symbols, and a renewed commitment to the healing process. Spurred by sensitive and insightful popular books, like Carlos Castañeda's "studies" of Yaqui Indian spirituality, there is a growing interest in the shaman. And as we've said, the shaman is the fullest expression of Magician energy in human life. He signals new possibilities for achieving greater wholeness as individuals, and as a species. With him present to locate and steward sacred time and space, perhaps we'll finally find a place where "all shapes . . . live together like one being."

5

UNDERSTANDING
SACRED SPACE
AND TIME

A CENTRAL DYNAMIC OF THE MAGICIAN'S WORK IN the world is his location, consecration, and stewardship of sacred space and time. With the Magician's help we see that space and time are not uniform. Space and time are lumpy, not smooth and homogenous. There are places and moments that carry an extraordinary emotional charge. The Magician adventures into these charged places and times, and shows us how to experience them in a positive and regenerative way.

Arnold van Gennep was the first to talk about this heterogeneity of space and time. He noticed the phenomenon in the course of his studies of the anthropology of primitive peoples,

maybe
but
w/
Paths
Beyond
Ego

Facing the Mystery: Sumerian Statuette from Tello

(beginning twenty-first century B.C.)

That is late for Sumerian?

specifically in the context of their *rites de passage*. He observed that these rites, elaborated and dramatized by religious rituals, marked one of the major life transitions of all human beings—from childhood to adulthood.

Mircea Eliade identified these adolescent rites of passage as more specialized instances of what he regarded as the primary, all-pervasive impulse of all human life. He called the dynamic by which human beings continue to move forward throughout the course of their lives "initiation." Joseph Campbell popularized Eliade's idea of the initiatory process, and framed the idea with others from the field of depth psychology in his book *The Hero with a Thousand Faces*.

Victor Turner added further understanding to our anthropological conception of the *rites de passage* to which all our lives are subject. Though scholars once defined the rites as taking place in the passage from childhood to adulthood, they soon confirmed what is actual human experience: that the initiatory scenario is played out again and again throughout our lives, at different stages, from birth to death, and perhaps beyond.

Initiation into a richer, deeper, more mature way of being human always occurs in sacred time and space. Eliade noted that premodern peoples all recognized the heterogenous, multidimensional nature of reality. According to him, these peoples experienced two basic forms of reality. The day-to-day form Eliade called "profane," hence the other—the mind-bending, gut-wrenching form—was termed "sacred." Because "profane" now carries so much negative baggage, we will call this familiar reality "ordinary." Likewise at times we will call "sacred" reality "extraordinary."

There is a fantasy common to our times which equates "sacred" with "pleasant." The well-known Christian hymn "In the Garden" is an older version of this same fantasy. But an experience in sacred time and space is often anything but

107

pleasant. To a primitive, any time is "sacred"—of the Gods—if it is out of the ordinary. They believed the world was always running down, and needed periodic infusions of sacred energy to remain in existence. Thus their forays into sacred space offered not merely an initiatory experience, but also a concrete way of helping the world to stay alive.

Extraordinary reality does at times become wonderful—if it doesn't kill us. But it is often at first disorienting and terrifying. All of the deep spiritual traditions know this, as do those few brave individuals who undergo an analysis, or some other form of in-depth, self-reflective psychotherapy. We can move into extraordinary reality in several ways, and once inside of this sacred dimension we encounter a variety of serious psychological perils, which like a snake's venom offer a potential for healing along with their particular dangers.

Turner identified two kinds of sacred space. The first he called *liminal*, from the Latin word for threshold, *limen*. The second he called *liminoid*, by which he meant quasi-liminal. From a psychological perspective liminal space is initially deconstructive. It dissolves our previous expectations as to ways of experiencing ourselves and our relationship to the world. Then it offers us a new vision of ourselves and our relationships. We are regenerated, recreated almost from the bottom up, as new, more fully integrated and mature people.

Liminoid space on the other hand may refresh us and recharge our batteries, but it will not transform us. Idyllic vacations take place in a kind of liminoid space. They are truly out of the ordinary but do nothing to change our lives.

Sacred space and time always carry a charge of Libido. Bearing an uprush of unconscious archetypal material, sacred reality can devastate an Ego if not adequately contained and managed. Before it becomes healing—which it does only under optimal conditions, when stewarded by a magician—it makes a person crazy. We all know the craziness of contact with the sacred dimension, from the death of a loved one, the loss of an important job, or a separation or divorce.

There is no way to live a human life without occasional excursions into extraordinary reality. Ancient peoples were aware of this, and they ritualized their "crazy time," hedging it around with ceremony and physical and psychological boundaries. When a person suffered a loss, he was made taboo. His neighbors avoided him. They knew he was likely to be acting erratically, and so wanted no part of his energy—after all, he was particularly susceptible to being possessed by animal spirits. By these means the energy was contained, so that it could be transformed, with the help of a tribal shaman, into a regenerative energy rather than a destructive one. Inadequate insulation of the Ego, and inadequate management of the powerful forces of sacred reality, lead to chronic liminality and insanity.

The ancient Sumerians had an interesting way of illustrating and restructuring their recognition of those moments when a human life moves from ordinary into extraordinary reality. The Oriental Institute of Chicago houses a remarkable collection of Sumerian statuettes. There in the darkened halls, after passing through a reconstruction of the Babylonian Ishtar Gate, one encounters a collection of strangely posed figurines. These representations of Sumerian men and women (circa 3000 B.C.) stand in an attitude of prayer, legs together, hands clasped before them, composed and centered. All of their energy and attention is directed at one unseen reality.

Their most startling attribute—more arresting even than their intense concentration—is the expression in their eyes. These are crazy eyes, eyes filled with wonder and terror. They are huge, wide open, staring unblinkingly at something we cannot see. We can imagine what they are looking at, because we know that these statuettes represented actual individuals, and were placed in the hearts of the Sumerian temples, in the midst of sacred reality. The statuettes aspired not merely to symbolize, but actually to be the souls of those men and women. Kept in the continuous presence of sacred space and time, they served to infuse the energy of the extraordinary into the day-to-day lives of individuals as they pursued their mundane desires and wishes outside the temple precincts.

The expressions on the faces of these statuettes, especially their eyes, graphically portray how human beings respond to "crossing the threshold" into the extraordinary domain. The same dual response of terror and wonder is present in the expressions and body language of modern people undergoing a psychotherapeutic process. The same communication with the ineffable occurs as these analysands lay bare the foundations of their souls in order to be transformed.

In the premodern world sacred space was never created. It was always discovered by some unusually gifted, intuitive person. That person was the magician, who was skilled at interpreting omens and signs from the divine beings who dwelt just behind the veil of the material universe. Here and there, as they broke through that veil and revealed themselves, the magician was present as a witness.

Ancient cities were sacred spaces, usually roughly (and sometimes precisely) circular by design, with the palace-temple complex always located at the circle's center.[1] Thus the King dwelt at the organizing center, from which the created world radiates. Sacred mountains, sacred trees, and inner sanctums all were the "power spots" through which an energy exchange took place between the various dimensions of reality. The center was always bounded and contained by impregnable walls or "magic circles" or some other device designed to separate ordinary from extraordinary time and space.

All of our experience of sacred space and territoriality is really a projection of our own inner realms onto the outer world. All of our encounters with "crazy time" and the demons and angels that inhabit it occur within our own psyches. Thus in order to find our own individual centers we need to be able to access the inner Magician. When we allow ourselves to be guided by his wisdom and his technological expertise, we can each find our way to the center of our own inner realm. Every man has the right, and the responsibility, to do this.

THE DYNAMIC STRUCTURE OF SACRED REALITY

The three stages that follow the constellation of the Magician archetype have been described by all the scholars of initiation. Eliade speaks of a wearing down of profane time, the entrance into sacred time, and then the reenactment of archetypal cosmogonic processes.[2] Campbell speaks in parallel of the Call, the Belly of the Whale, and the Return.[3] Using more technical language, Turner describes structure, liminality, and the reconstruction of structure (or status enhancement).[4] The following figures will illustrate how these different terminologies of the initiatory scenario clearly map onto one another; they are three different ways of saying the same thing.

Other traditions offer the same insight. There are three phases to initiation into Zen Buddhism. Zen masters teach that before enlightenment, a mountain is only a mountain. During enlightenment the mountain is no longer a mountain. After enlightenment, the mountain is once again only a mountain. The initiation ends with a return to the ordinary. Though every cherished notion may for a time be completely overturned, the facts of the world do eventually reassert themselves once a strengthened, wiser Ego is formed.

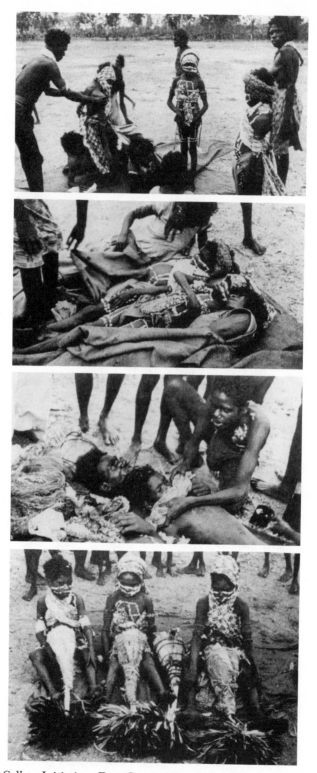

The Call to Initiation: Four Stages in an Australian Aborigine Rite

Figure 1

THE ARCHETYPE OF INITIATION

PHASE I	Pilgrimage PHASE II	PHASE III
Ordinary Consciousness/ Life-World Morbidity	Ordinary Consciousness/ Life-World Destruction; encounter with transcendent power and its agents	Reconstitution of Ordinary Consciousness; Life-World in renewed, reintegrated form
van Gennep: Separation	Transition	Incorporation
Turner: Structure I—Preliminal State I	Antistructure—Liminal Transition—Communitas (varying degrees of communitas, whether liminal or liminoid)	Structure II—Post-liminal State II
Campbell: Familiar Life—The Call Tyrant Holdfast	The Descent into the Zone of Magnified Power	The Return with Boon that Restores the World
Eliade: Profane Time/Space I World Deterioration (the terror of history)	Sacred Time/Space Journey to the Center	Profane Time/Space II
Freud: Fixation-development off of schedule	Return of the Repressed	Attainment of a more mature psychosexual stage
Contemporary Occultists Significance Hunger Malignant Discouragement	The Quest Ordeals, etc. Danger of pseudoinitiation and chronic liminality	Adepthood-empowered for Creativity and Significant Service
Crisis (e.g., loss of spouse through death or divorce) Realization of need for Analysis (before therapy session)	Grief Process Analytical environment as vessel or container (therapy session)	Reintegration and new Adaptation Post-Analysis Adaptation (after therapy session)
Call to worship	Sacred Time/Space	Reentry into Daily Lives

Invocation | Confession | Benediction | Recessional

Submission, resignation, surrender of autonomy, denial of agency, degradation mechanisms

Exaltation (relative)—status enhancement, reappropriation of enhanced autonomy, affirmation of agency, status dramatization

Figure 2

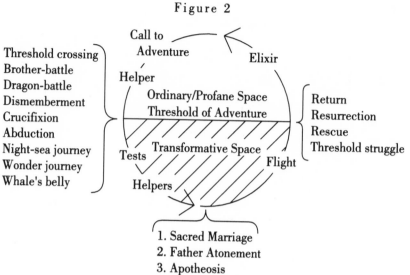

Threshold crossing
Brother-battle
Dragon-battle
Dismemberment
Crucifixion
Abduction
Night-sea journey
Wonder journey
Whale's belly

Call to Adventure

Helper

Ordinary/Profane Space
Threshold of Adventure

Tests

Transformative Space

Helpers

Elixir

Return
Resurrection
Rescue
Threshold struggle

Flight

1. Sacred Marriage
2. Father Atonement
3. Apotheosis
4. Elixir Theft

Figure 3

TURNER'S CATEGORIES RELATED TO THE CULT EXPERIENCE*

PSYCHOSOCIAL STATE PRIOR TO TRANSITION	TRANSITION	PSYCHOSOCIAL STATE AFTER TRANSITION
MOVEMENT THROUGH NORMAL TRANSITIONS		
Partiality	Totality	Partiality
Heterogeneity	Homogeneity	Heterogeneity
Structure	Communitas	Structure
Inequality	Equality	Inequality
Systems of nomenclature	Anonymity	Systems of nomenclature
Property	Absence of property	Property
Status	Absence of status	Status
Distinctions of clothing	Nakedness or uniform clothing	Distinctions of clothing
Sexuality in marriage and family context	Sexual continence or community	Sexuality in marriage and family context
Maximization of sex distinctions	Minimization of sex distinctions	Maximization of sex distinctions
Distinctions of rank	Absence of rank	Distinctions of rank

Figure 3

TURNER'S CATEGORIES RELATED TO THE CULT EXPERIENCE*

PSYCHOSOCIAL STATE PRIOR TO TRANSITION	TRANSITION	PSYCHOSOCIAL STATE AFTER TRANSITION
Just pride of position	Humility	Just pride of position
Care for personal appearance	Disregard for personal appearance	Care for personal appearance
Distinctions of wealth	No distinction of wealth	Distinctions of wealth
Selfishness	Unselfishness	Selfishness
Obedience only to superior rank	Total obedience	Obedience only to superior rank
Secularity	Sacredness	Secularity
Technical knowledge	Sacred instruction	Technical knowledge
Speech	Silence	Speech
Kinship rights and obligations	Suspension of kinship rights and obligations	Kinship rights and obligations
Intermittent reference to mystical powers	Continuous reference to mystical powers	Intermittent reference to mystical powers
Sagacity	Foolishness	Sagacity
Complexity	Simplicity	Complexity
Avoidance of pain and suffering	Acceptance of pain and suffering	Avoidance of pain and suffering
Degrees of autonomy	Heteronomy	Degrees of autonomy

EXAMPLES OF APPLICATIONS IN MODERN INDUSTRIAL SOCIETIES

Period prior to significant personal loss	Period of mourning—grief process	Reintegration into society after grieving is complete
Settled period of early adulthood	Midlife crisis	Entry into middle adulthood
Period prior to difficulties in early adult transition	Entry into a cult (normal liminality)	Return to ordinary life outside the group
	-or-	-or-
	Remain chronically liminal, unable to reenter structure	Status hierarchy of the group begins to function for the individual as structure

*Adapted from Victor Turner, *The Ritual Process* (Ithaca, N.Y.: Cornell University Press, 1977), p. 106. Used with permission.

Figure 4
DEVELOPMENTAL PERIODS IN THE MASCULINE PILGRIMAGE*

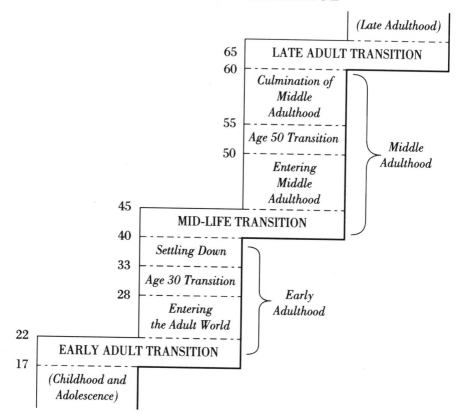

*From Daniel Levinson, et al., *The Seasons of a Man's Life* (New York: Alfred A. Knopf, 1978), p. 57. Copyright © 1978 by Daniel J. Levinson. Reprinted by permission of Alfred A. Knopf, Inc.

Stage One—*The Call*

The call to initiation can come at any time. Look at the beginnings of myths and fairy tales—they almost always begin with a call. Jack plants a magic bean, and the stalk grows high into the sky. He knows that by climbing it he'll reach the land of the giants. Now Jack can heed the call and climb up the

From Boy to Man: Circumcision Among the Australian Aborigines

beanstalk—or he can ignore it and go on with his life as if nothing has happened.

Jungians believe the archetypal Self is always trying to get our attention.[5] The Self engineers all sorts of attempts to call us into initiation. The urgency of the calls increases at certain phases of our lives when our Ego structures are particularly inadequate to face our changing circumstances. The Self's methods of calling us send us into crisis, and we are forced to attend to the message. Of course we may be (and most frequently are) completely unconscious of being led by this process. *But to the archetypal Self, life is quite simply a continuous process of initiation, a series of deaths and rebirths.*

There are two basic kinds of a call into the initiatory process. The first is directly linked to our life-cycles (see Figure 4). In adolescence, the call comes to boys and girls in part because of the suddenly accelerated release of sex-specific hormones. This call is to accept adult feelings, interests, and responsibilities. In premodern societies the initiatory call is celebrated and embraced by well-known puberty rites, van Gennep's original *rites de passage*. Boys were separated from their mothers and isolated in special structures created for the purpose. They were then initiated into manhood by the tribe's ritual elders.

The use of terror and physical mutilation, either scarring or circumcision, was one important aspect of a boy's initiation. The inculcation of wonder and awe through the teaching of the tribe's sacred myths is another. Alternatively, the boys were driven out into the wilderness on vision quests. They faced physical danger and even the possibility of death. A girl's initiation occurs differently; at the time of her first menstruation, she will often be set apart and instructed by the wise old women in the mysteries of womanhood. A girl's passage is easier to place, since it occurs with a definite physical event; perhaps the ceremonies marking a boy's passage into maturity are more elaborate because the event needed to be created. The primitive tribes who hold these initiation ceremonies realize that human beings need to die to their old selves before they can be born anew.

Marriage, childbirth, retirement, and death are other life-cycle occasions marking the entry into, and exit out of, sacred reality. The Hindus charted these major life changes, and every mature man looked forward to the time when he could retire to the life of a yogi, in order to prepare himself for death and his next incarnation.

All of us can attest to the disorienting and unnerving effects important life changes have on us. Even when the change is positive—passing through puberty, having a first sexual experience, graduating, getting a first job, having children—all are occurrences that leave us in a strange new landscape of feelings and perceptions. A man who has witnessed the birth of his child sees the world through different eyes from those he had at the moment of the child's conception. Those who have retired from a life's work see themselves and others in very different ways than they did when still in the thick of it.

Life-cycle changes can be gut-wrenching and mind-bending. But when the call to initiation comes to us through *trauma*, the second form of the call to become fulfilled, it can be emotionally and cognitively even more difficult to handle. Often the Self will initiate a life crisis without the Ego even being aware of the fact. A man is going along with his life, things seem to be going pretty well—he has a loving wife, a middle-class life-style, his kids are thriving in school, and there looks to be a promotion on the horizon. And then, pow! He comes home one day to find a note on the refrigerator that his wife has left him and has taken the kids and the checkbook.

After experiencing a tear in the seamless fabric of his consciousness, a man realizes that everything that had seemed so certain is not certain at all. He begins to challenge his assumptions. As one by one they are stripped away, he tumbles head over heels into crazy time.

We all live with the fantasy that we can control our lives. If we have enough willpower, so we think, we can make time stand still at our happiest moments—and then unforeseen disaster strikes. In a few vital moments, the world changes from a secure and supportive place into something alien and surreal.

Grief over a loss sheds a whole new light on everything. We find depths within ourselves which had previously remained hidden and repressed. A forbidding new world shatters our illusions of omnipotence. We are forced to submit to a radical realization of our helplessness and our finitude. Suddenly our plans and dreams are crushed as irrevocably as houses are tumbled in earthquakes and farmlands are smothered in toxic volcanic ash.

Every time we reach a crisis of real proportions, we go over the first threshold. This stage parallels what ritual scholars call "stripping," or "ritual humiliation." This is where the first ordeals are faced, and where the Ego realizes the forces it is up against are far greater than expected. The fears faced by the Greek initiates into Demeter's mysteries were engineered to bring this realization about.

Our terror and primal panic come into play as we cross this threshold. We may take comfort in the realization that terror is a foundational part of most calls. The terror that is registered in the eyes of the Sumerian statuettes lies like a sleeping dragon at the base of all human souls. In the wind of this terror old Ego structures are blown apart. The "I" we had thought of as strong, stable, and consistent is laid waste in a moment.

There are people who seem not to be unnerved by their major life crises. They manage them with hardly a whimper, and never with the odd look in the eyes that signals the onset of crazy time. Maybe a man does handle things well when the crisis is upon him, and then falls apart privately later. Or perhaps he never does fall apart. His life rigidifies. His speech becomes clipped and short, as if choked off. His eyes lose their luster.

A man like this has refused the call. He has become what Joseph Campbell calls the "tyrant holdfast," who rigidly clings to an outmoded Ego-consciousness, and who dies psychologically as a result. We can see this in the retired man who spends all his time at the local tavern, retelling the same old jokes and stories, unable to face his inevitable fate. He is unable to move into the rich period of self-reflection which Jung tells us lends vitality to old age.

The Call of Death: Osiris in the Form of a Bull Transports His
Worshiper to the Underworld (from an Egyptian coffin in the British
Museum)

When we see a neighbor deal with a loss as if nothing has
happened, it may be precisely because nothing has happened.
He may be so locked out of his emotional soul that he was able
to feel nothing. A crisis that can be handled well hasn't been
handled at all. A crisis demands change and suffering, and a
rigid response does no one any good.

If a man comes upon an initiatory phase in his life,

perhaps a mid-life crisis, and he doesn't recognize it as potentially initiatory, he can end up less of a man than he was to begin with. The crisis can cripple him. If he gets the right guidance during his crisis, he can become much larger than before. But to accomplish this he must die to certain aspects of himself. If he is unwilling to let those aspects go, he reduces himself—by rigidifying the old myths of his life, and not accepting the new ones offered him by his unconscious.

A man moving into extraordinary space and time often begins acting out his sexual impulses. The ancients kept temple prostitutes in recognition of this. A man may have grown comfortable and complacent with his wife, when suddenly he meets someone new. He pursues his new affair at all costs, putting his job, his status, and his marriage in jeopardy. His old structures are unexpectedly dissolved, and he finds himself floundering in deep water. Most often what he is trying to do is hold on to his youth, and deny the reality of his approaching death. And so he finds himself suddenly abandoning the social expectations his old persona has led everyone to expect.

There is an important truth to recognize concerning the acting out of sexual impulses. At bottom an extramarital affair is a spiritual quest. A misdirected quest perhaps, but a quest nonetheless. A man who starts sleeping around is looking for spiritual renewal. He is looking in the wrong place, but probably because there are no ritual elders available in his life to guide him.

The same is true of any kind of acting out. The atmosphere in a bar or a honky-tonk is almost sacred—in that particular social situation there is a frank, perhaps forced attempt at communal cheer. Every person is treated as an equal, and all are searching for some sacred connection to the wellsprings of life. This simple truth should mitigate our feelings of moral disapproval, for though an alcoholic is tragically mistaken in the means of his search, he is a searcher nonetheless. When a Jesus or a Buddha is able to love any person, regardless of their sins, it is because of a realization of what the sinner is attempting.

Social norms and expectations are dissolved in sacred space and time. With this dissolution comes a rapid rise in anxiety. The escalation of anxiety levels indicates that previously unlived material from the deep unconscious is pressing up against the repression barrier, and threatening to erupt. When a man feels the pressure of a call from the unconscious building up, he needs to find a safe and contained way of being in extraordinary reality. He needs boundaries, and someone to help him steward those boundaries, and insulate his Ego against the powerful instincts, needs, and memories that threaten to overwhelm him. He needs to be enabled—and it is the Magician who will help enable him—to let his repression barrier dissolve. Then he can integrate the material that wells up from beneath it.

He must submit to a process that has begun anyway. The Greeks who undertook the mystery rites knew they would somehow be terrified, and they submitted themselves to that fact. Novice monks and nuns of many spiritual traditions submit to having their heads shaved, a mortification that symbolizes a willingness to submit to psychospiritual rigors as well.

The prospective analysand submits himself to a schedule of fixed meeting times, locations, and fees before work begins. In the Eastern religions people are more accustomed to guru-student relationships. Our culture is wary of such relationship dynamics, and rightly so. But if we wish to be led for a time, we must accept a leader.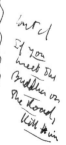

If a man is not to become a tyrant holdfast, he must acquire true humility. Humility helps him to submit his Ego to the liquefying and deconstructing effects of his own unleashed unconscious. In traditional societies it was the older men who ritually humbled a boy, showing him, at times with brute psychological and physical force, that his Ego was not in fact the center of the universe.

While humiliation doesn't always allow for a state of true humility, it is sometimes regrettably necessary to humiliate an arrogant Ego. Thus ritual humiliation is often a part of initiations of all kinds. A basic psychological rule is that an Ego that cannot learn humility on its own will, in fact, find some means of humiliating itself. And the degree of untransmuted infantile grandiosity indicates the degree to which the grandiose Ego must be humiliated.

People often sense their own need for humiliation, and go off unconsciously looking for humiliating experiences. They may turn to alcohol or drugs in a primitive attempt at self-abasement. In the absence of the rituals ancient peoples used to confront the greatest modulator of grandiosity there is—death—modern men often only flirt with their own mortality.

Men who cover their bodies in tattoos, cut themselves with knives, or burn themselves with cigarettes are involved in this same search for submission. Men who torture others are unconsciously mutilating their own grandiose selves, projected onto their victims.

Suicide is related to self-wounding and scarification practices. The suicide's Ego has misunderstood the call of the Self to die to its old ways of being, feeling, and thinking. In the absence of a spiritual sense of how to hear this call, the Ego takes the message literally. Unable to withstand devastating unconscious pressures to end the Ego's present orientation—which the Ego may regard as the only possible way of living—an individual may end his life.

Looked at from this perspective, it is not so surprising that suicide rates are highest among teenagers and the elderly. These two periods of life, perhaps more than any others, are times of upheaval and transition. The suicide has been unable to find adequate containment in his crazy time, and consequently he cannot bear the terror and wonder of his own extraordinariness.

The Magician is on intimate terms with death. He knows that death always precedes rebirth, and rebirth ultimately is his goal. The high suicide rates in our modern culture reveal a lack of magicians and ritual elders among us. Yet there are still a few wise men who understand the mysterious connection between life and death, and the vital importance of submission for the salvation of the soul.

Stage Two—*The Belly of the Whale*

The belly of the whale is equivalent to what St. John of the Cross called "the dark night of the soul," and Turner called *liminality*. When we are taken to a condition of liminality, we have been made, like it or not, to heed the call. The tyrant holdfast has been outmaneuvered by the growth potential of the Self, and the Ego is immersed in the unconscious.

We feel that there is no escaping the largely unpleasant material now brought to our attention. Our shortcomings, repressed desires, and shadow sides are exposed. At this fateful time we may withdraw our projections from others, and admit our own less than ideal attributes. In this liminal space we experience what psychologists call "the return of the repressed." Painful memories, unresolved childhood developmental issues, unfinished business with our hidden grandiosity—all rise to the surface in painful succession.

This is when some individuals suffer a psychotic break. Benign, nurturing Aunt Suzie "goes off her rocker," and someone finds her months later in another town, living with a young man. Or a Presbyterian elder comes home from

The Belly of the Whale: Joseph in the Well; the Entombment of
Christ; and Jonah and the Whale (page from the fifteenth-century
Biblia Pauperum, German Edition, 1471)

work, loads his shotgun, and blows himself and his family
away. None of the neighbors can explain, in the newspaper
interviews that follow, why such a quiet man would behave
in that way.

And of course in terms of ordinary reality his actions are
inexplicable. We come to expect his familiar persona to be
always in place. But when an individual meets the return of
the repressed in extraordinary reality, anything can happen.
When a murderer defends himself, claiming the Devil has
prompted his actions, we are inclined to scoff—but the Devil
is one of the faces commonly given to the unconscious forces

that erupt in sacred space and time. Deprived of life, those parts of ourselves we have repressed become very angry.

Unresolved childhood rage can burst forth with an almost cosmic intensity. The passion for life which we deny ourselves can emerge in a murderous frenzy. Those talents, hatreds, enthusiasms, and potentials we have never lived out, but have projected onto others, come pounding on the doors of our repression barriers. Smoldering neuroses become psychoses. Pervasive suspiciousness becomes florid paranoia. Naïve tenderness becomes pathetic dependence and maudlin sentimentality.

If we maintain an observing Ego down in the belly of the whale, we may experience the oddly pleasant sensation of "merging" with others. Always temporary, and never as uncomplicated as it at first appears, merging occurs when we let down the boundaries of our fragile Ego structures. In sixties parlance we "let it all hang out."

This blissful merger with a group of others also immersed in liminality Turner calls *communitas*. Communitas was often attempted in the United States and Western Europe in the sixties. Young people founded communes, encouraged everyone to "make love, not war," and practiced free love among their own ranks. Sensitivity groups were initiated in an effort to find a way to structure and evoke communitas, and many new religions were established in this era.

Communism was based on an attempt to impose communitas on whole peoples. The communist experiment was doomed to fail, even if the internecine political warfare that plagued the movement had never existed. Communist leaders were attempting to restructure a profane society using an antistructural phenomenon present only in extraordinary reality. While societal norms and personal Ego structures are temporarily dissolved in liminality, a return to ordinary reality demands a return to Ego structures, however artificial they may be. Sacred space and time must be left behind in order for individuals and their societies to exist at all.

One man in his late forties entered analysis complaining of the artificial constraints put upon him in both his work and personal lives. He was a college professor, the father of three children, and he felt locked into a "straitjacket routine" with his colleagues and his wife. Too many people in his life were withholding and not spontaneous. He longed for his student days.

He mentioned an experience of communitas, which was for him the high point of his life. During a Christmas vacation in his senior year, he followed the urging of some hippie friends and left on a long pilgrimage to a "sacred mountain" in Arizona. He had done this as a lark. Normally reserved and structured, he had decided for once to do something spontaneous.

The "far out" religious group he traveled with had a bus painted with peace signs and flowers. Along the way they drank heavily and smoked pounds of grass. They shared the intimate details of their lives, and relived with each other important moments from their childhoods, as well as their secret loves, hates, fears, and hopes. The pilgrims made love with each other in various pairings, without jealousy or possessiveness.

The analysand, though a stranger in the group, found himself joining in freely. He was warmly welcomed by one and all. There were no barriers, no status distinctions; he had stumbled across the proverbial big, happy family. "We were all one," he said sadly, but still—after so many years—with a trace of the old glow. "Why can't the world be that way?"

He compared his past experience on the bus to a present-day faculty party. "The first thing anybody asks you at one of the parties is, 'What do you do?' And depending on what you reply, they peg you. They nail you. You know—'Oh, he's an assistant professor of whatever. He must be making x thousand dollars a year.' They think they've got you figured out when you tell them what you do. What about who you are? Why is everybody so concerned about your rank in the pecking order?"

The answer to his question was and is because we live in community, not communitas. We live in a structured society. We spend most of our time in an ordinary reality, in which what we do for a living, where we make our home and who we make it with are our primary concerns.

Sacred space and time look very crazy to the structured Ego. And structure is something human beings need, because it reinforces the Ego, not to mention the orderly functioning of society. To an outside observer, someone undergoing deconstruction and regeneration is a loose cannon, dangerous and definitely to be avoided. We all have experienced watching someone at a painful crisis, a divorce perhaps, turning to his friends and being met by subtle avoidance behaviors and disapproval. The friends who give him a cold shoulder do not wish to be reminded of the weaknesses in their own marriages. The fear is that even proximity to someone in the Belly of the Whale marks you to be swallowed next. Extraordinary states bear a "psychic contagion," and this is why ancient people used boundaries and taboos to contain them. Extraordinary reality threatens to undo us.

When we are in sacred space and time, we need to get a fix on a central point, some stable and unchanging reality around which we can rally our beleaguered psychological structures. In the psychotherapeutic process, for example, we need to be able to "fix" on our therapist. He or she can temporarily become for us an *axis mundi*. The therapist catches and holds, under the best of circumstances, our projection of our own hidden Selves.

The therapist, the regular time of our sessions, and the

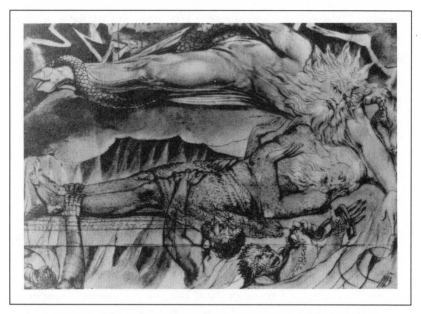

The Dark Night of the Soul: "With Dreams upon My Bed Thou
Scarest Me and Affrightest Me with Visions"
(drawing by William Blake)

space of his or her office all become stabilizing influences,
constituting the boundaries and containment we need in order
to process the revelations of the unconscious, while continuing
our daily lives. We create a kind of communitas with the
therapist. We make of the therapist a kind and loving parent,
with whom we can share everything without fear of rejection.
And in the bounded space of the psychotherapeutic process,
we must be able to suffer fully, celebrate fully, and modulate
our impulses in life-enhancing ways.

Containment is an important part of the optimal experience in the Belly of the Whale. The psychotherapeutic process
is of course not the only place this containing can take place.
Analysis will never be available to more than a small minority
of a minority social class. Even those who are not deterred by

the expense may avoid analysis because of social bias. In many places in the country therapy is still thought of not as an opportunity for personal growth, but as the last resort of a crazy person.

What are the other possibilities of finding a containing guide? A marriage partner can offer containment, though this is rarely successful. A relationship as intimate as that may not necessarily be strong enough to withstand the eruptions of rage and other archetypal material that occurs in crazy time. And sometimes the rage is directed specifically against the marriage partner—which makes for a confusion of transferences that the most skillful of analysts would be hard-pressed to manage.

It is becoming rare, too, that any modern profession will offer this containment. Once professions were themselves "callings." Now most professions have been reduced to careers. Success is measured only by gains in income or status. Interestingly there are plenty of young doctors and lawyers ready to abandon their jobs. They are disgusted by the lack of a vocation, and instead of ritual elders they find they are working for older but nonetheless immature careerists. The young do their best to guide themselves, but this is an inadequate answer to the problem.

In the sixties the government promised to offer containment. Mental health facilities were to be ubiquitous and inexpensive. Now most of the patients from these facilities are sleeping in the streets.

Religious communities can provide ritual containment, but because most establishment religions have been thoroughly modernized, even this possibility is unlikely now. A modernized religion either does not acknowledge that extraordinary space and time exist, or does not think them vital to the process of human psychological growth. Many modern clergymen look askance at parishioners who are in the midst of life transitions. And few have any understanding of themselves as ritual leaders; they have forsaken the call to be true initiatory spirit guides.

But if our desire for guidance is keen enough, we will find it. It may not come from the expected, or even the ideal, direction; still it seems to be true that the Self always finds some way to carry out its agendas. Nonetheless we must make every effort in this society to offer some means of initiation, and the containment it requires.

While extraordinary reality can be terrifying, it is also regenerative and transforming. When we can be guided through it by a magician figure who is familiar with sacred space and time, we gradually consolidate a new set of Ego structures. We may be led by the archetypal Magician energy itself—the "inner guides" of the hypnotherapists, the "power animals" of the shamans—or we may find a therapist, clergyman, or other to guide us. We come to develop a vital Ego-Self axis. By constellating the *axis mundi* within ourselves, we connect to a Self of unfathomable richness and complexity. We may soar, as shamans do, when the unutterable beauty of the Self opens to our wondering gaze.

As the dark night of the soul begins to lift, and the heavy weight of sorrow and fear begins to dissipate, we may feel a kind of ecstasy. Some analysands report feeling, like mystics of all epochs, "at one with all things." Although this is a beautiful feeling, there is a danger to luxuriating in it because the reorganizing Ego, still contaminated by infantile impulses, often interprets the feeling in grandiose terms—"*I* am all this! *I* know the truth! *I* am saved!" The ecstasy leads to a religious conversion for some. Unfortunately, when inflation occurs in this way, it is a short step from "*I* have seen the light" to "*you* have not"—and the hysterical intolerance that results.

The vision presented to the Ego in this crazy time within the psyche should not be literalized. The Ego may believe itself to be a hero, since it is the focus of so much archetypal energy. A state of possession occurs, exactly like what was once identified as demonic possession. But the demonic is not the only force that can possess us. We can be possessed also by the light, which then becomes *itself* the darkness.

The Magician is the master of spirits, though, and he holds the keys to the initiatory gates at the thresholds of sacred space and time. He can help us keep our wits about us. He helps to insulate us from the power of the other archetypes, but uses their energy resources to aid us in life-enhancing ways. Interestingly, the shaman always keeps his Ego-consciousness in the midst of a deconstructing visit to the unconscious. He is a good role model for us to follow as we journey into the sacred realm.

Stage Three—*The Return*

As Joseph Campbell reminds us, we face enormous difficulties getting back out of sacred reality. There is such a thing as *chronic liminality*—in which an individual is caught forever in limbo, unable to pull himself back together to resume a life in the world. Charismatic religious leaders and grandiose politicians are sometimes unable to distinguish themselves from the Self they have witnessed. Hence when a man styles himself, through an almost unimaginable unconscious inflation, as the "führer" or "maximum leader," he has left a healthy part of his Ego behind in the extraordinary dimension.

Such a man returns to the mundane world with some enhanced consciousness, and internal "alpha male" status, but no sense of his own limitations. He walks and talks among us, but we can look in his eyes and see he is caught in that other world. His eyes are glazed. They bear an unnatural light. They may carry even a godlike aura in them, but they are not humble. They are the eyes of a man whose Ego has been "overcooked."

Sooner or later a man such as this will fall. He has been

The Magician's Return to the World: Moses Before the Children of
Israel in Egypt

"cooked" too long in the pressure of sacred space. Like Shah
Pahlavi, Noriega, Ceaușescu, Hitler—he will not be able to
carry sacred reality for long. He is the minister who burns out
after a year of proselytizing. He had the fantasy for a time of
being a savior, capable of anything. He is too close to the
"flame," the archetypes, and their energy soon exhausts him.
He is the assertiveness training participant who can't come
down off the high he found in his weekend workshop. After
alienating everyone at the office, he ends up collapsing at the
drinking fountain. And he returns to one workshop after another, believing them to be his only way to feel truly alive.

There is an opposite possible danger threatening the man
who leaves the sacred dimension. If he leaves too early he may
be "undercooked." He is the man who goes to see a therapist

after some crisis, has a few useful insights, and then quits, believing himself now to be back on track. Unlike the addicted analysand who continues with his therapy two or three times a week—for life!—the undercooked man is locked into an unconscious fantasy of omnipotence. Sooner or later he will end up in the consulting room again, after another crisis based on the same problems.

The best way to negotiate a successful return to the world is to be helped with establishing, while still in the Belly of the Whale, new structures and behaviors. By enacting these in his imagination, the adventurer is able to modulate the grandiosity of his visions. He will then find ways to embody his sacred revelations in his ordinary life. The Bible rightly tells us that "without a vision the people perish." It is equally true that with nothing but visions, and unrealistic plans for implementing them, people languish.

Vital to all successful initiations is the archetype of the Magician, and the human men who carry out his tasks. It is to these men that we now turn.

THE WAY OF THE MAGICIAN: THE RITUAL ELDER AS STEWARD OF HUMAN WISDOM AND TRANSFORMATIVE PROCESS

THERE ARE CERTAIN "POWER SPOTS" IN THE world that the Magician recognizes, as do the mortal men embodying his archetypal energies. The exact location for the Holy of Holies in Jerusalem was revealed to a magician. A magician was the one to discover the arrangement for the megaliths at Stonehenge. Past magicians were led, often by one of their power animals, to the exact location of a break in the earthly plane, through which sacred energy poured into the world, either from the underworld or the heavens above.

Power Spots: The Magician in His Magic Circle—Faustus and
Mephistopheles

In this sense the biblical Jacob was a magician, for as the
legend recounts, he happens to fall asleep on a rock which is
at the foot of a divine "ladder." He is visited there by a
descending "angel," with whom he wrestles until dawn. He
forces this spirit to bless him—a shamanic feat—and he consecrates the place as a power spot forever after.

Carlos Castaneda's books explore power spots in detail.
He has Don Juan, the Yaqui *brujo*, instruct him in the intricacies of finding his own power spots. Don Juan tells him he
must try many spots. He must try sitting cross-legged here,
and now there, and now in another spot, until at last he feels
centered. Then he will be on his spot. And Don Juan explains
that once he is on his power spot, nothing can destroy him.

Castaneda does report feeling a difference between various places. In some he feels vulnerable and off-center, and in others, he feels deeply connected to the resources of power within him.

Finding a power spot is not simply a matter of finding a place that feels comfortable, perhaps because it is familiar. Rather it is a matter of deeply intuited sensitivity to those places and times where the material world becomes "transparent" to the Spirit, to borrow a term from theologian Paul Tillich.

In the book (and movie) *The Last Temptation of Christ*, Nikos Kazantzakis has his Jesus go out into the wilderness following his baptism. There he must find his identity and his calling. Like any magician, psychic, or medium—like anyone sensitive to unseen energy patterns—he finds his spot. Then he draws a circle around himself in the sand. The demonic visions of temptation he has cannot break into his circle. The spot he has found protects him.

Magicians never invent or create power spots. They only discover them. Once a spot has been recognized by a magician, he will often build an altar, pillar, or pole atop it, or leave a statue of the god who appeared to him there, or mark out a boundary. This boundary can be as simple as Jesus' circle in the sand, or as spectacular as Imhotep's massive, ornate Saqqara wall.

An altar placed on a power spot serves to mark an *axis mundi*.[1] Along this central point the chaotic energies of the profane world can rush into extraordinary space. And the boundary helps to keep the energies of the sacred and profane worlds discrete—to protect the profane world from being overloaded with sacred energy, and to shield people from unintentional travels into what can be a crazy reality. If sacred space were poured freely into the profane world, it would be contaminated by it, and lose its energy.

As magicians have always known, keeping a place sacred is difficult. For all its power, sacred space is elusive and tentative. It cannot be willed to remain intact, any more than it can be commanded to appear—it is always a hierophany, a sudden, unforeseen appearance of a god. Although the great shamans could move in and out of sacred space at will, even they could not fully control extraordinary reality time. A shaman's task was not to control but to maintain those places where sacred and profane worlds met. He was to keep the boundaries in good repair, and keep the center fresh and strong. The rest was up to the divine powers.

The magician meets his task by meticulously following ritual prescriptions, often ones that have been handed down for generations. He keeps himself attuned to his spirit guides and their directives. He is a true steward of extraordinary reality. His ultimate calling is to conduct his fellows into, through, and out of power spots. He is himself a spirit guide.

He demands that those who have been called to enter extraordinary space observe appropriate boundary rituals. Recall that when Moses encountered Yahweh at the burning bush, he was required to remove his shoes "because the ground whereon you stand is holy." The approach to any temple in the ancient world was accompanied by similar rituals of cleansing and purification. The Hebrew high priest could enter the Holy of Holies only after he had been ritually purified, and then only once a year, when the *axis mundi* was active.

We have emphasized the crazy side of extraordinary space and time. But it is important to remember that truly liminal space is potentially transformative. Many times a man will recognize that he is in a transforming space, even without the benefit of a cognitive framework with which to understand it.

A middle-aged man who for years had nurtured his mystical sensitivity took his first trip to Mexico. Even before he left he felt his trip would include a spiritual experience. What kind of spiritual experience he did not know. He spent several days in Mexico City, enjoying himself very much, but feeling none of the spirituality he had expected. Then he drove out of the city to the ancient site of Teotihuacán.

Teotihuacán is a vast ruined temple complex, built by an unknown civilization of Native Americans before the time of Christ. It was the first fully developed large urban center in the Americas. He walked down the long Avenue of the Dead, lost in the almost palpable silence of the place. He became aware of the faint sound of Indian flutes wailing in the distance. Though the place was thronged with tourists, he felt more and more removed from the contemporary scene—he was lost to a magical world that danced and vibrated just behind the outer forms of the profane world around him.

He climbed the huge Pyramid of the Sun, and got a view of the whole plateau for miles around. This was a powerful experience for him, but not what he had imagined. He became conscious that he was searching for a spot where he could be in the center of the feelings that were welling up within him. His feelings were of great beauty and stillness, and of longing; he had a sense of a quiet dynamism and spirit.

He climbed the steps of the Pyramid of the Moon. About halfway up, he stopped suddenly. He sat down. He had found his spot. He felt lifted and gently suffused with updrafts of energy. His soul seemed to open up to him, along with the soul of the place itself. For several hours he sat there, hardly moving. The experience changed his life. Leaving the ruined city, he vowed to himself that ever after he would live his life in the spirit he had encountered there—with quiet intensity and authenticity, with spirit, and with an unsuspected aesthetic sensitivity. His inner Magician had guided him into, through, and out of transformative space and time.

The poet Rainer Maria Rilke had a similar extraordinary experience in a garden. In retrospect he located the impetus for his masterful *Duino Elegies* in the insights he gained from the experience. He wrote a third-person description of the event which bears examination.

> He remembered the hour in that other southern garden (Capri), when, both outside and within him, the cry of a bird was correspondingly present, did not, so to speak, break upon the barriers of his body, but gathered inner and outer together into one uninterrupted space, in which, mysteriously protected, only one single spot of purest, deepest consciousness remained. That time he had shut his eyes, so as not to be confused in so generous an experience by the contour of his body, and the infinite passed into him so intimately from every side, that he could believe he felt the light reposing of the already appearing stars within his breast.[2]

The dissolution of the physical boundary we see here is common to the extraordinary experience. It is one reason why journeys into sacred space can be so disorienting to the unprepared psyche, and why guides are so helpful during these crisis times. Rilke's moments in the garden transformed him; he developed a deeply spiritual and original understanding of the universe, which was weakened only by his inability to support an embodied relationship with a woman.

LIMINOID SPACE AND TIME

Often people unconsciously seek out sacred space. They feel a growing restlessness, out of a sense that something wonderful is going to happen. Or the sense is of foreboding and anxiety instead. They start looking for initiation. They go looking for paradise—in Las Vegas, the Caribbean, or Europe, whatever their fantasy prefers. Some join the Peace Corps, or work in an inner-city church. Some get entangled in extramarital affairs, start taking drugs, or hook up with a fringe cult. They may involve themselves with genuinely crazy, even psychotic people. They look outside themselves for an elixir to transform them.

What is happening to them is that they are hearing the call to enter liminal space. As the biblical authors describe it, the call is to "repent," and be transformed. But more often than not instead of finding liminal space they land in liminoid space. *While liminoid space can be refreshing, it does not produce transformation.* It may bring pleasure without a reorientation of the personality as a whole. Or it may bring suffering without insight. It always disappoints to some degree, because without any lasting change, when we exit liminoid space we feel let down.

Rock concerts provide liminoid time and space for some. The lights, the crowd, the musicians and their music, the alcohol perhaps and the drugs, evoke for a time a giddy paradise on earth. Maybe we share a temporarily ecstatic state of consciousness with those around us, even with perfect strangers. Maybe dancing in the aisles and passing the joint around brings a fleeting state of communitas. But when the concert is over the experience quickly fades. The next hungover morning, the magical musicians begin to fade from memory, their living images soon replaced again by the more familiar images of their album photos. And it may seem difficult to remember what all the fuss was about.

Experiences such as this are potentially liminal. They are certainly sacred—for they are taking place in extraordinary space and time—but they do not transform us. For the moment they are energizing and refreshing. But come the next work day, they are buried by routine. What makes the difference between a liminal and a liminoid experience?

The Magician. Robert Plant, Willie Nelson, Perry Como—however accomplished as stage magicians these performers may be, they are not authentic spirit guides. They celebrate and evoke the liminoid, but they do not try (nor would they be able) to lead us any deeper. Their business is to entertain people, not to transform them.

Unfortunately most who work in the professions that should be helping to regenerate people are no more interested in guiding transformation than entertainers are. Most modern ministers have virtually no understanding of the power of ritual and symbol. True to their iconoclastic Protestant heritage, they reject such things as "superstitious devices." But ritual prepares and orients the psyche that has been called to enter crazy space. Without it, and without some means of understanding the symbols and images that occur there, the psyche can only lose its bearings.

It is only when the Magician isn't functioning well in the psyche that you don't experience the symbols. You have signs. A sign is something to which literal meaning is attached. A symbol refers to meanings beyond itself; it opens onto a wider dimension and contains a surplus of meaning. When the images sent by the unconscious are interpreted by the Ego as signs only, the images lose all their importance, and can no longer be a useful guide to personal psychic problems. To interpret a symbol as a sign represents a failure of the imagination, and a malfunction of the Magician.

In summary, many religious leaders no longer understand or accept their roles as ritual elders and spirit guides. They believe a little training in a pastoral counseling technique qualifies them to heal. They have little sense of the depth and power of the human soul. And they are so busy attempting to appear normal to their congregations that they forfeit the mystique that must attend the ritual elder before any real transformation can take place. It seems the modern religions will go to any lengths to denature their teachings—from the banal, "modernized" mass of the Catholics to the rationalized "historical" Jesus of the Protestants and other secularized contemporary religious practices.

In occult communities, the adepts are usually as under-cooked as their counterparts in the established religions. Though purportedly more appreciative of sacred space and time, its boundaries, and the mystique of ritual leadership, the unfortunate fact is that many occult leaders are in a "magician inflation." They naïvely believe they have "mastered" the spirits. Their inflation disqualifies them for the serious and risky task of stewarding others through sacred reality.

The casualties of minority religions, charismatic Christian movements, even the assertiveness-training workshops are legion. So many have been hurt rather than helped because there is a disastrous dearth of mature ritual elders in our society. People seeking self-transforming, liminal experiences encounter only liminoid ones. And when a would-be adept leads seekers through processes he cannot control, does not understand, and therefore cannot steward, the seekers often end up under- or overcooked. Rather than freeing souls caught in various forms of psychopathology, these "spiritual leaders" deprive people of healing (and often their earthly goods as well).

THE ANALYST AS MAGICIAN

Many modern clinical psychologists, psychotherapists, and psychiatrists are equally in the dark about issues of sacred space and time. And though a Jungian analyst's theoretical background should leave him responsive to these issues, there is no guaranteeing it will. Until a therapist understands the

Jung

vital significance of the magician's role—an understanding predicated on an adequate access of the inner Magician—he or she will be able to do very little more than comfort people. Transformation demands an extraordinary context.

Some psychotherapists speak wanly of "frame" issues, and believe they understand about boundaries. But we have to turn to Jung to find a clear conception of the alchemical sealed vessel necessary for psychotherapeutic processes to effect lasting change. Jung believed the analyst to be a "psychopomp," a conductor of souls. He knew therapeutic sessions in themselves could be occasions for sacred space and time. The whole course of an analysis could be understood as taking place in an extraordinary reality, over a period of years.

Of course on the deepest level extraordinary reality lies within any analysand's organizing center, which Jung called the Self. Within us all are natural psychological boundaries which protect the Self from the profaning effects of the rest of the psyche and of the outer world. In turn the psyche and the created world are normally protected from the numinous power of the Self. The Self functions much like the God of traditional religions, noted Jung; if approached too closely it will utterly overwhelm uninsulated Ego structures.

The analyst's job as magician begins as he insulates the analysand's Ego against the powerful unconscious contents that erupt during the extraordinary time of the analytic sessions. The analyst supports the Ego's boundaries against these archetypal contents, and also contains them by keeping the analytic work in a structured time and space frame. In addition the analyst must hold the analysand's projection of the still unfamiliar Self. The analyst becomes for a time the *axis mundi* of the analysand's psychological world. Eventually an analyst helps his charge to realize that the true center is waiting within the unconscious.

The analytic process can be seen as a kind of "reparenting," as some therapists call it. People engage in a psychotherapeutic process essentially because parents fail to provide their children with adequate ritual leadership. The first magicians we encounter in our lives are our parents. We look to them to hold and contain us, see and hear us, and keep us safe during our emotional storms. We need them to contain our anger, and hear our feelings without judgement or rejection.

The problem is that throughout history parents have been unable to adequately perform these tasks. For one thing few parents ever access the Magician for their own needs, and so are in no position to act as magus for a child. Maturation also requires liberation from numinous projections onto the parents. Thus it falls to the psychotherapist to accept judiciously and consciously his client's parental transferences and archetypal projections. After accepting them he can help his client adventure into those psychic chambers where the inner Magician resides. Then the essential task of removing king and queen transferences (projections) from the parents can be completed. As the individual opens to the mythic realm of the "King and Queen in the Other World," he is liberated while the all-too-human parents can be forgiven for their myriad failures.

THE MAGICIAN WITHIN

Ultimately it is the Magician within, in the service of the Self, who guides all of our initiatory experiences (psychotherapeutic and other). The Magician holds the keys to the gates at the boundaries of extraordinary space and time.

To facilitate understanding, we have represented extraordinary reality as a uniform dimension, forming along with the profane dimension the whole of the universe. But in fact extraordinary reality is more of a collection of different complex, highly nuanced states. It involves the whole of the unconscious geography, personal and collective, studded with various dynamic, feeling-toned structures. A human consciousness can stray into any one of these structures and become trapped.

In fact Jungians talk about the many "rooms" of the unconscious. The structures they describe include the Shadow, the Anima and Animus, the various complexes and a whole host of archetypes—some predominantly masculine, some feminine. Hypnotherapists talk about entities of nearly infinite number which may appear in the psyche and "possess" the personality.[3] Other psychologies speak of introjects, inner "objects" and "imagoes." Heinz Kohut examined false self and true self configurations. Erikson presented the different inner conflicts present in instinctual modalities. Recent trends in psychoanalytic theory are moving in directions which support Jung's pioneering vision of the deep structures of the psyche.

Depth psychologies increasingly attend to the figures from dreams, visions, fairy tales and science fiction, mythology and folklore; it has become general knowledge that these figures are denizens of the unconscious. A great teller of fairy tales like Tolkien believes fairies are real, living in another dimension and dreaming of humans. From Tibet to the Yucatán the ancient religions believed there were levels and dimensions to be encountered both in the underworld and in the heavens.

What does all of this mean in terms of the inner Magician? It means that he—and his mature expression, the shaman—has access to the whole terrain of the human unconscious. He knows the passwords that can take the Ego in and out of these magical realms. He can voyage inside himself without getting lost, or falling under the enchantment of any one place or structure in sacred geography. It is the Magician who wrote the Tibetan and the Egyptian Books of the Dead, giving advice to departed Egos for the negotiation of the fearful inner landscapes of the afterworld. He wrestles with demons and power animals, and is on intimate terms with complexes; he uses his knowledge of these structures to keep himself free of them. With his mercurial agility he can cross any particular unconscious boundary, and so it is he who keeps a man's immortal soul free and aids other members of the human community in both personal and social liberation and transformation.

Remember, each of the fully expressed archetypes of mature masculinity must be balanced by and incorporate influences from the other three. The Magician must be balanced by the dynamic structures of the King, Warrior, and Lover; together the quadrated structures of the masculine Self make a complex whole. The cohesive masculine Self is composed of these four archetypes, but transcends them. The four archetypes, therefore, must interact in a mutually enriching and regulating way. In conjunction with the other three archetypes, the Magician becomes an essential component of the Generative Man in his empowered wholeness.

PART 3

THE UNINITIATED MAGICIAN: MALFUNCTIONS AND SHADOW FORMS

THE MASTER OF
DENIAL:
THE INNOCENT ONE

THE USUAL JUNGIAN CONCEPTION OF THE SHADOW
is of an "alter ego," a subpersonality which resides in the
personal unconscious, and which stands in opposition to conscious behaviors and values. The Shadow's attitudes are exaggerated, in direct proportion to the exaggeration of the Ego's
own attitudes. This idea is very similar to the law of physics
that states that "for every action there is an equal and opposite
reaction." Jung believed a person's primary task to be the
integration of Ego and Shadow opposites; as this is attempted
the whole personality makes a creative advance toward psychological wholeness and individuation toward maturity.

The Nazi: "Squire" Göring Among the Villagers of Mauterndorf

It is generally assumed that the Shadow is built around undesirable character traits and impulses. But in fact the Shadow is organized around all split-off traits, including desirable ones. Even the darkest Shadows hold hidden gifts, abilities, and wisdom in store for the Ego. The problem is often that the Ego is so filled with righteousness it will not admit Shadow offerings. Some Shadows may even be filled with light, as a predominantly negative, destructive Ego will have a compensatory Shadow that is positive and creative. Such appears to be the case with Adolf Hitler, whose Shadow provided him with a maudlin sentimentality concerning children and animals.

Jungians also recognize a part of the Shadow that goes beyond the dynamics of the individual psyche. This is known as the collective shadow. Among other things, the collective shadow holds values and attitudes at complete variance with those of a people's collective consciousness. The various hatreds between races, nations, and religions arise as one group projects its collective shadow on another.

Beyond this there may be a collective human shadow, which positions itself in opposition to any particular social or ideational norms. This is the shadow that stands in opposition to the most fundamental human values—those that have remained uniform and universal throughout our history. Social injunctions against murder, stealing, and other common crimes are opposed by this deep shadow, which has been personified in religious writings as Satan or the Devil. In psychological terminology it is the "antilibidinal Ego." It is our belief that the antilibidinal, life-denying Ego is related to unconscious and unmodulated infantile grandiosity—this grandiosity is the window through which the "devil" enters a human life and possesses it.

Our own contribution to the Jungian understanding of the Shadow is in our discovery and explication of the Shadow's bipolar split. Each side of the bipolar split plays shadow to the other, and the bipolar system as a whole plays the shadow for the archetype in its fullness. Thus "Shadow" in our schema does not mean merely a personal unconscious element that stands in a simple relationship of opposition to either the Ego or a particular archetype. It is a more complex structure than that, and has therefore a more complicated relationship between its poles, and between the poles and the archetype than previously believed.

In order for the archetype to be accessed by the Ego, the bipolar Shadow must first be integrated as far as possible. Only at that point will the bipolar system be transcended, and each pole's gifts made available. Each pole must be made "conscious" of the other, through a process of active imagination.[1] Each pole must integrate the other, according to the Ego's directions; the Ego is responding to promptings coming directly from the Self, as well as from the particular archetype as an emissary of the Self. When the bipolar Shadow no longer obstructs a mature expression of the archetype, the archetypal system functions optimally and its energy is made available to the Ego.

We call the passive pole of the Magician's Shadow the "Innocent." A childish naïveté is a characteristic of the passive poles of all the archetypes. The innocence of the Shadow Magician is always feigned—just as the King's Weakling is dishonest about his tyrannical impulses, and the Warrior's Masochist disguises his sadistic aggressive impulses. Barely concealed beneath the Innocent's repression barrier is a terrific cunning, and technically refined manipulative skills.

The Innocent only appears to be ignorant. He seems to be naïve, and to lack a power drive, but he is only hiding his true colors. When pressed by a therapist in a psychotherapeutic situation, the Innocent will often respond with petulance, evasiveness, or veiled irritation. When questioned further he will mechanically respond, "I don't know, I don't know." Such a refusal to own his own aggressive and manipulative impulses can be very trying for a therapist. Sometimes these resistant denials take up many hours that could be spent on insightful therapeutic work—especially if the therapist is unfamiliar with this subtle form of magician malfunction.

We see this same behavior in the man who surreptitiously works against his boss, by complaining incessantly and spreading office gossip. When called upon by his superior to answer for his behavior, the Innocent in a man will answer, "Who, me?" His surprise and indignation will be only partly feigned. The Innocent is the manipulating man who manages consistently to come home late on garbage nights, though he knows how important it is to his wife that he be around to take the garbage out. If confronted about it, he may burst into a self-righteous rage: "You know sometimes I have to work late! I'm wearing myself out for you and the kids. Who makes the money around here anyway?" Or he may gaze at his wife with baleful eyes, profoundly wounded by her accusations. And partially he *is* innocent, as far as his being largely unaware of acting out his hostility. But just beneath his repression barrier, his Shadow knows the truth perfectly well.

The man possessed by the Innocent claims not to understand himself, his relationship dynamics, or the consequences of his behavior. He believes there to be no Magician energy residing within him, and he projects his manipulative Shadow onto others. His boss, he thinks, is overly demanding and unreasonable, and attempting to manipulate him. His wife he likewise believes to be invasive and persecuting. Other people he sees as being withholding, and into "power trips." As far as he can see they are out to get him.

There was a man in a church's adult study group who held up the opening prayer because of an intense private discussion he was having with the man beside him. When asked to finish the conversation so that the class could begin on time, he withdrew into a petulant silence, and refused to participate in the class's opening deliberations. Later he claimed not to understand what the class was talking about when the discussion turned to exploring how to handle angry feelings. He proudly proclaimed, "I never have an angry thought towards anyone."

Two classically defined personality disorders offer examples of the Innocent's claims not to be manipulative, or cognizant of his anger.[2] The Dependent Personality Disorder and the Passive/Aggressive Disorder both are manifestations of the Innocent.

In the Dependent Personality Disorder, the Innocent experiences others as being at the center of things. Others have all the power, technology, and knowledge. The dependent believes he lives to please others. He avoids asserting himself, because consciously he thinks if he asserts himself he will be abandoned. Given the depth of unconscious anger behind this disorder, if the dependent were to assert himself he would probably also express a lot of this anger, as well as his frustration at being passive and dependent. His unconscious anger might very well be alienating to others. Careless, unconscious self-assertion might therefore realistically cause others to abandon him.

This man frequently denigrates himself and his accomplishments. He is self-effacing, and he can't take a compliment. Often ingratiating, he sugarcoats the veiled demands he makes on "powerful" others, lest they withdraw their good will from him. He falls all over himself in an attempt to present himself as completely harmless. Most of us recognize him as untrustworthy. Sooner or later we know he will knife us in the back out of his envy for the imagined power we hold over him.

All of the strategies of the dependent man are attempts

to manipulate others into caring for him and attending to his needs. His apparent helplessness and his whining do, at least initially, elicit nurturing and caring feelings from others. Eventually, though, his dependent coping strategies become tiresome. When they backfire, his protestations of innocence and ignorance are met with skepticism and disbelief.

Dependent men are very threatened by their repressed feelings of hostility, and their manipulative motives. As the repression barrier begins to break down under pressure from this unwanted, hidden hostility, the dependent experiences a rapid rise in his anxiety level. In fact, there is a fundamental anxiety which is experienced whenever one's shadow threatens to become conscious.

Many dependents experience "separation anxiety." As those he looks to for support withdraw from him, the dependent suffers his worst nightmare. Because he is caught in the passive pole of the Magician's Shadow, the dependent also feels a chronic dread of responsibility—of new responsibilities in particular. Frequently he will short-circuit when asked, at home or in the office, to take on a new task or role. Status, because of its attendant duties, is the last thing he wants. Like the Trickster (the active pole of the Magician's Shadow) he does not want to move into the adult realm of making worlds. He prefers to sit on the sidelines, criticizing and denigrating the efforts of others, trafficking in a cheap hopelessness.

Dependent men have a deep-seated tendency to develop severe depressions, which can, in extreme cases, result in catatonia. This is the logical extreme of the urge to withdraw from the world.

The other major personality disorder exhibited by the Innocent pole of the Shadow Magician is the Passive/Aggressive Disorder, sometimes called the Negativistic Pattern. This disorder is also manifested by those caught in the Shadow Warrior's passive pole. The passive/aggressive pattern arises

159

exactly as it does in the Shadow Warrior, when the repression barrier is failing, and the coping strategies of playing "innocent" are failing too.

When the repression barrier fails, an underlying rage over the Ego's extreme feelings of dependency and passivity begins to rise to the surface. The Shadow suddenly reverses its customary polarity, in this case moving toward the active pole. But unlike the Warrior's Sadistic eruptions, which are often violent, the Shadow Magician's passive aggression is rarely so overt. The aggression is palpable, but it is disguised somewhat by the Magician's talent for secretive, elusive behavior. Passive/aggressive moves are frequently made on a verbal or an intellectual level instead of a physical one.

In both of the above disorders, which so often appear together that it can be difficult to separate them, there is a hysterical denial of manipulative motives. In extreme cases the Innocent will even deny the presence of manipulative motives in others. This man believes "everyone is basically good," and cannot imagine a person really harboring any ill intentions toward him or anyone else. He simply cannot absorb the import of the nightly news. If his illusions ever do come to be shattered, then his self fragments as well!

This man also tends to be naïve about his own sexual motives, as well as the motives of women. He is one type who tends to be implicated in cases of sexual harassment. The Innocent's reaction is generally to be frightened, astounded, and morally indignant at the charges, because he is so divorced from an understanding of his own unconscious desires. What he considers "friendliness" is "misread" as a sexual advance, by women who actually are reading his unconscious motives better than he is himself.

The Innocent has serious difficulties in extraordinary space and time. He cannot execute even the first requirement of his stewardship role. Either he cannot locate transformative

The Mentor: Cro-Magnon Magician as Initiator into the Mysteries

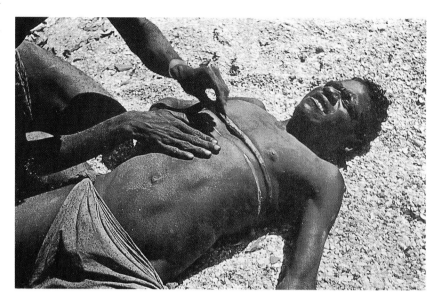

Scarification

Black Elk Before the Six Grandfathers

Jesus the Magician Raising Lazarus
(fourth century A.D. gold glass plate)

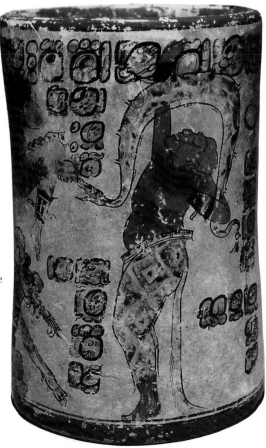

Visions: Maya Dancer with Snake
(polychrome vase from Altar de
Sacrificios, Petén, Guatemala,
400–800 A.D.)

On the Shaman's Journey:
Elijah Ascending

Peter with the Keys to the
Kingdom: Bas-relief from a
Nineteenth-Century Church

space and time, or he mistakes it as being located in others. The Innocent often believes his *axis mundi* to be in another person. Unwilling to access his inner Magician, he projects the archetype onto some "magical" other. Through his passivity, he allows that other to locate, define, and steward his life structures. If someone else is willing to do this for him, the Innocent limps along reasonably well—but left to his own devices he is totally lost.

For example, there was a young man who frequently succumbed to an underlying malaise. Returning home from work, he would be overcome by a vague feeling of panic. Unsure what to do with himself, he would usually collapse on the couch, turn on the TV and do absolutely nothing. His apartment was a mess. He never dusted or cleaned. His furniture was old and in need of repair or replacement. His walls were unadorned. The few plants he had were dying. He usually ate frozen dinners, but when he did bother to prepare something, he left his unwashed dishes in the sink for weeks.

Then he began a relationship with a bright, vivacious woman who lived in his building. Thereafter he almost never went home to his own apartment, but instead went directly from work to his girlfriend's place. She provided him with a center, a structured "space" to be in. She set the agenda. Now he had things to do when he came home.

On those rare occasions when he did spend time in his apartment, he immediately felt his accustomed anxious lethargy. He also felt profoundly uneasy about being so dependent upon his girlfriend for a sense of direction, or what he called "an orientation, a compass point." He reported that he dreaded the Saturday mornings when he had not slept over at his girlfriend's and she had not scheduled the day with him. He would wake up, climb out of bed, take a shower, and then feel totally dispirited. He was actually afraid of all the free time he had ahead of him.

To him, the free time was featureless. Like the space in his apartment, it was blank, directionless, and frightening. Without the space and time his external magician organized for him, he was left to his terror of a homogenous, meaningless, lifeless void. This void is the same mythological chaos which ruled before the Gods established a center and organized a world around it. Space and time, without a possible sacred dimension, is simply nonbeing.

What this dependent man needed was to access the Magician in his fullness, and follow the lead from his own masculine depths into locating, consecrating, and stewarding the extraordinary space and time occupied by the Self within him. If he had he would have come to know and be comfortable with himself in his vital, life-giving depths. He would also have come to know and steward, as the technician of his psychic energies, his own psychological boundaries. He would have felt strong, safe and contained, rather than suffering another person's well-intentioned "invasions" of his own space and time.

The Trickster is the opposite pole of the Shadow Magician. We now turn our attention to him.

8

THE TRICKSTER:
THE DETACHED
MANIPULATOR

I N A SENSE ALL OF CIVILIZATION IS A PRODUCT OF the Magician's work, under the supervision of the King, and protected and promoted by the Warrior. It is certainly true that our modern age is the age of the Magician—with all its specialized professions, rapidly advancing technologies, and increasingly deep soul-searching and self-reflection.

However, it is also an age in which the Magician in his "power shadow" form has run amok. The Shadow Magician has overseen the creation and deployment of enough nuclear weapons to destroy every human being on the planet, and all but the most primitive and hardy life forms, many times over.

right to Jacob. Then Jacob gave Esau bread and the lentil soup; and he ate and drank and rose up and went his way.
Thus Esau threw away his birthright.

Jacob Tricks Esau

His labors have also led to the careless pouring of toxic materials of all kinds into an ecosphere that is now showing signs of comprehensive deterioration. He has helped refine the capacity of certain individuals to lie, cheat, and steal on an international level—through an artful combination of psychological insight and sophisticated media technology. The unbridled scramble to acquire material goods and personal wealth, at the expense of millions of powerless people, is directly attributable to the Trickster, the active sociopathic pole of the Shadow Magician.

Ours is a world in which "solid" and "stable" businessmen and administrators label artists and other sensitive types as "crazy," then turn around and coldly direct the pollution of the environment and the starvation of millions. Few of these men recognize that fear, hate, and envy control their reaction to more sensitive men, who have a healthier erotic connection to the world and other human beings. In our world Madison Avenue attempts to convince us that our love for others is measured by the amount we spend on them, and those engaged in the lucrative "helping" medical, psychological, and legal professions raise the cost of their services so that the people who need them most are effectively excluded. These too are signs of a veritable rampage of the Shadow Magician in his Trickster form.

There are still teachers in the public schools who pigeon-hole their poorer students on the basis of ethnic and cultural background, despite the growing body of evidence arguing against limiting children in this way. The moral tone these teachers take is indicative of the subtle emotional sadism characteristic of the active pole of the Shadow Magician. Some teachers persecute even their obviously gifted students out of barely concealed hatred and envy. In the world of higher education there are many professors who delight in intimidating students who "dare" to question them too closely about their emotional detachment, deconstruction of meaning, and sociopathic behavior.

Some therapists, psychiatrists, and analysts withhold from their clients the very insights that are vital to the healing process. There are physicians who will not level with patients about a terminal condition, thus depriving them of the time and the capacity necessary for making personal decisions about how best to live the end of their lives, and provide for surviving family members.

There are also those shadow technicians of human suffering who make their livings wringing the last possible dime out of the bereaved survivors. Related to them are the technicians of hype, of style, of commodities and futures, stocks and bonds, real estate and defense contracts, who have manipulated their respective markets in ways that have impoverished

1. Because of their sociopathy, the acquisition of a
me, for example, is now far beyond the reach of even
........income people.

So many technologists are so malignantly self-serving that they spend their lives blithely furthering the growing gap between the world's "haves" and "have nots." These are the men responsible for acid rain, for the syringes and the oil found polluting our planet's oceans, for the wanton destruction of our irreplaceable rain forests, and for the ozone-destroying production of CFCs. Of course, to the extent that we all benefit from their machinations and do not actively oppose them, we are all responsible for the consequences of their exploitation.

Drug lords, victims of their own infantilism and greed for power, are among those who are most possessed by the active Trickster pole of the Magician's Shadow. Their wealth far exceeds the legitimate needs of any human being. Their technology is centered on the production, refinement, and shipment of the life-threatening substances that poison our children.

In the same psychological predicament as these unfortunate men are the financial "wizards" who use the economic system for their own ends, and give it nothing in return. The men who participate in the genocidal programs of the world are also caught in the cold enchantment of the Shadow Magician. The members of Germany's Nazi party, Russia's Stalinists, China's Communists, Cambodia's Khmer Rouge, and similar contemporary movements in Iran, Iraq, and Latin America (where there are those who still labor, centuries after the Spanish conquest, to eradicate Native American populations) have all demonstrated a willingness to use their technologies to wipe out other peoples.

These shadow magicians do not stop at manipulating people to serve their own ends. In many cases it is Mother

Earth herself they wish to hold in thrall—and Father Sky. The Trickster works to exploit them and uses his powers to destroy anything that looks to be establishing a creative order, or attempting to follow the basic, life-enhancing rituals of initiation into a richer and fuller life.

Men possessed by the Trickster are detached from the common concern for the welfare of others. And manipulative detachment is, as we will see, a hallmark of the Magician's "power shadow." These men are not erotically connected to the larger world; they do not experience the world of flesh-and-blood people, or of human feeling. By being withholding and secretive these men prove themselves to be cruel and sadistic. Exploitative and flagrantly perfidious, they destroy the worlds others are trying to build.

The Trickster differs from the Innocent in that he generally recognizes his manipulative skills, and revels in them. While the works of the Trickster can be manifest in any form of psychopathology, some personality disorders seem to be blatant expressions of his presence.[1] Among these are the Narcissistic Personality Disorder, the Schizoid Personality Disorder, and the Antisocial Personality.

The Narcissistic Personality Disorder is one form of the "independent" personality type. A man possessed by this disorder seems to be exactly the opposite of the dependent man. But as always in the bipolar configurations of dysfunctional coping styles, the two are closely related. The narcissist's independence is an exaggerated compensation for his feared, hated, and repressed dependency. Often men who crave and seize power do so because of their own desperate fear of their weakness. This same phenomenon can also be an aspect of the Shadow Warrior.

Theodore Millon notes that "for the narcissistic type, self-esteem is based on a blind and naïve assumption of personal worth and superiority." Note Millon's use of the word *naïve* in association with the narcissist. This points up the intimate connection there is between the active and passive poles of this shadow formation. Also it makes plain that for all his relative awareness of his urge for power, the narcissist is fooled in any self-appraisal by a basic naïveté.

He often tricks others into believing lies about his effectiveness and power. But he is often tripped up by himself—his habit of lying keeps him from telling the truth even in situations where the truth would benefit him.

Characterized by this naïve, inflated self-image, the narcissistic manipulator, Millon writes, "displays pretentious self-assurance and exaggerates achievements and talents." He is seen by others as "egotistic, haughty, and arrogant." He also demonstrates "interpersonal exploitiveness." He takes others for granted, using them "to enhance self and indulge desires." He "expects special favors and status without assuming reciprocal responsibilities."

The narcissist's "expansive imagination" leads to "immature and undisciplined fantasies," and he often lies in order to "redeem self-illusions." Furthermore he displays a "supercilious imperturbability . . . except when [his] narcissistic confidence is shaken." Otherwise he "appears nonchalant and coolly unimpressionable." His social conscience is lacking, as he "flouts conventions of shared social living" and "reveals a disregard for personal integrity and the rights of others."

Sad to say, this clinical description of the narcissist all too often matches our real-life experiences with bosses, coworkers, and mates. Many are the religious and political leaders on the world scene who fit this portrait of a dysfunctional psyche. We all have our lists of "candidates" who would offer telling examples.

Closer to home is the narcissistic therapist. This is the man who makes snap judgments about a counselee's dreams. He prides himself on making a quick diagnosis. Posing in an impressive leather chair, the narcissistic therapist makes certain that he is clearly in charge. Though he may express a belief that the individual psyche needs a therapist as an ally and a spirit guide only, he actually believes that he holds the key to an individual's healing. After one session he pretends to know (and with an inflated sense of self, may actually believe he knows) exactly the diagnosis and the necessary course of treatment. His magician inflation is easy to see.

This is the "guide" who uses the sessions we are paying for to try out his latest pet theory. He takes up our time and money with tall tales of past glories and clients he has "cured" because of his astounding expertise. He may even take our session time to talk about his own marital problems, or personal hassles with fellow clinic staff members. As he does so he displays what he supposes is wit and charm, as well as the brilliance of his interpretations—again, at our expense. He will often seek to exploit his clients sexually and will fight the establishment and enforcement of codes for ethical practice.

If we catch him in an interpretive error or inconsistency, instead of admitting it, backing up, and rethinking the issue, he will pass his mistake off as our misunderstanding of his comments. He avoids engaging in vital reflection upon issues of countertransference. However, if we press him, refusing to countenance his arrogance, we may well fracture his narcissistic confidence and thereby risk his rageful attack on our "resistance."

In flagrant disregard of the evidence we present to him, and in an act of great emotional brutality, he will attack, rather than ally himself with, our growing sense of integrity. Because he insists upon his own interpretations he will sacrifice our right to a sense of joy and consolidating wholeness. The narcissistic psychotherapist, like all other narcissists, is interested in his own sense of superiority. He is not really interested in our healing, and he will not tolerate our taking charge of the process. He will end by attacking any life-enhancing and world-building structures that take shape within us. And he will do so under the guise of knowing more than we do. He would have us believe he has insights into human nature we do not have, and which he cannot share with us because we lack the necessary intelligence or credentials. He is, unfortunately, well represented in all schools of psychotherapy and psychoanalysis.

The Schizoid Personality Disorder is another face of the Trickster. Millon reports that the schizoid "displays emotional and cognitive deficits that hinder the development of close or warm relationships." He reports that people caught in what we call this crazy space prefer "to concentrate their energies on hobbies such as stamp or rock collecting, mechanical gadgets, electronic equipment, or academic pursuits such as mathematics or engineering."

When schizoid men seek out treatment they frequently report feeling cut off from their own lives, as if living behind "a glass wall." Millon writes that their relationships "seem to have been emptied by a massive withdrawal of the real libidinal self." The schizoid manipulator is cut off from erotic, libidinal connection with the outside world. While trying to deprive others of joy and enthusiasm, they destroy their own capacity for a rich life. Every facet of life becomes reduced to the level of the "mechanical gadgets" they spend their free time tinkering with.

Here the Trickster is manifest in his avoidance of the intimacy and mutuality required for human community. Instinctual energies are not coordinated for community and cosmos (world) building. They are expressed in ways which isolate and alienate—and which ultimately dehumanize both the individual and those to whom he might relate.

Finally, the Antisocial Personality is the most aggressive expression of the anti-cosmic, anti-structure attitudes of the personality possessed by the active pole of the Shadow Magician: His defiant rejection of the masculine tasks of Kingship is almost total. The King's embodiment of divine law as justice has become for him his claim to be a law unto himself. The King's willingness to sacrifice himself for inclusive nurture has been replaced by the sociopathic Trickster's willingness to exploit and cannibalize all others *with extreme prejudice*. The epidemic in the production of these personalities in our culture is a direct result of our failure in providing ritual leadership for human initiation—both masculine and feminine.

It is no wonder that a world like ours, very much in the grasp of the Shadow Magician, is a world in which human beings feel cut off from the wellsprings of nature. In our sterilized, mechanical technosphere, we feel out of touch with other living things.

The ancient shamans led the hunters of their tribes in the pursuit of game, always mindful of the sanctity of human and animal life. They felt close to the spirits of the animals they killed, and prayed to the slain animal for forgiveness. Today we have no similar conception of animals—to us they are not living, breathing beings, with feelings and spirits. Instead we think of there being a number of exploitable beasts in the world, and the trick is to be the best at exploiting them. Our only "direct" contact with animals is with the cellophane-wrapped meat we find displayed in chrome and glass cases, dyed a blood red, luminous under an artificial light.

Is it any wonder we alienate an alienated sky with the CFCs we discharge from our mechanical spray cans? Once that sky was alive with Gods and Goddesses. The rain was once the life-giving semen of a benevolent ally. Now it is the bitter tears of a fouled civilization.

Are our machines killing us? Are we allowing lifeless silicon chips to make of our lives a logical exercise? The schizoid scientist looks to his computer for a metaphor for the psyche, and the rest of us are cowed into agreeing with him. *He must know better than we, we reason; he's the technician, the professional.* Mary Shelley's *Frankenstein, or the Modern Prometheus* stands as the prescient moral fable of our age. Through his black magic Dr. Frankenstein makes a man out of disparate pieces. His experiment goes haywire because of his complete insensitivity to the feelings of the unfortunate being he has created. The outcome of the story is a dire reminder of the effects of a technology prematurely unleashed upon the world by the morally immature.

We do not wish to disparage the professions that draw heavily on the schizoid tendencies of the Left Brain. There are men who work tirelessly and helpfully in them. *However, it is worth the warning that a world caught in the power shadow of the Magician is not only a world in danger, but a world whose continued existence is in doubt.*

Jung was deeply concerned about the trend toward life-lessness and mass society he saw in the unreflecting rush into technological culture. He warned that the collective Ego has become arrogant since the Enlightenment of the eighteenth century, and has assumed a position of "god-almightiness." He predicted that the collective unconscious, cut off from the world of nature and of instinct, would not long tolerate pretensions to godhood. The collective unconscious, he warned, was bound to retaliate on a massive scale against the collective Ego's narcissistic and schizoid relationship with nature. He believed that we would have our own "Promethean debt" to pay to the world of instinct, by suffering a great catastrophe.

Why is there a Trickster present in our biological makeup at all? He does fulfill a purpose—of deflating our hollow pomposity, and embarrassing us with it. When serving life, he is a kind of inner prophet, who calls us to account for our arrogance.

The movie *Batman* turned out to be nothing more complicated than a Trickster parable. Batman's Trickster is embodied by his archenemy, the Joker. In one scene the Joker is merrily enjoying a diabolical parade down Main Street, when Batman flies overhead in a flashy, expensive jet. With all his cannons firing Batman can't hit the Joker, who is standing in plain view in the middle of the street. But the Joker raises a pistol and shoots the million-dollar jet out of the sky. This is a clear picture of the Trickster's role in bringing us down to earth!

Often we give our power away to people we imagine to be better than we are, smarter, more vigorous, or more in charge. The Trickster's task is to find out to whom we are giving our power, and then interrupt the idealizing transference. He puts us in all kinds of awkward positions until we realize we have no choice but to reclaim the unlived aspects of ourselves.

The man possessed by the Trickster, in contrast to the Innocent-dominated man, may be able to find extraordinary space and time, in his work and within himself. But it will be liminoid space and time, not liminal. His narcissistic and schizoid attitudes will prevent him from genuinely being transformed. Because he has not found liminal space himself, he will be unable to take others into it, through it, or back out of it. What knowledge of hidden secrets he does possess, as we've seen, he withholds from those who come to him seeking some kind of initiation.

He may, however, have located the boundary of truly liminal space and time, and there he may position himself as a false guardian of the threshold. There he will sadistically hurl the unwary pilgrim into the abysmal darkness. He may catapult his would-be initiates into the center of the "fiery furnace." Unable or unwilling to help them insulate their disoriented Ego structures, he will be unavailable to aid them in containing the return of their repressed impulses, avoiding danger, discovering their own *axis mundi,* or getting a hand when they need to get back out of crazy time and space. Either he will yank them out prematurely, so they remain "undercooked"—or he will let them burn to a crisp. Through his narcissistic naïveté, and an inflated sense of capacity, he may do these pilgrims irreparable damage rather than helping them. We see this Tricksterism often among self-appointed New Age "shamans" who claim to have been recipients of shamanic initiations but who in fact are merely possessed by the Shadow Magician and his inflation.

Here is the group leader who allows the group process to get out of control. Perhaps this happens through his genuine ignorance, or perhaps he derives from this a secret sadistic delight. The moment a member of the group discloses more about himself than the group can handle, the group may react with moralistic judgments, or hysteria and alarm. The disclosing member immediately discovers that he is not safe. He feels shame and anger, and he has a right to—he has been betrayed.

Here too is the leader of the spiritual community who, because of his own pretensions, leads trusting novices into insufficiently consecrated "magic circles," evoking "spirits" and "demons" beyond his control. They often make a feast of the novices' hopes and aspirations, and perhaps their sanity as well. Here we are reminded of Merlin, who started Arthur on his career of world building, but who "forgot" to tell him the prophecy about Lancelot and Guinevere!

We believe that neither the human psyche nor our society can survive if it continues in a state of possession by the Shadow Magician. Sooner or later, the Shadow Magician who seeks to manipulate life and love, to withdraw from the realm of feeling into a sterile caricature of a sacred reality of his own devising, and to avoid the task of world-building must—like the Wizard of Oz—be released from the deceitful sham of his

existence. The magician line of development must be actual-
ized in a mature way if the four powers of the masculine
psyche are to find wholeness and balance in their expression
in a mature masculine self. Let us turn now to the challenge
of masculine magician initiation.

PART 4

Becoming A Shaman: The Challenge Of Masculine Magician Initiation

9

THE SHAMANIC POTENTIAL IN CONTEMPORARY MEN: THE CHALLENGE OF MAGICIAN INITIATION

MAGICIAN ENERGY IS CALLED FOR IN ALL AREAS OF life, in the professional and the personal sphere. As an energy resource that helps us to organize our psyches, the Magician is indispensable. His energy allows us to live our lives as mature men, consciously and intentionally, and with deep self-reflection.

We've examined what a shortage there is of men willing to embody the Magician to help others through their crises. But there are men out there who are doing this, and they are doing this very well. It's like the proverbial story of the dog that could walk on his front legs. The fact that he can't walk

Einstein

very well isn't as important as the fact that he's walking at all.

Many of those who enter helping professions are looking for help themselves. They are in tune with the Magician because they've been trying to access his energies for their own lives for years. Ministers, therapists, and college psychology majors often do not realize until their training is almost finished that help is really what they were after, and when none was available they became helpers as a substitute.

Helpers who do not realize this have yet to pass the second threshold, back out of the Belly of the Whale. They often begin a career with the zeal of the prophets, because their connection with the archetypes themselves is still so direct, and unmediated by strong Ego structures. The phenomenon of helper burnout soon results. The fantasy of being more than human collapses, and the human does soon after.

It can be helpful to remember the lessons of some of the world's great spiritual traditions. An important one is that the enlightened man is ordinary. He has crossed the threshold into the third stage of initiation and has returned to ordinary space. *Because a man is extraordinarily charismatic does not mean he is enlightened. Like Moses coming down off Mount Sinai, he shines, and he does not know he is shining. And like Moses, his proximity to the numinous may cloud his judgment as to what course of action to take. When choosing a guide, choose him carefully.*

One of the wonderful consequences of *The Power of Myth*, the series of television interviews between mythologist Joseph Campbell and Bill Moyers, is that so many men were painlessly guided to the Magician energy. While no substitute for a flesh-and-blood ritual elder, Campbell did manage to convey his love for mythology to a wide audience. So many men have been called stupid somewhere along the line that they are loath to ever pick up a book. But with the series whetting an appetite for mythology, many of these men are beginning to read again—discovering their undeveloped magician potentials.

Campbell is an interesting example of a modern magician. The Lover and the Magician were clearly the guiding energies in his life. When he speaks with Moyers of Warriors and Kings, he speaks with annoyance. He doesn't like religions of the King or the Warrior. He likes those that emphasize the Magician's wit and both the compassionate and erotic traditions of the Lover.

The Lover values everything, and doesn't want to choose. The Lover is inherently promiscuous. And so Campbell offered us his joyful mythic promiscuity. He loves all the myths of the world, and he wants everybody else to love them too. Bill Moyers was his perfect foil, since he accesses more of the Warrior and King energies of his personality. Between the two of them all four of the archetypes of mature masculinity were brought together, and this, besides the subject matter, helped make the series so popular among men.

Campbell was as far from perfect as the rest of us, and a lot of his Shadow material was exposed in the press after his death. There aren't any perfect men in the world. We have to learn to accept the gifts a man can bring us, and deal compassionately with his failings. His failings should by no means be dismissed, but they should not be used to dismiss him either.

Campbell was a magus whose dying gift was one of inspiration. He got a lot of people excited about myths and the human psyche. Many people have now begun to realize that the world of myth is real, and that we are real to the extent we participate in the myths. They are taking Campbell's message to heart—that now it is time to take all the stories, and use them to build a new, workable planetary myth, one that accepts tribal diversity but transcends tribal limitations in the quest for an Earth Community.

Campbell is one image of a flawed but vital modern magician. It will be worthwhile to consider what a truly mature contemporary magician might look like. We'll begin by considering the characteristics of the shaman, the individual who we believe most fully embodies the archetype of the Magician.

THE SHAMAN AS KNOWER

The shaman is the knower of hidden truth. He gains his knowledge by excursions into sacred space and time. He is an adventurer in the realm of the spirit. He undertakes his journeys outside of ordinary reality initially in an effort to heal and integrate himself. He may not be conscious of this as a motivation—in fact, he may refuse this interpretation. But anthropologists have often noted that the budding shaman is called into the spirit's realm by physical illness and/or psychological distress. And the sacred spaces shamans describe are clearly the healing structures of the psyche.

Once within the imaginal realm the shaman learns its sacred geography. He comes to know the strange inhabitants intimately, and can see and speak to them, where "normal" people can only, at best, intuit them. Once the shaman has become familiar with these inner spaces, he can enter, traverse, and exit these imaginal worlds at will. Through ecstatic flights of the spirit, he ascends his "central mountain," or his "world tree," and can travel either upward to the heavens or downward, into the underworld, along the *axis mundi*.

He learns to draw power from the undifferentiated realm for his own psychic system. He is one of death's intimates, and can stare into the abyss of darkness without escape into denial. Like a high-wire artist, he learns to balance inner forces, and thus becomes adept at accepting and transcending the opposites of the profane world—death and life, darkness and light, activity and receptiveness. He can find the *axis mundi* in his psyche, and so can serve as the manifest center for others. His animal, instinctual nature and his spiritual strivings are brought into a delicate harmony, with neither voice subordinate to the other.

Confucius

Whoever can survive the power of the divine realm has developed an adequate "Ego-Self axis." The shaman has insulated his Ego structures from the high "voltages" of the dynamic structures in the collective unconscious. He learns to be an expert at containment—of his own Ego, of his inner angels and demons, and of the inner voyage as a whole. Because of his psychological facility, he is the successful embodiment of the "observing Ego."

His capacity for movement into and out of sacred reality endows him with an exceptional capacity for creative problem solving. And when a shaman draws on Lover energy as well, he becomes the creative poet, the singer, the artist and the myth maker.

The shaman's tools for evoking altered states of consciousness have been objectively explored in recent years by anthropologists and psychologists. Of primary importance are intensifying visualization techniques—akin to Jung's active imagination exercises—used to picture unconscious contents in vivid detail. In addition the shaman may subject himself to extreme temperatures, or use sensory deprivation techniques to get beyond bodily distractions. He may use hallucinogenic drugs, although this practice is relatively rare. Finally, and universally, he uses auditory stimulation. This is usually in the form of rhythmic drumming. Some researchers believe the drumming may amplify natural body rhythms, such as the heartbeat and certain brain wave frequencies—the same frequencies that are linked to altered states of consciousness.

A traditional shaman is, of course, an anachronism to most moderns. We must find a way to develop new appropriate expressions of shamanic potentials in a postmodern society. There are, as we have seen above, contemporary men who are accessing the energies of the Magician. Let us review again some of these ways in which men today are embodying these potentials.

The contemporary man who accesses these energies enters the sacred spaces of energy fields—from electrical to libidinal—in order to gain firsthand knowledge of their workings. Any world that underlies and gives rise to the material world and the realm of human behavior is ground for his study. He examines the clockworks of the universe, inside and out. He comes to recognize patterns of force that others do not see. He learns to decode mysterious information, whether he is a weather researcher investigating the interactions of fronts or a counselor listening for evidence of the repressed elements of his client's personality.

Though a technical specialist in his field, the contemporary shaman is enough of a generalist to formulate a more encompassing world ethic. He avoids a too-narrow focus on his work, and accepts responsibility for happenings in the outside world. Only those caught in the Shadow energies of the Magician are myopic, limited by their fascination with their own expertise.

Unfortunately most men trained in a technical field are encouraged to be myopic. Consider the engineering student who has one or two electives in the whole of his four- or five-year university course. Because our society is now completely dependent on the knowledge of specialists, the time it takes to learn a specialty precludes learning anything else. As a consequence there are legions of doctors, plumbers, scholars, and lawyers who remain cultural barbarians outside of their fields. They know little of the universe as a whole, of human cultural history and psychospirituality, and thus have no means for forming a coherent and sophisticated picture of the world. These undeveloped individuals don't penalize only themselves—their ignorance inhibits them from contributing their best efforts to our faltering society. We've put a corporate ladder in place of the ancients' ladder to the stars; our monoliths are the ungainly towers on Wall Street.

In traditional societies the shaman always had a larger worldview. Thus the modern who is adequately accessing his shamanic potentials will have wide-ranging interests. He will be deeply concerned about society as a whole, and about his planet. He will be seeking ways to implement the moral application of his insights, in different arenas—legal, political, philosophical, or scientific. He is the kind of man who is committed to an inclusive community, joining and leading other citizens in their efforts to fight global warming, world hunger, pollution, the destruction of the ozone layer, and other planetary problems.

Because his ultimate goal, in whatever career he follows, is to contribute to healing through stewarding his knowledge, the contemporary shaman keeps abreast of the latest developments in his area of specialty, and in general human knowledge too. He doesn't believe his education ends with his last year of school, but continues to study his interests for the whole of his life.

If he happens to be an academic professional, he will find himself continuing to deepen his involvement with the intricacies of his subject. He may be a New Testament scholar who returns at fifty to further linguistic studies—the better to be able to parse out a particular pivotal biblical text. Or he may be a philosopher who repeatedly examines the processes of his thoughts, looking for the moment he moves beyond the bounds of his argument or school of thought. Or he may be a mathematician, worrying his equations until they yield up their numeric secrets—opening us to new conceptual universes.

With the inward focus of their energies, academics are often labeled "absentminded professors." Though they appear to be—and frequently are—detached from the world, these men have an erotic connection with realities we hardly dream of. With some justification they view themselves as

187

mental pioneers, adventurers into the extraordinary spaces of the mind. After all we call their best efforts "breakthroughs," as if they were punching a hole in the limits of our knowledge, and leaving for the rest of the species a new fund of available wisdom.

This is an important embodiment of shamanic potentials in contemporary life.

The contemporary shaman sifts carefully through his professional and personal life for any evidence of irrelevant or destructive behaviors. The Magician is, however, the archetype of introversion and reflection. The man who is under the Magician's sway can fall into the trap of wondering whether he doesn't spend too much time wondering. But the man who successfully embodies his shamanic potentials, accepting his energies but not letting them take him over, is vigilant, incisive, and alert. He quickly gets to the heart of problems others can't fathom. He sees beyond the trees to the forest. Often he will understand people better than they understand themselves.

He makes time to be alone with himself, with his thoughts and feelings. By doing so he maintains communication with his own unconscious. Others gravitate to him, because of his inner order and calm. He sees the shadow in himself and others, and faces the reality of death. At the same time he lives out of a deep inner joy, knowing that ultimately life triumphs over death.

His understanding connects him with the Center, and lends authenticity to his words and deeds. He may have an aura about him of great depth. Others may feel him to have an unseen presence attending him, of extraordinary consciousness. Unusual insight shines in his eyes. Some may experience the unsettling feeling that he can "see right through" them.

Because of his center, he is not easily drawn into the chaos of family disputes, or of clashing personalities in the workplace. He observes things carefully when they begin to fall apart, and thinks strategically before he speaks or acts.

Rigidity is a hallmark of any psychopathology. The man accessing his shamanic potentials can recognize within himself the seeds of all the major personality disorders. However, he remains relatively free of possession by them, thanks to the strength of his Ego structures, and his resulting cognitive and emotional flexibility. His reactions to difficult situations are structured, but creative. He experiences potential calamities as opportunities to learn new coping skills. And since he has worked to understand his childhood wounding, he has learned to take responsibility for what he is not responsible for.

Although he is deeply reflective, he tries not to obsess about issues. Rather he evaluates all the information he has at his disposal, with an aim to implementing a decision. He listens to his advisers and to every voice in his psyche, like a good board president, and then acts with as much wisdom as he can muster.

A fifty-five-year-old man entered analysis while in his second year of divinity school. Lacking any experience in depth psychology, this man didn't realize how deeply he was drawing upon the energies of the Magician. He started therapy feeling like "a jack of all trades, and master of none." He had had a host of jobs, even potential careers, any one of which could have led to a decent life's work. He had painted and plastered; worked in a warehouse, a frame shop, and a car dealership; taught college theater; been a school counselor; run his own business—and now he was preparing for the ministry. He had three master's degrees, but had never wanted to get a Ph.D., because that level of commitment to a limited topic had seemed too confining.

Now he was an impoverished student again at fifty-five, and he began feeling like a failure. But as he explored this sense of failure in analysis, a deep pride spontaneously emerged, along with a conviction of real accomplishment. The Magician energy within this man, as an emissary of the Self, conveyed the triumphal self-assurance that his professional life had been anything but a failure. In fact the variety of his experience had been profoundly enriching.

As he talked in greater detail about his life experiences, it became clear that he was not at all a jack of all trades. Indeed he was a true master of several. In one dramatic session it became clear to him that an inner wisdom had guided him in ways that helped him avoid too narrow a specialization. As a result he was provided with an enormous repertoire of knowledge—technical knowledge in his several fields of study, and most important a rich knowledge of himself, and of other people. Unconsciously using a favorite word of the medieval alchemists, he said it seemed that he had been hard at work for fifty-five years laboring on his "opus." Now it seemed to him his range of experiences gave him an unusually rich background for becoming a real spiritual leader.

The Magician was this man's governing archetype. Like the ancient shamans, he had been moving into and out of different psychological spaces. Throughout his long and often arduous life of inner and outer adventure, he had acquired both the knowledge and the technology of psychospiritual power. With this realization, things began to shift into focus for the analysand. His life began to manifest a purposefulness which before had been hidden just below the level of awareness. He was now more capable of living his life consciously and intentionally. With now a conscious accessing of his shamanic energies, his capacities increased, along with the pleasure he found in them. Today he is a highly respected parish minister in the Chicago area.

THE TECHNICIAN OF POWER

We have seen above that traditional shamans were technicians of power and used that power for personal and social healing. Once the shaman had healed himself, he could begin to help heal others. After the initial and decisive integrative event, a traditional shaman was never self-involved. As the technician of power, his several efforts were always intended to help others.

The shaman's role as chief priest at seasonal festivals emphasized his psychospiritual leadership; his knowledge of sacred reality was his chief weapon against his people's ill health. He mediated also between the sacred and divine worlds, whenever mediation was called for. By his ministrations he led people into death—symbolically, at festivals, and actually—and helped his people through that dreaded portal into life renewed and life eternal.

He worked at curing his people's illnesses using the initiatory scenario. Of course he formally initiated the boys into manhood, following the prescribed ceremonial rituals. But he also initiated the sick into a deeper, richer understanding of themselves—so that they might gain insight into the underlying psychospiritual causes of their symptoms. As part of his healing ministry, he often interpreted his patients' dreams. More unusually he helped them communicate directly with the spirits that were afflicting them.

When the situation warranted, he would intercede directly with the spirits. Thus he was the mediator between his people and other forms of reality. Often this mediating role involved very real dangers for him. He would take physical "poisons," and psychologically malevolent "spirits," into himself, and struggle with them there. The self-sacrificial as-

Navajo Healer

pect of the shaman's healing technique has become the most vital aspect, in Christian theology, of the salvific effect of Jesus the Magician.

Because he was uniquely entrusted with all of these skills, people looked to the shaman to construct and conserve the myths by which the community lived. He educated his people in their own heritage, affirming their natural and societal ideas of stability and order. His people believed that his recitations of the myths of origin were in themselves healing and regenerative. As the primary repository of the myths, he was allowed some leeway to change them, to accommodate the changing times.

We want to emphasize here that every one of man's functions can be seen to be evoking, contain accessing archetypal energies. He accomplishes these tasks ꞊ first for his own sake, but finally for the good of his people; eventually he helps others do the same.

In what ways does a contemporary man become, like the shaman, a technician of power? Any man working with material technology is accessing the Magician to at least a superficial degree. More interesting to us are the psychological ramifications of drawing on the Magician as technician of power. Many of these characteristics apply directly to the practice of psychotherapy. But they also apply to any man—regardless of any diplomas, certificates, or titles—who is attempting to live, and to help others to live, a more intentional and psychologically healthy life.

Because of his own experiences with extraordinary space, this man values the psychological "spaces" of other people. By honoring their inner worlds of thought, fantasy, feeling, and symbol, he helps them value these dimensions of their own being more fully. He appreciates their various ways of picturing to themselves their joy and pain, their hopes and fears, and by doing so he helps to lead them into these inner spaces. The very act of beholding a person helps to heal, mirror, and contain him, and the modern shaman does an excellent job beholding others. He does for them what their parents often could not or did not do for them as children.

Most of us, tragically, have had our inner worlds devalued, criticized, or ignored by our parents. We learn from this to be less than fully present in our minds and feelings. We discredit whole layers of our personalities to please our parents. Thus we leave large areas of the psyche undeveloped, and sometimes even hostile to our conscious identity. This inner "dis-ease" is the cause of many of our psychological, relational, and physical illnesses later in life.

The contemporary shaman, however, helps us to feel worthwhile and self-validated by listening to us, and empathizing with our position. He may not agree with our interpretation of events, because he may have a wider perspective than we have. But he honors our feelings. He will not try to talk us out of our feelings, however exaggerated or inappropriate they may be. Rather he will say something that mirrors us, like "It must be really painful for you to feel this way." Or if the feeling we need to have mirrored is positive, he may say, "That's wonderful! I'm so happy for you." In short, he offers others "empathetic attunement."

This man will be devoted to helping himself and others arrive at the truth in any given situation. He has careful decisions to make, about how much truth to reveal and how best to reveal it. His interest is not in saying something wounding, but something helpful. There will be times when he will have to be firm. Parents, psychologists, and teachers are often called upon to perform this juggling act of affirming another's efforts to arrive at the truth, but gently countering any denial mechanisms that are getting in the way. The rewards are many for those who can work through their defenses, until they see the deeper and more accurate truths the modern magician sees.

This man is an important facilitator in the initiatory processes of the individuals in his life. He works to balance and reconcile the opposing personalities of family members and employees. If his job demands interaction with environmentalists, he works to do justice to his company's concerns and the interests of the living planet as well. If he is a psychotherapist, he works to help clients integrate their warring subpersonalities. Whatever his career, he works to integrate various perspectives and levels of reality, hoping to help those around him find their true centers.

There are many times when standing for the truth is

hazardous to the modern magician's health. Socrates and Jesus both learned how much public denial and hostility are centered around the truth. They had to stand, as have many after them, with no support but their own integrity; finally they were struck down for their moral courage. While the man who is appropriately accessing the Magician will not "cast his pearls before swine" by injudiciously speaking truths in a hostile environment, he will nonetheless stand publicly for the things he believes in. He is willing to risk his job, if an important truth demands it, or risk losing his marriage, his children's affection, or even his life.

When he needs to be, this man is self-sacrificial. When he risks his well-being he does so intentionally. His considered risks are taken without masochism. He draws the poison out of others not to relieve them of their responsibilities, but to ease the burdens on their overloaded Ego structures as they struggle for increased maturity.

There is a moving depiction of a shamanic self-sacrifice in the movie *Star Trek II: The Wrath of Khan.* Toward the end of the film, the Starship *Enterprise* has been mortally crippled after a duel with an enemy. There is only one way to save the ship and its crew. This involves a suicidal mission to be undertaken by someone who has a complete technical knowledge of the ship's power resources. While others gather in the bridge, feeling completely defeated, Spock slips quietly from the scene.

Spock has been the shamanic figure throughout the series, and in the movies that followed. He is a reclusive, mystic contemplative, the knower of truths far beyond the comprehension of his human companions. As chief engineering officer, he is also the technician of power.

Soon Captain Kirk is called to the ship's power system. He finds Spock there, sealed behind a transparent energy shield at the ship's reactor—its sacred core. Spock's body is seared. With his bare hands he has repaired the damage, making the necessary connections and then burning up from the eruption of energy that followed. Separated by the transparent wall, Spock and Kirk both slump to the floor. With tears in his eyes, Kirk asks his dying friend, "Why?" "The good of the many outweighs the good of the few—or the one," Spock replies, placing his hand on the wall in the Vulcan sign for blessing. "I am now, and I will always be, your friend."

At the funeral service Kirk speaks of Spock, whom everyone had regarded as being without feeling, as perhaps "the most human" of all the beings he has known.

The contemporary shaman, at his best, also has a strong connection with the Lover and the King. He is erotically connected with others. In his self-sacrificial mode he performs the greatest act of all. Without masochism, bound to his people by tremendous love, he will, if necessary, lay down his life for them.

The self-sacrificial therapist draws out his client's anger and distrust, recognizing the client's need to engage in temporary transference dynamics. As a parent he invites his children to let him have it. As an activist he may invite the hostility of those who repress their own sense of guilt. He evokes our hidden shadows—when he deems it to be necessary—in order to bring things out into the open, where they can be struggled with and overcome.

The man who organizes his community against drug pushers, who confronts those shopkeepers who sell drug paraphernalia, who marches on City Hall to demand more police patrols and who then takes on the rage of the drug sellers and users he is putting out of operation, is the contemporary shaman. He is the whistle-blower at the power plant who exposes faulty construction practices. He is the minister who preaches against his congregation's habits of gossiping and hate-mongering, thus bringing that spiritual poison down on himself.

Like his traditional counterpart, the contemporary shaman conserves and transmits the norms and values of his
particular specialty—and ideally of his culture as a whole. For
the most part he teaches his students the fundamental and
foundational practices in his field, the perennial wisdom. He
takes his part in cultural continuity. He may be the art instruc-
tor who insists that his students learn thoroughly the insights
and techniques of the old masters before they strike out on
their own. Or he is the master carpenter who insists his students become adept at the handling of basic tools—hammer,
nails, and saw—before advancing to power tools. As a responsible teacher of theology, he insists his students learn the fine
points of the arguments of the historical and systematic theologians who form the bedrock of the Christian intellectual
heritage before they attempt experiments in "constructive"
theology.

At the same time he is himself a seasoned innovator. He
encourages originality in his advanced students, but only in
the context of inherited traditions. With their creativity anchored in major traditions, their originality takes an intelligible form. And as he comes more and more under the influence
of the Lover, he will depart increasingly from established
norms, leaving his innovations to the generations to come.

In summary, the shaman within every man has three
essential responsibilities in the total psychic system. The first
is to serve as a conduit between the Ego and the unconscious.
He locates, consecrates, and stewards the Ego-Self axis, the
inner *axis mundi* from which the psyche gains stability and
dynamism, and around which it revolves. The second major
responsibility is to empower the Ego to actualize the promptings of the Self in everyday life. This involves moving the
ideas from extraordinary reality into concrete, embodied facts
in the ordinary realm. During this activity the psyche—and
particularly the Ego—learns the value of submission, insulation, and containment. Third, the inner shaman must steward

197

the existing mythology of the individual psyche, while at the same time discerning new mythologies as they emerge from the unconscious.

This final task involves enactment, first in the imaginal realm, and later (after refinement and careful consideration) in the realms of social and community life. The assumptions we live by are not thrown away lightly by the Magician within. He tries to make sure we are moving beyond them, as he discerns and evaluates the new directions in which the Self is heading. He tries to ensure that the unfolding of the life of an individual man is as elegant and fullfilling as it can be.

If a man has his Magician on-line, he will embody structure and wisdom as he moves forward—in terms of both his knowledge and his proficiency as a technician of power. He will share his knowledge with others in order to further the healing and initiatory processes taking place within the human community. But how is a man to achieve this mature level of functioning as a human magician? Traditionally, humans have referred to the process of learning to steward innate powers as that of *initiation*. Let us turn now to the challenge of masculine initiation in general—and to the task of Magician initiation in particular.

FOUR MASCULINE POWERS, SEVEN STAGES OF INITIATION

Before we conclude this chapter with an outline of the content of a masculine Magician initiation, we want to invite your reflection on the stages involved in a man's initiation in any of the four powers of the masculine Self. If a man is to become capable of accessing his magician potentials and expressing them in leadership as a ritual elder, he needs more than a few simplistic ideas about initiation and ritual forms. *Rituals, including initiation rituals, were always designed to create or facilitate a certain result in and for the participants.* This means that one needs to have an adequate sense of the task to be achieved before beginning to formulate ritual practices. In traditional tribal and other premodern cultures around the world it was accepted that masculine initiation was not a simple process involving only one transition. Indeed, different cultures presented different theories with regard to the number of stages of initiation required for maturation as a magician. Probably the most widespread emphasis was upon seven stages of initiation. After much reflection on the emphases of tribal cultures in the light of contemporary psychology and Jungian psychoanalysis, we want to suggest a way of thinking about the stages of initiation that can be seen to apply equally to each of the four "lines of development" of the masculine psyche—to each of the four masculine initiations:

1. *In the first stage of initiation in a particular power or masculine potential, the individual cannot experience the power in question as a part of his own resources.* In fact, the individual is so out of touch with the energy or psychospiritual capacity that is lacking that he experiences its absence as a vague uneasiness, emptiness, or longing, with accompanying anxiety, depression, or compulsive behaviors. It is in a psychospiritual situation such as this that the archetype of initiation is constellated and the individual becomes, as discussed elsewhere, a "Quester." He doesn't quite know what he lacks or what he is seeking, but he has begun his "night-sea journey."

2. *In the second stage of initiation, the individual manages to locate the "golden" qualities he longs for. At first, however, he can only experience the potential or quality in projected form in another person, object, or institution.* From

a psychoanalytic perspective we say that he experiences it in what is called an *idealizing transference* to another person. The achievement is that of finding the "lost" part of the Self. The remaining challenge is to internalize it, master, and steward it.

3. *In the third stage of initiation, the individual begins to experience the quality or power in himself.* This is usually a powerful experience and one that quickly leads to what Jungian psychologists call "inflation." Others have called this stage one of "unconscious incompetence." Jung often referred to this as the manifestation of a "mana personality." One is flooded with the raw archetypal power of the archetype being accessed and quickly comes to believe that one is embodying its essence. *In short, one is at least briefly "possessed" by the archetype, unaware that the spell will be broken as soon as the truth of the demands of development of the potential become obvious through a confrontation with the reality of ordinary life.* This is seen often today as men go on their vision quests, encounter the archetype, fantasize themselves as the new bearers of the "golden feather," and return to society offering themselves as shamanic visionaries—usually with an old or new "tribal" revelation. This is a common and dangerous phase on the path of maturation of magician potentials. There are parallel expressions in the other three masculine powers.

4. *The fourth phase of initiation is that of developing the courage to face the ordeals that are necessary in order to achieve initiation in the masculine power being sought.* This has been called a stage of "conscious incompetence," and is what some psychologists have called "achieving the depressive position." It is truly an achievement because the individual has now gotten past his denial and is beginning to acknowledge the challenges he faces in development of the quadrant

of the psyche in question. Now the individual has gone from troubled lack of consciousness of the power to delusional possession by it and now to the much more difficult task of realizing how much work must be done to develop it to a mature and functional level.

His task at this point is to confront his shame and sadness in a constructive way that allows him to avoid simply giving up in a disillusioned depression—usually leading to a continued denial of the developmental challenges being faced. Here he is struggling with the task of developing "true humility": *knowing his limitations and getting the help he needs in the journey.* Here he must locate the master teachers and submit to the discipline and costs involved in the struggle for mastery.

5. *The fifth stage of initiation marks the achievement of a basic or journeyman level of competence in the masculine potential being developed.* This stage has been called "conscious competence," and marks the consolidation of a "good-enough" functioning in a particular sector of the Self. Shadow expressions of the archetype are lessened to a significant degree and anxiety about this area of one's life begins to recede while self-esteem begins to manifest in this "quadrant" of the soul. While one may not feel ready to be a teacher or mentor of others quite yet, one is on the way to a higher level of mastery, idealizes others less, and is more capable of admiring needed mentors. This process continues while one is doing the remaining work needed to achieve adequate balance of the opposites in the soul and become more cohesive and empowered in all four quadrants of the masculine self.

6. *The sixth stage reflects the stage of mastery of the innate power manifest in this particular quadrant of the masculine Self.* This has been called the stage of "unconscious competence." At this level the master of the power has been

able to integrate the potential in question into the "flow" of his functioning so that it *appears* effortless, natural, and un-contrived to others. Recent brain research has documented that there is an actual change in brain function once this level has been achieved. Here we find the discoveries of contemporary science again confirming the assertions of ancient wisdom traditions with regard to the potential of initiatory process. Utilizing the masculine power in question has now moved to a level characterized by a spontaneity and effectiveness heretofore lacking.

7. *The final stage of initiation in a masculine power—the "seventh degree initiation"—is that of the individual's ability to steward the power for the widest, most inclusive human community known to him.* This is, without doubt, the most critical of the developmental tasks facing us. Adlerian psychologists have long emphasized the importance of what they call the *psychology of use* rather than a *psychology of possession.* By this term they are addressing Alfred Adler's belief that the real question of psychological health and human maturation is whether we can bring our potentials and capacities into the service of "social interest"—of the widest possible human community. *How, in short, do we use the abilities and competencies we have developed?* There are millions of men who have "sixth degree" initiations in several of the quadrants of the masculine self. *These men are highly competent warriors, magicians, perhaps even lovers—but have not yet begun to see that their remaining and most critical challenge is one of stewardship for the community of Earth.* Human spiritual traditions have provided us with many images of this level of initiation. In the Magician line of development, a common image of the capacity to steward Magician potentials for liberation and healing in the human community is, as we have already seen, that of the shaman.

We want to emphasize that this "seventh degree" of initiation is a possibility in each of the quadrants of the human self. It is a human species potential—coded in our evolutionary heritage and one that we must keep in consciousness as men and women as we face the challenges of the most critical time in human history. *Without accepting the challenge of this "seventh degree" of human initiation in the four quarters of the soul we will be unable to facilitate the global transformation which is in the balance in our time.*

Before turning to our discussion of the *means* for empowerment in the Magician sector of the masculine Self, we want to outline the *tasks* of the masculine Magician initiation—those of building and empowering the Magician structures of a man's mature masculine Self.

THE TASKS INVOLVED IN A MAGICIAN INITIATION: AN OUTLINE

We have discussed above the bipolar shadow of the Magician archetype. It is, of course, very important to be able to recognize the manifestation of detached manipulation and denial in oneself and others. But it is not enough to grasp the dynamics of the bipolar Shadow of the Magician archetype. *A man's Magician initiation must be reflected in a number of positive qualities, values, and achievements that influence the way he lives and his attitudes and involvements in the wider human community.* In the following discussion we present a few keys that may be used to recognize maturation along the Magician line of development. These "keys" should help you in the task of discerning how you are doing in your struggle toward full empowerment in this sector of your psyche. We recommend that you reflect in depth on the following questions:

1. *An initiated man should be able to claim the intellectual birthright that has been bequeathed to him by the two-million-year-old man within him.* Barring irreversible brain damage, a human male is capable of developing cognitive capacities and wisdom far beyond the level that our contemporary specialists in "education" lead us to believe. Reflect on the following questions: Was I taught by my family system or society that I was "stupid," a "retard" who "just could not learn"? Did my family or society convince me that I had a hopeless "learning disability" that made attempts at further study useless? Often in families the siblings are split into the ones for whom Magician development was permitted, even encouraged, and those for whom intellectual endeavors and successes were off limits. There are many men who have not achieved their high school diplomas or college degrees because of this curse on their Magician potentials by their family system, or their social location in a racist or classist society. Others have avoided graduate school or other continuing studies because this sector of their psyche has never received a blessing by significant others. *American culture in particular is highly anti-intellectual and the impact of television is leading us further into the erroneous belief that anything worthwhile can be communicated in a "sound bite" and learned with little effort.* Increasing tribalism, ethnocentrism, sexism and racism in educational circles, are discouraging the study of huge sectors of our human cultural and intellectual trust. Though he may have to go against the popular assumptions of educational professionals and the prevailing strictures of political correctness, *a man should be empowered enough in this sector of his selfhood to claim his right in principle to access to the entirety of the human cultural, intellectual, scientific, and spiritual heritage—from every human race, culture, and spiritual tradition.* Every man should be empowered to take himself seriously as a human mind—one with the

capacity to participate in and contribute to the cognitive universe represented by accumulated human knowledge and wisdom.

2. *An initiated man needs empowering access to his Magician potentials without allowing them to possess him and drive him compulsively into isolation, detached reflection, and other passive modes that remove him from genuine embodied involvement and commitment in his social world.* Do I tend to retreat into isolation when things are not going well for me? Do I avoid putting adequate energy and time into the cultivation of friendships and love relationships? Do I retreat from the world into my head through compulsive study or intellectual work? Do I tend, therefore, to assume a voyeuristic position in my life-style? When the Magician archetype is having too much powerful but unconscious influence on us, it tends to push us into compulsive detachment and into roles, both social and vocational/professional that both facilitate and mask such unconscious Magician possession. For example, academics, psychotherapists, and religious leaders often have chosen their careers under the powerful unconscious influence of this archetype and continue compulsively to live their lives largely in Magician space. In this situation, the demands of the body, relationships, and public responsibility often are ignored.

3. *An initiated man will have developed the capacity of the Magician sector for "bullshit detecting" without allowing it to drive him compulsively into a marginalized, cynical, and nihilistic relationship to his world. Though he can "see through" sham, pretense, and his own denial, he will retain his ideals and continue to formulate his constructive vision of—and plans for—both self and world.* Am I a practical jokester who cannot get serious about anything or a nihilistic cynic who cannot see anything of sufficient value to get excited

about or to fight for? If you said yes, the corrosive Trickster elements of the Magician sector of the psyche are "deconstructing" both your self-esteem and your possibility of building a world (the mythic "cosmos") that is worth living in. Beneath the surface this is a retreat into one form of a grandiose "Magician inflation" that disdainfully rejects even the possibility of significant, even decisive constructive action in the world.

4. *An initiated man will develop his Magician potentials to access his capacities for self-understanding—for knowing himself, his patterns, his Shadow tendencies, his strengths and weaknesses, the primary agendas for struggle in his movement toward wholeness and full empowerment as a man. He will do what is necessary and pay the price of moving toward mature awareness of the psychosocial dynamics manifest in himself and in others.* Have I experienced repeated patterns of failures and disappointments in my personal and/or vocational life which I do not understand and which I have not made a disciplined and concerted effort to investigate, understand, and change? Have I let the expense and time commitment of individual and/or group psychotherapy discourage me from such efforts toward understanding and transformation? If I have problems with substance abuse or other compulsive behaviors, have I avoided the opportunities for development of the inner Magician offered so effectively by the many 12-Step programs around the world?

In terms of our system of understanding the male psyche, we can ask the questions in this way: Do I understand at a basic level the positive and negative potentials of each of the four sectors of the masculine psyche—King, Warrior, Magician, Lover? Do I understand where I am strong or weak in these sectors? Can I take the diagram of the masculine Self in Appendix A of this book and shade in the areas where I have achieved basic mastery and mark those where I still need more work? Do I have a plan for facilitating my continued empowerment in each of the four quarters?

5. *An initiated man will not be easy prey for the simplistic, totalistic, and tribal visions offered by the spiritual, political, or ideological charlatans of his day. He will not allow "true believers" of any totalistic pietism to narrow his view of either the human past or the human future. He will find other means to manage his anxiety without surrendering the freedom of his mind to ideologues.* Am I a credulous "true believer" in a fundamentalistic sect, whether ideological, political, psychological, or religious? Fundamentalists of all kinds are on the ascendant around the globe today. There are fundamentalist Jews, Christians, Muslims, Hindus, Buddhists, Native Americans, and so on. In psychology there are fundamentalist Freudians, Adlerians, Jungians, Kohutians, Kleinians, and so on. There are fundamentalist Democrats and Republicans. There are even fundamentalist "deconstructionists" and so-called "postmodernists," who claim to be standing against such fundamentalisms but in fact are fueling the current intercultural fragmentation and growing malignant tribalism. The task of seeing through the unconscious Magician inflation of all contemporary fundamentalisms is a growing task that faces us both personally and politically.

6. *An initiated man will not allow himself to ignore his moral and spiritual responsibility for the stewardship of his cognitive, intellectual, and academic achievements. He will struggle resolutely against the prostitution of his mind by antisocial and unjust political and economic interests which are the enemies of an inclusive human future.* How am I doing at stewarding my knowledge and mastery of the human scientific, cultural, and spiritual trust that has been bequeathed to me by my human ancestors? Am I squandering it

in trivial pursuits? Am I hoarding it and manipulating the power I have gained through it solely for the selfish interests of my merely personal agendas or those of my social class, race, gender, guild, or professional in-group? Do I try to keep my technical knowledge esoteric so that the "masses"—the ordinary men and women of the human community—will have to buy it from me at inflated prices? Or am I seeking every possible means to make the liberating and healing benefits of this knowledge and mastery truly accessible to the widest possible inclusive human community?

7. *An initiated man will not seek to avoid the painful effort of study, of the intellectual and spiritual preparation that will be required if he is to assume his full role as a human ritual elder for an inclusive human community.* Have I begun and am I persevering in the studies necessary for me to be a responsible participant and leader in a post-tribal, interracial, interfaith inclusive EarthCommunity? Some would have us believe that initiation in the Magician sector can be radically simplified and achieved through a few relatively undemanding ritual or devotional practices. *Unfortunately, this is another quite prevalent form of Magician inflation which offers the lazy man's dream: an easily acquired, anti-intellectual, pseudo-Magician certificate.* These offers of weekend workshop Magician/shaman initiations come in all brands from Apache to Sufi, from Baptist to Buddhist. Certainly they often do an effective job in regressing us into the direct experience of the Magician archetype, the archetype of initiation, and *liminal* or *liminoid* space. The good news is that there is a rich, multitribal, multicultural heritage for us to touch and to steward—and many who will help us learn the various tribal offerings. *The bad news is that the requirements of responsible Magician development in our critical time leave no place for a new simplistic tribal pietism that turns*

*aside from the requirements of intensive studies to p.
ourselves for being responsible citizens of an inclusive
tribal community.* These studies must include broadening
awareness and understanding of major world mythical and
spiritual traditions as well as the insights from the human
sciences necessary to understand the human psychological and
spiritual unity that underlies these varied traditions. *This is
not a task merely for those who would like to style themselves
an intellectual elite. Ordinary men from all walks of life are
now pursuing such studies and sharing them with each other
and with their communities.*

In short, have I done the work necessary to prepare
myself to be a Ritual Elder for my family, for other men and
boys, for my wider human community? *We cannot finally
delegate our Magician responsibilities to those who offer
themselves as credentialed "professionals" either as academ-
ics/educators, psychotherapists, or religious leaders. We must
assume our own involvement in and responsibility for the
ongoing moral and spiritual guidance, celebrations and rites
of passage in our personal, familial, and communal lives.*
The completion of a "vision quest," a Master of Divinity
degree, a doctorate in psychology or psychiatry, is no guarantee that a man has done the initiatory spiritual work necessary
for functioning as a human ritual elder. A great shaman once
gave us the key litmus test on this issue: He said, "You shall
know them by their fruits." Are people liberated, empowered,
and healed by their presence or not?

We should apply this test to ourselves as we assess our
development in this area. Perfectionism is a demonic mirage,
not a realistic standard. A man with a "good enough" Magician initiation will become—as did his forebears in tribal
cultures—a responsible Ritual Elder for his people. He may
not make his living by providing such leadership—but like the
Apostle Paul, he may offer it in the service of a larger, inclu-

sive vision. He may express this leadership in personal and family ritual and celebration, in men's groups, in leadership in religious groups, Scouting, recovery, and through many other community organizations. *What is certain is that he will provide liberating, empowering, and healing ritual leadership for his people. He will steward his shamanic potential for the Earth Community.*

10

THE SORCERER'S APPRENTICE: ACCESSING AND MASTERING MAGICIAN POTENTIALS

JUNG BELIEVED THAT WHEN WE VIEW OUR LIVES from a perspective "outside" ourselves, outside, in other words, normal Ego consciousness, we tend to become aware of an invisible center. In his essay *Dream Symbolism in Relation to Alchemy*, he notes:

> We can hardly escape the feeling that the unconscious process moves spiral-wise round a centre, gradually getting closer, while the characteristics of the centre grow more and more distinct. Or perhaps we could put it the other way round and say that the centre—itself virtually

the knowing self?

The Buddha (Sārnāth, fifth century A.D.)

unknowable—acts like a magnet on the disparate materials and processes of the unconscious and gradually captures them as in a crystal lattice.[1]

This invisible center is, Jung tells us, the archetypal Self, around which all individual psychic material is organized. The Self is the *axis mundi* of the psychic world. Out of chaos it organizes a personality, and then turns it to face the cosmos.

Jung pictures the Self as a mandala. A mandala is a ubiquitous image of the complete Self, a circular or square-shaped image of totality. The Sanskrit word *mandala* comes from the Tibetan Buddhist tradition. Mandalas are incredibly complex circular paintings of the cosmos done by monks.

Throne rooms, palace-temple complexes, the great urban centers throughout our species' history, sacred circular spaces like Stonehenge and other magical sites all ultimately represent the organized and balanced Self within every man. The same creative order found in an individual exists within the collective psyche of humanity as a whole—waiting to be discovered and embodied.

A man usually turns to reflect upon his life at some point during its second half. When he does this, he may look back and see the patterns and structures of the energies that shaped him. These were present even before he identified them, moving his life in a Self-determined course. He may see the extraordinary space and time he carries at the center of his psyche, which erupts from time to time, moving him through transitional states. His life, he may notice, has in effect been spiraling ever closer to a consciousness of its essence. After encounters with his Shadow, his Anima, and all his other complexes, neuroses, and archetypal energies, he reaches finally his invisible, profoundly mysterious center. If he has been able to answer the calls that have come to him—in trauma and disappointment, crisis and craziness—then he has passed through a deeply self-healing and integrative process. He has been initiated into the fullness of his archetypal Self—the Diamond Body within.

ACCESSING TECHNIQUES

By learning to access the archetypes of mature masculinity appropriately, we enable ourselves to become "generative men." Appropriate access involves allowing the inner Magician to insulate our Ego structures, and maintain the boundaries between those structures and the enormous energies of the archetypes. Then the Ego may tap into those energies safely, and use their specialized forms of life-force for more fulfilling, committed, and creative living.

Generative men are world makers. They consciously choose to become part of the solution, not the problem. They enable our societies, in small ways and large, to become genuine stewards of all systems of life on Mother Earth and under Father Sky.

Contemporary men can access the Magician energy using exactly the same methods they use to access the other archetypes of mature masculinity. In preceding volumes we have detailed these methods. In *The King Within* we laid out the techniques of objectification, imaging, and active imagination work in its various forms—including the various forms of prayer and meditation.[2] The psychotherapeutic process can also be useful. We emphasized the importance of bonding with other men, and of reading biographies of great men who, with all their flaws, embody some aspects of King energy. In *The Warrior Within* we wrote of dream interpretation and active imagination dialogues as techniques for achieving access to the archetypes in their fullness.[3]

The same techniques need to be engaged in by the man

who wants to get beyond his possession by the bipolar Shadow of the Magician, and move toward a life-enhancing accessing of the Magician. Like the shamans of old, such a man will need to access the knower and the technician of power within himself in order to help initiate himself into a more integrated, conscious, and intentional way of being. Ultimately, again like the ancient shamans, he will access the Magician in order to help others make their own lives more meaningful and generative.

There are two further techniques to emphasize in the accessing of Magician energy. Let us recall the example of the enervated young man who felt disoriented and lost in his own apartment, and who needed his girlfriend to provide him with an organizing center. This man was obsessional about two related "normal" forms of human behavior. He reported his preoccupation with the placement of objects: on his desk at the office, on the tables in his home, on his dresser. In fact, whenever he was called upon to set something down—his coffee cup, his pen, a dish rag, or a piece of paper—he would get physically "stalled" while deciding where to set it. Only once he found a spot that "felt right" for the object could he set it down. Finding the right spot left him feeling greatly relieved.

Numbers were his second obsession. He counted the number of times he puffed on his cigarette, the number of times he sipped his coffee, and the number of strokes he used to brush his hair.

His first behavior was a way of trying to find his own center, and "orienting" his own feelings in relationship to his own inner and outer world. Once this was pointed out to him, he was instantly released from his anxiety over this quirk. *He was able to appreciate that his obsession with object placement had been a useful first step in finding a center for himself.* And over a period of time, as he began to gain more inner structure, these centering behaviors greatly diminished. They eventually subsided to the level on which other people habitually operate when trying to arrange furniture, or style their hair, until the look is "right."

His obsession with numbers was again understandable as an attempt to center, this time using a kind of internal mathematics. There is a very common Jungian conception of the importance of numbers to the psyche, particularly in terms of odd or even values. As any mathematician will tell us, numbers are symbols. Jung believed numbers are one of the symbolic systems we use to picture psychological processes and structures to ourselves. Basing his ideas on the dreams and preoccupations of his analysands, and supplementing these with insights from the ancient traditions of numerology, Jung noted that even numbers tend to stand as symbols of wholeness and centered stability, and odd numbers represent incompletion, and dynamic forward movement.

Thus even numbers represent the psyche at rest, in a self-integrative phase. Odd numbers show the psyche in the process of venturing outside itself. This is readily comparable to the fundamental processes of systole and diastole—and of the inhalation and exhalation so important to integration in the Eastern mystical traditions. The phases of the initiatory process reflect this pattern. After an expansive enhancement of status, the initiate moves onto a structural plateau (even numbers) and then moves again into a dynamic period of liminality (odd numbers).

Jung developed quite an elaborate interpretation of psychic processes in terms of numbers, which we will not recount here. It is sufficient only to note the feelings the young man had about the odd and even numbers he used in his counting rituals. He felt secure and centered if his routines ended on an even number, and restless when he ended on an odd one—encouraging a forward-moving dynamic as he searched for another number to resolve the "incomplete" feeling the odd numbers gave him. After being made conscious of the ways his counting rituals tapped into his inner psychological structures and energies, he was able to accept them without anxiety. And again as his inner structures consolidated, his counting rituals tapered off to the level at which most people unconsciously engage in them as normal visualization.

We tried an experiment to engage the young man's apparent sensitivity to numbers and locations. Taking a cue from Don Juan's instructions to Carlos Castaneda, we suggested the young man try an exercise. He tried it during one of his featureless Saturday afternoons, when he naturally had a significant amount of time to be by himself in his apartment. As suggested, he didn't turn to his TV or his stereo, but offered instead a prayer to his inner Magician. Then he sat cross-legged on the floor and waited, without moving, to see what feelings he would encounter in that spot, and what numbers might occur to him. He recorded the numbers and his feelings in a notebook he carried with him.

He moved around the apartment, trying one spot after another. He made a map of the entire floor area of the apartment, trying to find the "power spot" or places at which he felt most centered, powerful, structured, and alive. These "sacred spaces" he would then be able to enter at will in the future, whenever he felt the need to get in touch with their particular feeling-toned character as an expression of his inner Center.

Of course on a certain level what he was doing was mapping his own inner structures and energies. He found the exercise immensely stimulating and reassuring. It did two things for him simultaneously. *First of all, it gave form to the previously unstructured space of his apartment.* He was able now to orient himself immediately when he walked through the door. Secondly, as his analysis proceeded, he was able to see how his external map was the projection of his own inner geography.

He had in fact discovered one special space, near the west

wall of his living room. There he felt his inner *axis mundi* most powerfully constellated. He began structuring his activities around different hours, noting the differing feelings aroused at one hour or another. He plotted the rise and fall of his energy levels, the onset of his feelings of malaise, and the beginnings of his feelings of vigor. Eventually all of these discoveries were integrated into the rest of his analytic work, and the young man became more attuned to the extraordinary regenerative spaces and times he carried within himself. By using ancient shamanic techniques, he had gone a long way toward successfully accessing the Magician within himself.

FIVE STAGES TO ACCESSING
THE MAGICIAN WITHIN

David Feinstein has outlined "A Five-Stage Model for Fostering a Revitalized Personal Mythology" in an essay on shamanism.[4] It offers an excellent technique for invoking the inner Magician, and for using Magician energy for the purpose of self-reflection and personal transformation. We've drawn heavily on Feinstein's method, though using a slightly different vocabulary, in the following discussion.

Stage One—
*Recognizing when a guiding myth
is no longer an ally, but an enemy*

As we become sensitive to our psyche's processes, we will discover many instances in which the "guiding myth" is not working. We find that the dysfunctional family patterns we were taught, the "old tapes" that may convince us we are less than worthwhile, that we cannot succeed or be happy, are getting in our way. Old ways of experiencing ourselves, and the meaning of our lives, are no longer valid. Transitional experiences often prompt our awareness of unusable guiding myths. Traumatic events, life crises, separation and loss—as well as positive events, such as job promotion, marriage, the birth of children—all may shake our life habits to their foundations.

An increasing sense of dissatisfaction, anxiety, or depression may also signal that we are beginning to outgrow our old identities. An obsession with ritualized behaviors, as in the case of the young man described above, may inform us that we are being called into extraordinary reality, in order to be initiated into further knowledge of ourselves and of our lives.

If we are accessing the Magician adequately, we will recognize what such unsettling, sometimes disastrous events portend. We will allow our inner Magician to reveal the Self's demands, which move us ahead in our spiraling journey to the Center. Reflecting deeply, we may discover that our formerly sustaining life-myths are holding us back. If this is our finding, then we must recognize these old myths to be our inhibitors, even our mortal enemies, and no longer our allies.

Stage Two—*Bringing conflicting myths into consciousness*

As we become more aware of the old myths by which we have lived our lives, we will also find other impulses registering in our consciousness, gifts from the knower within. We may have other images for our lives, repressed hopes and visions to explore, and paths to take out of our pasts. We need to attend carefully to these evanescent impulses, and explore them as consciously as possible. We will need to use active imagination techniques and other methods of imaging and objectifying in order to do this. When we can hold new and old myths side by side in our consciousness, bearing the painful tensions of their opposition, we can begin to explore the full meaning of each.

Stage Three—*Evoking a new mythic vision*

We begin then to amplify the images, feelings, and visionary patterns that we find welling up from the unconscious. Through active imagination dialogue, dream interpretation and amplification, we will seek a greater and greater clarity from the emerging images.

What are they saying to us? What new meanings do they offer us for our lives? What directions are they pointing us in? And as we gain a more coherent vision for ourselves, we will discover the implications the vision has for our acting in the world—for our vocation or mission in life.

There is a stage in the psychotherapeutic process called "enactment," and this is the time when possible courses of action are mulled over and rehearsed in the imaginal realm. Whatever new vision a man has been given, he must imagine very specifically how it might look in terms of his actual life. It might be he is called upon to make a career change, a physical move, or a change in his patterns of relating to others. He needs to refine the vision in a dialogue with the unconscious. This way he can find realistic strategies that he can implement in order to embody the extraordinary in the ordinary. Drawing on the energies of the Magician, he makes himself the mediator between the various levels of reality in his own life.

Stage Four—*Committing to the new myth*

If engaged in a psychotherapeutic process, we can make this commitment in the form of a contract with our therapist. If not we can make our contract directly with the Magician, and beyond him, with our true Self. In this contract, we will commit ourselves to a step-by-step plan for taking action to embody our new myth in our daily lives. We will commit, as far as possible, to bring our heaven to earth, as we incarnate our divine energy in our daily human lives.

Stage Five—*Embodying the new myth in our daily lives*

Once we have made the contract, we will need to fulfill it no matter how painful or taxing that may be. Old patterns of thinking, feeling, and behaving die hard. Complexes and neuroses are amazingly resilient. When we least expect it, they find ways to reassert their rigid, life-denying power. Shadows are incorrigible and intractable. They cannot be overcome simply by an act of will. They cannot be banished by good intentions. Dysfunctional patterns will fight for their lives. Thus we must exercise the shaman's hypervigilance and self-discipline. We have to establish the boundaries we have contracted for and defend them, as the angel guarded the boundaries of the Garden of Eden with his flaming sword. We will draw our "magic wands"—our phallic power in its Magician form—to insist upon our new Ego structures, and protect our fragile Ego-Self axis.

Old patterns tend to urge regression with the force of a tidal pull. Because its activity is unconscious, this regressive undercurrent is particularly dangerous. But if we are committed to a new vision of ourselves in the world, and we work to embody our new myth, we can complete our initiations successfully. We can call upon the Technician of Power to move us from immaturity to maturity.

Eventually we will move to a position of strength from which our Ego can gain access to all four archetypes of mature masculinity. For as Blake doubtless discovered on one of his shamanic excursions into the collective unconscious:

Four Mighty Ones are in every Man;
a Perfect Unity
Cannot exist. but from the Universal
    Brotherhood of Eden
The Universal Man. To whom be
Glory Evermore Amen.[5]

DEVELOPING THE

SHAMAN IN THE MALE PSYCHE:

A CONCLUDING SUMMARY

For thousands of years, human sorcerers have engaged in the use of mystification and "mumbo jumbo" as a part of their cultivation of their "magician persona" while practicing their craft. Some have interpreted this as just another expression of the tendency toward deception and manipulation often observed in practicioners of this social role. We believe, however, that there may be another explanation for this use of dramatic technique in the functioning of the Magician/shaman. *Since most persons, past and present, tend to underestimate the sheer scope and difficulty of an adequate Magician initiation, human magicians may have used their theatrical techniques to maintain interest on the part of their pupils for the years of fatiguing study required to become a master magician.* We must remember that in many human cultures prior to modernity, one did not expect to achieve the maturity required for the role of Ritual Elder before the age of forty at the earliest. Our time requires an equal amount of seriousness on our part. In some ways, the task of the post-tribal Magician initiation is more challenging than ever before in human history—and more important for the human future.

In the preceding volumes of this series we have presented

various means of accessing the four powers of the male psyche, many which are applicable to work with each of the different archetypes. We have reviewed some of these in the above discussion. But before concluding our reflections on the enormous challenge of a Magician initiation adequate for our critical times, we would like once more to summarize some of the most helpful means of developing in this critical area of masculine maturation.

1. *Schedule into your life times of retreat and reflection on a regular basis.* Just as "garden time" for the Lover aspect of the Self must be carefully scheduled and protected, the sacred space of contemplation and transformation must be carefully located, accessed, regularly utilized, and protected from external demands. There is no way that one can give adequate energy to the task of one's Magician development without such set-aside space and time.

2. *Begin to work toward finding and ritualizing your own sacred places and times for inner work.* These can include special retreats away from home, planned on a regular basis, as well as set-aside spaces and times in one's home and daily schedule. The more disciplined you become in this ritualization of space and time, the more your Magician functioning will be empowered to serve the other sectors of your selfhood and life.

3. *Work toward a disciplined utilization of dream interpretation and active imagination.* An excellent practical guide to both of these means toward self-knowledge is Robert Johnson's excellent book *Inner Work*. There are no more powerful means for developing an ongoing relationship with the Wise Man within us, and Johnson is a master of the art. You may want to seek out a competent therapist to assist you in your journey until you feel capable of continuing the quest under the leadership of your inner guides.

4. *Begin to keep a personal journal as an ongoing container for your inner work.* Seek out the Intensive Journal Workshops developed by Ira Progoff. Progoff is a Jungian analyst who quite rightly believes that the utilization of insights from depth psychology cannot be limited to the analyst's consulting room. He has developed an in-depth journaling technique that provides a structured and intensive engagement with the great questions of meaning and vocation in one's life. There are ongoing series of these workshops that provide continuing opportunities for reflection and deepened insight.

5. *Find an ongoing men's group that is seeking to develop masculine potentials in its members and that is not afraid to experiment with creative ritualization.* Helpful resources here include Bill Kauth's excellent book, *A Circle of Men,* and the anthology *Wingspan: Inside the Men's Movement,* edited by Christopher Harding. Both include resource guides and helpful bibliographies for explorations in this area. Such an involvement will not only give you a container for ongoing exploration of personal and interpersonal issues, it will also give you an opportunity to serve others as a ritual elder. Practice in a men's ritual group will give you the experience, competence, and confidence you need before you will feel ready to offer leadership in widening areas of family and community life. One extremely important contribution of participating in a men's group on a regular basis is that it helps one avoid the chronic detachment that often accompanies exploration of the Magician sector of the Self. Another is that the "bullshit indicators" of the other men in the group will help you catch yourself when you begin to levitate to "never, never land," and the ongoing relationships and cooperation will keep you grounded. Finally, the containment and ongoing support of the group will aid you in getting past your own

denial, standing the pain of increasing insight, and mobilizing the courage for liberating changes in your life-style.

6. *Defy those who would shame your intellectual abilities or who would seek to limit the scope and/or depth of your studies. Claim the two-million-year-old mind that is your birthright! Shamelessly* build your personal library and let it make a statement to those around you. Let your investigations range from tribal culture, myth, and ritual to explorations in Eastern and Western philosophy and religion. In spite of the harangues of contemporary "know-nothing" ideologues, claim your right to study and learn from the intellectual legacy left us by Earth Men and Earth Women from all of the tribes of our Home Planet. *This includes the intellectual legacy of Western civilization.* You have a right to benefit from the tutelage of an E. D. Hirsch into the requirements of literacy today and to penetrate the metaphysical visions of a Paul Tillich or an Alfred North Whitehead. Do not let the new tribalism of some in our society today lessen your freedom to explore any regions of the sciences and humanities that are your human heritage. Follow your passion in your studies and do not hesitate to make sacrifices to make them a reality. Stewarding your intellectual potentials is not just "selfish." Your studies will increase the quality of leadership you can offer your community.

7. Finally, remember that the latest popular perspectives being pushed by the media, religious leaders, or the dominant academic "priesthoods" may not be helpful for the healing of our planet, the creation of Earth Community, or the development and implementation of a post-tribal, species ethic. Keep your "bullshit and cowshit" detectors in good repair. In the next few critical decades you will need them as never before.

Take, for example, the anti-Jungian bias in contemporary academic and religious circles. It is amazing to us that so many

225

would-be intellectual and spiritual leaders have not made the effort to get past simplistic stereotypes of C. G. Jung's work and its contemporary relevance. *Jung and his intellectual legacy in fact offer us one of the few large visions of the possible human—one that does not lose the magnificence and splendor of our species and its potentials.* Jung's tradition would have us bridge science and religion and look beyond tribal visions that divide us as a species. As one of the first truly postmodern shamans, he has left us a challenge to move to a new inclusiveness in our spirituality. After Jung, all tribal visions must be reframed in the context of an inclusive Earth-Community. *In short, mature shamans in the future must seek the wisdom and vision to be EarthShamans. Anything less will be a betrayal of our species.*

BECOMING AN EARTHSHAMAN: STEWARDING MASCULINE MAGICIAN POTENTIALS FOR A POST-TRIBAL HUMAN COMMUNITY

I F ANYONE EVER THOUGHT THAT KNOWLEDGE ALONE would bring spiritual or moral maturity, a careful study of the history of human culture would quickly shatter that fantasy. Images of the demonic, antisocial magician abound throughout the cultures of the world. Just as careful, disciplined development of one's Warrior potential does not guarantee that one will steward them in the interests of the human community, empowerment on the Magician line is equally susceptible to diversion into antisocial, egoistic pursuits. Con-

Accessing: Etruscan Magician at the Gates of Death
(rear wall of the Tomb of the Augurs, Tarquinia, 540–520 B.C.)

trary to contemporary romantic views of tribal cultures, medicine men "of high degree" have always been tempted to misuse their powers for manipulation, demagogy, and/or personal
economic gain. As we have seen above, living in "Magician
space" predisposes one to a heightened cynicism, even nihil-
ism in all areas of one's life. We touched briefly on some of the
negative expressions of Magician potential in our chapter on
the Trickster. Before we conclude our discussion, however, we
want to emphasize again that many of the unique problems of
contemporary culture can be seen as directly traceable to the
Magician inflation of modern intellectual and professional
elites. As we have seen above, this prevalent Magician inflation
has been manifest in the antisocial, tricksterlike abuse of
scientific and technical knowledge. Perhaps the most infa-
mous examples of this tendency were seen in Germany's Third
Reich where many of the most powerful intellects in German
culture were easily recruited into Hitler's brain trust. As if
ignorant of Goethe's *Faust,* they worked to develop the Nazi
propaganda machine and Hitler's new military technology including the V-1 and V-2 rockets. They provided scientific
expertise in designing the "final solution," even doing "scientific" experiments on the men, women, and children in the
death camps.

*We want to stress here, in conclusion, that this tendency
to use knowledge of all kinds in antisocial ways is a universal human phenomenon.* In another example, even the most
liberal and social-justice–oriented Christians often still develop sophisticated theologies that teach church members that
Christians are "the people of God." *This, of course, implies
quite clearly that non-Christians are not the people of God.
These well-meaning religious leaders are continuing to use
their knowledge to perpetuate a pseudospeciating influence in
the human community.* In a time when theological education
in America postures a great deal on the topic of "globaliza-

tion," the lack of emphasis on comparative religions in theological seminaries is a clear expression of this parochial, clearly tribal, insularity. *Fundamentalists of the different spiritual traditions are even more blatant examples of attempts to use knowledge not just to excuse but to promulgate spiritual narcissism, psychological splitting, and intergroup hatred.*

But it is not just our religious leaders who are playing "Shadow Magician." The greedy exploitation of medical knowledge by the American medical profession is an enormous dragon which our society has not yet even begun to face. Our inability to confront the greed of medical practitioners is no doubt a mark of the primitive level of our initiatory development in each of the four powers. But the role of undeveloped Magician potential in the public is clear. *We have an idealizing Magician-transference to physicians which is so archaic and unconscious that we cannot call them to account without experiencing unmanageable anxiety—therefore we avoid the moral and political responsibilities that face us in the area of health care.*

Understanding Magician inflation can also help us understand the behavior of our legal profession and professional politicians. Is it not ironic that those whose professed responsibility it is to steward our legal system are so flooded by Magician energy that legal tricksters now preside over the deconstruction of justice in our courts? *Contemporary public disillusionment not just with the legal system but with the entire political process is traceable in large part to the dominance of Trickster energy in both legal practice and professional political life.* This includes the employment of "spin-doctors" to enable candidates to lie more effectively and sophisticated techniques of deception to keep the public from becoming aware of the selling of the public trust to the highest bidder without reference to the consequences for the body politic. It is noteworthy to us that we tend, in the context of our disillusionment, to consider this situation a condition to be endured rather than a problem to be solved. This is simply another mark of our acceptance of masculine immaturity as normal and business as usual—and our inability to recognize and name monster-boy behavior when we see it.

The most important issue, therefore, is how we use our Magician potentials—are we stewarding them for the health of both selfhood and community or are we allowing them to possess us and push us under the influence of the Shadow Magician? We hope that the discussion above has empowered you toward the fullness of your Magician potential and toward effective stewardship of it.

THE KEYS TO THE KINGDOM

We have standing on a desk in our Chicago office at The Institute for World Spirituality a limestone relief sculpture, about six inches across, ten inches high, and an inch and a half deep. It is a relief carving of Saint Peter, one of the greatest magicians ever. The artist—apparently medieval—has cut deeply into his material, so that Saint Peter appears to be remarkably free of the surrounding stone.

The apostle is sitting in semiprofile. His bearded face is turned toward us, and his head is surrounded by a halo—a symbol of his enlightenment, and of a mind aglow with divine energy. He sits on his padded chair like a draftsman before his drafting table, or like an engineer, or a secretary, a designer, or any of us really, sitting before our typewriters and computer screens. He sits in a paradigmatic, archetypal position— straight-backed, with a slight slope in the shoulders, and one foot resting slightly ahead of the other.

Saint Peter is sitting under an ornate arch. His chair, and

the bulk of his body, effectively blocks this entrance to the inner world lying stretched out behind him. That arch is like a gate, or a portal into the vast boundary wall found everywhere and nowhere between here and now and there and then.

The old magician is wrapped in a Roman cloak. His eyes are bulging, wide awake, like the eyes of the individuals in the Sumerian statues. They are filled with the terror and wonder of the witnessed sublime. His left hand is raised, and one finger of this hand holds his left eye open wider, as if to say "Behold! I see you! Do you see me? Everything is in the eye of the beholder. If you wish to pass through this gate, which I guard here against those who sit in darkness, then you will have to be able to see! Only if you can see will I allow the crossing of this threshold!"

In his right hand Saint Peter holds a key. His key is every bit as big as a scepter, a sword, or a magic wand; it is the key to heaven—the key that will unlock the gates of the paradisal realms and dimensions, so that the initiated may pass. This same key can be used to unlock the dungeons of hell and free the captives.

This ancient archetype sits here, a symbol of the Magician's best efforts to teach, inspire, nurture, and empower. He is the guardian of the threshold between ordinary time and space and those extraordinary worlds from which we descend, and to which, according to the mystics, we will return. Here sits the locator, consecrator, container, and steward of sacred space and time, saying to us, like all great teachers, wise men, poets, and prophets: "Look! Wake up! See more deeply. Know, as I know! And then, I will unlock the doors for you. 'In my Father's house are many rooms. I have prepared a place for you!'[1] 'As we were, so shall we be. Weep no more. Follow me!' "[2]

APPENDIX A

DECODING THE
DIAMOND BODY:
BEYOND JUNG

I N THE FOLLOWING BRIEF DISCUSSION WE WILL
show how we believe we have furthered Jung's work on the
deep structures of the Self. Our work builds upon his fundamental metapsychological assumptions.

Many Jungians have forgotten the nature and depth of
Jung's commitment to the *quaternio* and *double quaternio*
structures of the human Self. Jung believed that the human
preoccupation with quadration reflected a structural reality in
the collective unconscious. His best-known work on quadration is his typology—particularly in his explication of the four
functions of intuition, sensation, thinking, and feeling. Less

well known is his idea that the totality of the archetypal Self has been imaged clearly in the octahedron.

He presented his most extensive exposition of this double quaternio of the deep Self in his essay "The Structure and Dynamics of the Self" in *Aion*. Jung's intent was to articulate the various ways in which an octahedral shape of the Self may be shown to contain psychological insight (Figure 1). While he struggled mightily to make his case, many have found his exposition hopelessly opaque.

A few prominent Jungians have continued to search for the key to Jung's fascination with this particular octahedron. Others have adopted a similar octahedral shape to explain the deep Self, but have reinterpreted the meanings of the diamond's various facets and planes. Notable among these is John Layard's exegesis in *A Celtic Quest* (Figure 2). Layard suggests that an analysis of Celtic mythology leads to an octahedron that locates the archetypal Self in the lower pyramid and the human individuating Ego in the upper. The archetypal feminine joins the Self below. While somewhat more intelligible than Jung's study, Layard's ingenious interpretation of the diamond body has not become widely known for any clinical usefulness.

One more useful schema has been offered by Toni Wolff. In her essay *Structural Forms of the Feminine Psyche*, Wolff demonstrated how a feminine quadration could be seen to be expressed by more than typological distinctions (Figure 3). She delineates the four major feminine structures as the Mother, the Amazon, the Medial woman, and the Hetaira. Her work comes closest to anticipating our structural decoding, though her model has certain limitations. For a more thorough study of these, see Appendix C. Suffice it to say here that while she correctly sees these four forms as important feminine structures, she nearly misses their underlying archetypal dimension. In our terminology these dimensions are described

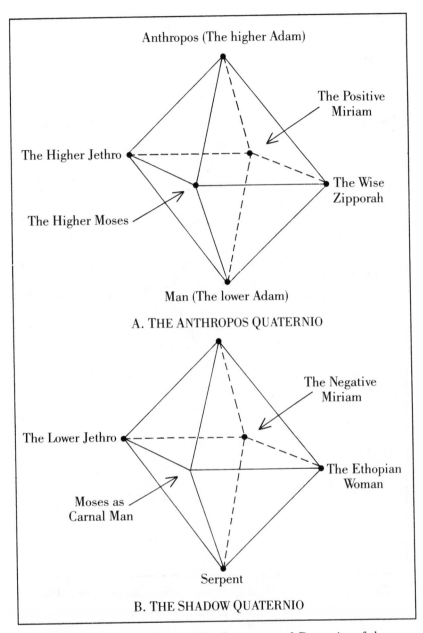

A. THE ANTHROPOS QUATERNIO

B. THE SHADOW QUATERNIO

Figure 1: From Carl Jung, "The Structure and Dynamics of the Self" in *Aion*, Volume 9, Part 2, of the *Collected Works*, p. 231.

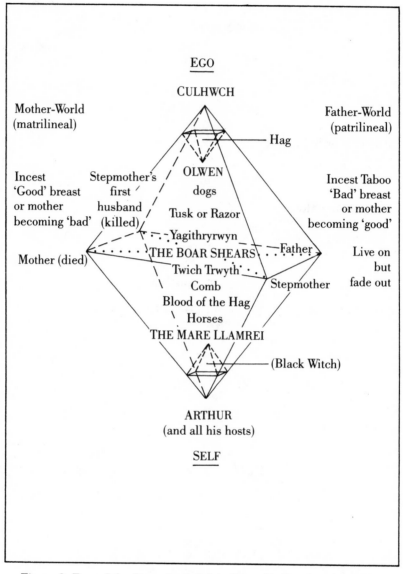

Figure 2: From John Layard, *A Celtic Quest* (Dallas: Spring, 1975),
p. 202.

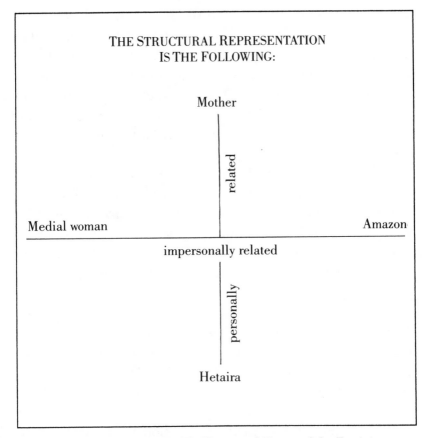

Figure 3: From Toni Wolff, "Structural Forms of the Feminine Psyche," privately printed for the Students Associations, C. G. Jung Institute, Zurich, July 1956, p. 4.

as the Queen, Warrior, Lover, and Magician. Wolff discerns aspects of the archetypes but describes for the most part traits of the feminine bipolar Shadows. Her model omits a necessary emphasis on balancing these four aspects in the movement toward individuation. Also she seems unable to interpret the dialectics that she correctly observes to exist between the Mother and the Medial woman, the Amazon and the Hetaira.

Ironically, we investigated these other models only after constructing our own. We did not approach this topic deductively, fitting psychological data into an a priori octahedral structure. Rather, we came to the double-pyramid model inductively, seeking to understand the shape our research findings seemed to be urging. Later we were astounded and gratified to find that others had struggled to decode the same diamond body.

Our model (Figure 4) has grown out of over twenty years of anthropological field research and clinical psychoanalytic process and reflection. If you examine this model carefully, you will note the two fundamental dialectical oppositions built into the psyche's deep structure. These are between eros and aggression (the Lover and the Warrior), and ruler and sage (the King/Queen and the Magician). Freud focused of course on the eros/aggression dialectic, and Adler on the ruler/sage (compare his work on superiority and social interest). Thus Jung was not entirely correct to ascribe Freud and Adler's conflict purely to typological differences. The two were focusing on different structural dynamics inherent in the deep structures of the Self.

We believe the human predilection for fourfold structures is grounded in an intuition of an inner quaternio. Each quadrant represents in a way a distinct "program" or biogram encoded with psychological potentials necessary to a cohesive and fully functioning human self. The King program contains the ordering and nurturing potentials. The Warrior program holds potentials for boundary foundation and maintenance, effective organization, action, vocation, and fidelity. Within the Magician program lie potentials for cognitive functioning, understanding, death, and rebirth. Receptiveness, affiliation, healthy dependency, embodied sexuality, empathy, and intimacy are all potentials characteristic of the Lover program.

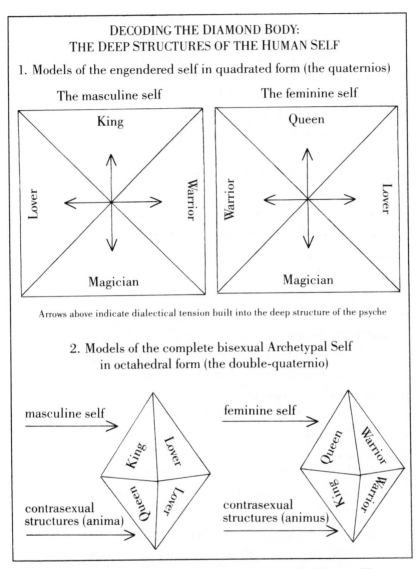

DECODING THE DIAMOND BODY:
THE DEEP STRUCTURES OF THE HUMAN SELF

1. Models of the engendered self in quadrated form (the quaternios)

The masculine self   The feminine self

King   Queen

Lover   Warrior   Warrior   Lover

Magician   Magician

Arrows above indicate dialectical tension built into the deep structure of the psyche

2. Models of the complete bisexual Archetypal Self
in octahedral form (the double-quaternio)

masculine self   feminine self

King Lover   Queen Warrior

Queen Lover   King Warrior

contrasexual   contrasexual
structures (anima)   structures (animus)

Figure 4: Adapted with permission from Robert L. Moore, *The Magician and the Analyst: Ritual, Sacred Space, and Psychotherapy.* (Chicago: Center for the Scientific Study of Religion, 1993).

All of these programs must be adequately accessed, then balanced one against another in a healthy dynamic tension, analogous to the tension of a well-functioning human musculature. Individuation and wholeness are not just esoteric concepts. The psyche has clear and discernible components available to it, which require deliberate sustained efforts to be attained, consolidated, and maintained. On the basis of our model, individuation requires development along four axes. This development counteracts the dialectical tensions built into psychic structure.

We chose the pyramid for our model because it most graphically illustrates the struggle involved in individuation. Individuation in this sense is the Ego's struggle to reunite the archetypal polar opposites at the base of each of the faces of the pyramid. (See pages 43 to 45 in Chapter 2.) *Wholeness is imaged in the capstone of the pyramid.* From the eye of illumination printed on our one-dollar bill to the temple on top of the Maya pyramids, we have noticed the support mythological traditions give to our intuited model of the goal of psychological and spiritual quest. *We believe we have been privileged to stumble, in the course of our research, across the actual encoded psychological structure underlying these mythic images.*

While the relation of the four foundational archetypes to Jung's theory of typology has yet to be researched, there does not seem to be any one-to-one correspondence. It seems likely that we will find sensation and feeling in the Lover's quadrant, and intuition and thinking in the Magician's—but typological theory neglects the other two quarters. Jung's insistence that Shadow work precede deep work on the Anima/Animus is, we think, clearly imaged in our model. Here the contrasexual is a realm as rich and diverse as that of the engendered Ego—yet deeper in the psyche and more difficult to understand.

Finally, we think our model helps make sense of the way in which male and female developmental challenges are simi-

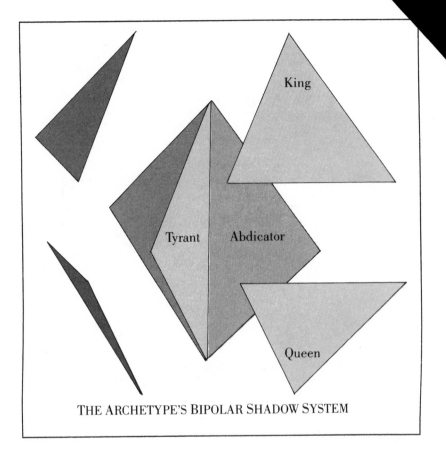

THE ARCHETYPE'S BIPOLAR SHADOW SYSTEM

lar—in the four powers there are to be accessed and integrated—and different—in their structural organization. This structural asymmetry will, we conjecture, help us understand gender differences in developmental trajectories, psychopathology distributions, and perceptual and communication styles. In short, it seems that Jung did in fact intuit the biomorphic form of the psyche's deep structures. We believe our model is a decoding of that structure, enabling us to relate research data from many different sources, and confirming Jung's assumption that the psyche is structured as an octahedral double quaternio.

ARCHETYPES AND THE LIMBIC SYSTEM

A CCORDING TO A NUMBER OF BRAIN RESEARCH-ers, most notably Paul MacLean, the limbic system (augmenting the more basic instincts of the underlying R-complex, or reptilian brain) is the seat of mammalian and species-typical instincts for all primates, including humans. Located in the paleocortical area, the limbic system consists of the fornix, hippocampus, cingulate cortex, anterior thalamic nucleus, amygdala, septum, the mammillary bodies, and associated hypothalamic areas. The paleocortex (as the term's Greek roots suggest) is the older brain, a region we share with other mammals. Ours is genetically configured particularly like the paleocortices of other primates.

Because the mechanism of evolution serves to develop new structures gradually, based upon older ones, there remain in our bodies any number of archaic structures that continue to fulfill their more primitive functions. One familiar vestigial organ, the appendix, no longer serves any apparent function (it is believed to have once aided the digestion of grasses) and because of this is now a frequent site of infection. The limbic system, however, continues in its inherited functions, and suggestively seems to be the locus for foundational archetypal structures—suggestively because this would appear to link human archetypes with the instinctive patterns of other species.

Paul Broca, in 1878, was the first to identify a large convolution common to the brains of all mammals as the "great limbic lobe."[1] In 1937 James Papez realized that this limbic system was the seat of the experience and expression of emotion.[2] Paul MacLean later developed the full concept of the limbic system.[3] MacLean came to believe the system was not only the center for emotion but also the integration center for correlating "every form of internal and external perception." It has, he claims, "many strong connections with the hypothalamus for discharging its impression."[4] While some researchers do not accept this notion, there appears to be no other neurological system available to play such an integrative role.

Within the limbic system are three primary subsystems:

1. the affiliative/attachment subsystem[5]
2. the autonomy/aggression subsystem[6]
3. the integrative/inhibition subsystem[7]

The affiliation/attachment subsystem, as the name implies, is almost certainly responsible for general mammalian tendencies to form social units characterized by nurturing, affection, and play. In humans and other primates these affiliative impulses may result in such complex psychological and social phenomena as reliance, dependence, and collaboration. The affiliative impulse seems to arise (along with each species's particular structures of affiliation) primarily in the cingulate gyrus.[8] MacLean has proposed that the concept of "family," for example, may be structured into the limbic system.[9]

Exploration, fear, defensive strategies, fighting, the acquisition of territory, the need for control (over the inner and outer worlds), and other self-definitive, self-preservative behaviors are a result of the autonomy/aggression instinct. This impulse enables humans to form cohesive selves through adversity. It may also give rise to the instinct to order society hierarchically.[10] The autonomy/aggression subsystem appears to be located in the amygdaloid complex.[11] There is evidence that in primates the amygdala plays a hierarchically ordering role for our societies.[12]

The third major limbic subsystem mediates the integration/inhibition instinct and is apparently located in the hippocampus and the septum.[13] MacLean believes this subsystem is the integrative center for the entire nervous system.[14] The hippocampus can be thought of as the gatekeeper of the limbic system, which system is the capital of the nervous system as a whole. Teamed with the neocortex (which brings cognitive functions into play), the hippocampus "gate mechanism" seems to be responsible for regulating, arranging, prioritizing, and modulating data from nearly every aspect of the nervous system. The hippocampus regulates alternating affiliative/attachment and autonomous/aggressive behaviors. When properly operating, this system regulates these competing drives to appropriately interact with any set of environmental stimuli, both inner and outer.

We believe that the four foundational archetypes we present in this series arise in the limbic system and are then elaborated and refined as they pass upward through the neocortex. This elaboration may be primarily achieved either by

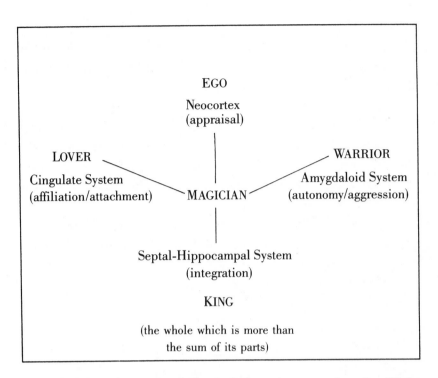

EGO

Neocortex
(appraisal)

LOVER   WARRIOR

Cingulate System   Amygdaloid System
(affiliation/attachment)   MAGICIAN   (autonomy/aggression)

Septal-Hippocampal System
(integration)

KING

(the whole which is more than
the sum of its parts)

the Left Brain's rational, logical functions, or by the Right Brain's intuitive, holistic mode. They may be given "humane" form especially in the frontal lobes, which seem to be responsible for empathetic and altruistic emotions as well as for refined cognitive processes. In order for the Ego to know and access any of the four major archetypes, it must experience a particular archetype as an asymmetrical composite of each of the others. In light of the brain research we've cited, a provocative correspondence suggests itself between the archetypal and the limbic systems.

It seems clear that what we call the Lover arises originally in the affiliative/attachment subsystem, and our Warrior arises in the autonomy/aggression subsystem. The Magician (which some other psychologies mistake as the Ego) arises in the integration/inhibition subsystem at its interface with the neocortical structures. We'd locate the Ego within the neocortex proper. This maintains the Ego's status as the apparent center of waking consciousness. Here it is separate from the Magician but initially at least more closely related to this archetype than it is to the Lover or the Warrior.

The King manifests as the integrated, mature functioning of all the neocortical and limbic subsystems. Though it seems to arise in the septal-hippocampal subsystem, it transcends this subsystem's gatekeeping functions. More than a regulator, the King embraces the Warrior, Magician, and Lover in an integrated, constituitive manner.

We have provided an elaboration of George Everly's diagram of the limbic system, including with it our four archetypes of mature masculinity.

APPENDIX C

ARCHETYPES AND THE ANIMA

I N THIS APPENDIX WE WILL SKETCH OUT SOME OF the structures and dynamics of the feminine psyche. Our particular interest will be in the Anima, the inner feminine element of the masculine psyche. We follow Jung in emphasizing that Shadow integration must precede serious work with the contra-sexual Anima or Animus. Implicit in Jung's approach is his understanding that integration of the personal Shadow solidifies the integrity of the Ego, and its achievement of a healthy psychosexual identity. Without a cohesive nuclear self, work with inner contrasexual structures can be confusing at best, and dangerous at worst.

We add to Jung's insights a description of the actual structural configurations of the contra-sexual Anima. The structure is similar for the feminine Animus (the inner masculine subpersonality in a woman), as we will make plain. As we've argued, the Shadow system involves both a personal Shadow and the bipolar Shadow of each of the four archetypes. After attending to the initiatory and integrative processes involved in mastering this Shadow system, a man can safely turn his attention to his Anima.

The aim of a relationship with the contra-sexual should not be to develop androgyny. Androgynous personalities entertain grandiose fantasies of "completeness within the Self." While there may be some genuinely biologically based androgynous personalities, as some brain research seems to suggest, for most men and women, androgyny is a masturbatory narcissistic stance, a kind of psychological hermaphroditism. For most people, any attempt to join the contra-sexual to the Ego results in a regressive merger rather than a mature complementary relationship. A merger with the Anima renders a man incapable of forming a mature relationship with his inner feminine energies, as surely as it skews his outer-world relationships with women. Jung believed that as a man's Ego grows stronger, his awareness of the contra-sexual as truly "other" will increase, until finally he can initiate what should become a lifelong relationship with his personified Anima through dreamwork, active imagination, and any other techniques he finds useful.

Contrary to what some contemporary Jungians claim, we believe the Anima is not an amorphous, ethereal "mood." The Anima has a dynamic structure that mirrors that of the masculine archetypes. As our diagram on page 250 (explicated in Appendix A) illustrates, the Anima is the feminine inverse of the four-faceted masculine archetypal pyramid. Turned upside down, the model becomes that of a feminine psyche. A woman's pyramid is composed of Queen, Lover, Warrior, and Magician archetypal facets, and her inverse pyramid is the masculine structure we've delineated. This masculine structure is her Animus.

Just as the masculine psyche demonstrates genetically determined archetypal patternings, the feminine psyche has its own distinct coloring. These masculine and feminine psychic systems each retain their distinct characteristics when operating as contra-sexual subsystems. Because of this we will quickly examine the deep structures of the feminine psyche, as they are the same as those in place in the male Anima.

Years ago Toni Wolff, a Zurich-trained Jungian analyst, described in *Structural Forms of the Feminine Psyche* four foundational personality types in women. These "forms" she called the Mother, the Amazon, the Medial woman, and the Hetaira. These forms parallel rather closely our concept of the four feminine archetypes, and by extension, the Anima. (See Appendix A.)

Wolff seems to us to have been very close to decoding the feminine psyche. However, her work includes a number of missteps which kept her from finally succeeding. Her first error was in focusing on the form of the Mother instead of the Queen. While it can be argued that the Mother (like the Father) is an archetype, the maternal and paternal forms are less inclusive than the King and Queen, and are more properly *aspects* of the royal archetypes than archetypes themselves.

The Queen is a numinous, mature structure, including and *exceeding* the Mother. The Great Goddess imagery of the ancient religions issues from the Queen's impact on the psyche. The Mother's focus, per se, is on a single family, where she is especially concerned with the needs of the infant human. The Mother is therefore less inclusively fertile than the Queen, from whom the earth itself derives its fecundity; and she is less inclusively nurturing, because the Queen nur-

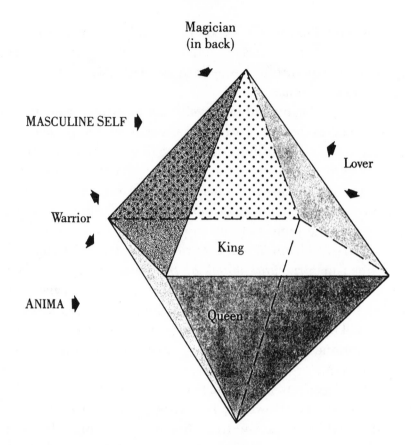

Magician
(in back)

MASCULINE SELF

Lover

Warrior

King

ANIMA

Queen

tures *the planet* she engenders, and not only children. And like the fully expressed King, the Queen encompasses each of the other three archetypes. Wolff excludes her other three forms from the Mother's influence.

Others might argue that the Mother does, in fact, integrate the feminine Warrior, Magician, and Lover. But to the extent that she does so she is approaching identity with the Queen. Though the Mother archetype provides a strong image of nurturing and blessing, she offers to a somewhat lesser degree an image of teaching and discipline (the Magician and Warrior) and, as Mother, no image at all of erotic love (the Lover). The Queen, however, provides images of all of these traits.

Wolff's second mistake is to weight the feminine Warrior with the culturally compromised image of the Amazon. In our system, the feminine Warrior is clearly related to Wolff's Amazon, but the legendary Greek form she's chosen often misdirects the aggressive energy that is this archetype's domain. Instead of using this energy in the service of the royal couple, supporting and extending the created cosmos, the Amazon of the myths all too frequently uses her aggression against males, even to the point of exiling her sons.

The fully expressed feminine Warrior helps a woman consolidate an independent Self by defining and defending legitimate psychological boundaries. The Warrior enables a woman to achieve other difficult tasks through strategic thinking, self-discipline, and hard work. But the feminine Warrior is not in any sense antimale. The Warrior does not misinterpret the battles she must fight as narrow tribal disputes, except in the legitimate defense of a woman's offspring. Where her children are threatened, a woman accessing her Warrior is programmed to react with swift and relentless ruthlessness. Otherwise, the woman in an axis with her Warrior correctly sees her battles as primarily personal efforts to establish a Self, and as transpersonal efforts to defend creation.

But by using the largely negative image of the Amazon, Wolff ends up really examining primarily the Shadow Warrior, in her sadistic expression. Possessed by the Sadist, a woman's fury is directed not only against men in general but against other women as well, and even against her own children.[1] A woman who allows the Amazonian Sadist to act for her in her life misses the potential benefits of the full expression of the feminine Warrior.

We hope the resources of the feminine Warrior will be accepted more fully into our culture. We would then see women engaged in a more active psychological and physical defense of themselves and their mates, as well as a fuller participation in the struggle against communal and global forces of destruction. There is evidence that our culture is increasingly learning to steward this energy—especially in the arenas of social and environmental reform.

The Hetaira is, like the Amazon, a culture-bound term. In ancient Greece the hetaira functioned much as the more familiar geisha did in Japanese culture—as a well-educated female companion and prostitute. But a prostitute is a manifestation of the Shadow Lover, no matter how well-educated. In Wolff's system the Hetaira displays both aspects of the Lover's bipolar Shadow, the Addict and the Impotent Lover. The Addict is operative in Wolff's claim that women under the influence of the Hetaira have a tendency to go from one man to another. The Impotent Lover is disclosed by the knowledge that psychologically a prostitute is often engaged in a fruitless repetition of her unsuccessful childhood attempt to gain her father's admiration and love.

The Hetaira seems to be a second-generation archetype, composed of fragments of more basic ones. She includes both poles of the Magician's Shadow—as a Manipulator she causes a woman to use men for their money and her own narrow interests, and as the Innocent One she lures a woman into displaying her naïveté about relationships. The Sadist manifests in a woman's underlying anger toward men. The Warrior's other Shadow pole, the Masochist, appears in her willingness to place herself in harm's way.

To the extent Wolff's final type, the Medial, approaches the concept of the shaman, it is an appropriate and full expression of the archetype of the Magician. It is Wolff's least limiting term.

Despite any other shortcomings, it is striking that Wolff's conceptualization of the archetypal dynamics of the *feminine* psyche agrees so closely with our own system of thought concerning the *male* psyche. We interpret this as a verification of our instinct to extend the concept of the quadrates psyche from the masculine to the feminine Self, and to the Anima and Animus.

To our way of thinking then, a woman's quadrated psyche functions just as does a man's. She balances the energies of four foundational archetypes—the Queen, Warrior, Magician, and Lover. The Queen guides a woman toward a centered calm, a sense of inner order she can extend into the outer world. She becomes gifted with the capacity to bless and join in fructifying union with the other members of her "realm." The Warrior guides a woman in self-discipline and self-defense, as well as in the defense of others. Her achievements are encouraged by the Warrior, and her sense of service to a Transpersonal Other reinforced. The Magician provides a capacity to introspect, to raise and contain power, to heal and to act as a mediator between the human and the divine spheres. Drawing on the Magician's powers, a woman may serve as a spiritual guide to others, especially in the task of initiating younger women into the mysteries of adult responsibilities and joys. And the Lover empowers a woman to be passionately and creatively engaged with all things, to be uninhibited sexually (playing and displaying) and profoundly spiritual.

Of course, the relationship between the masculine and feminine aspects of the Self are often problematic. For the Anima is a whole structure, and no man experiences it simply piece by piece, pair by pair. Just as he balances the energies of *his* four foundational archetypes, he must balance the four different signals that reach him from his Anima. It can be useful to separate out the different sources of these signals in order to distinguish their characteristics, so long as we remember that they operate as a whole.

The feminine energies beside each of the male archetypes give them depth and definition. But when a man is caught in one or more of the bipolar Shadow systems of the masculine archetype, he encounters *all* of the Anima's complementary

Shadow energies too. At the Warrior's *active* Sadist pole, for example, he will meet with the *passive* poles of the Shadow Anima, the Weakling/Abdicator, the Innocent One, the Impotent Lover, and especially with the Masochist. If he is Ego-identified instead with the Masochist, he will be confronted by the feminine Tyrant, the Manipulator, the Addict, and especially with the woman Warrior at her Sadist pole.

Relations between the masculine and feminine Warriors can be particularly strained. The only really successful mode for a relationship between them is as comrades-in-arms.[2] Otherwise the aggressive/aversive energies they each channel can be directed against the other, causing empathic breaks in man-woman relationships that are difficult to repair. A Warrior needs an enemy, and too often the masculine and feminine Warriors make enemies of each other.

A man who does not access the fully expressed Warrior (whose feminine counterpart is his comrade-in-arms) will tend to experience his Anima, and all the women in his life, in a split and shadowy way. He will see one aspect of the feminine as the Tyrant Queen—his sophomorically idealized and "virginal" mother. Women who are not like her he sees as whores, and we've seen what a complex mixture of Shadow elements a prostitute carries. The Tyrant Queen sends this man to his death to defend her. He, in turn, "fucks" a whore (rather than "making love" with her) in an act of revenge against his mother, overcoming "her" resistance with brutality. Here is the power issue the rapist fails to manage. He wants power over what he sees as an inordinately powerful, abusive woman. Perhaps his mother was physically or verbally abusive to him, or perhaps she was neglectful and uninterested. Such a man is of course not accessing his Warrior appropriately. Instead, he is a psychotic boy without any experience of his legitimate power.

Until a man becomes secure in his masculine identity, he

will remain a sadomasochist in his relationships with women. If he is not secure he feels that he is risking invasion by his Anima. He has yet to learn to respect his own legitimate territories as well as those of the feminine psyche, both within and without. The maturing male learns there is a space within him he can never invade, and that will never be "his." He must approach his Anima with respect. Once he learns to deal with this "other" with discipline and respect, he has the prerequisite knowledge necessary to deal respectfully with any "other," including the women he loves, other men, other species, and finally the Transpersonal Other we all need to serve.

The octahedral Self we diagrammed in Appendix A gives a good visual model for imagining these Anima dynamics. While it does not portray the vital interpenetration of the masculine and feminine structures, it does show how the contra-sexual system is contained *within* the total structure, and is in no way external to it. The two structures together form the "diamond body" of the great Self. Though it is in some sense merely a pictorial construct, it is an appropriately suggestive and allusive one. Like the implicit structure of a crystal, we each have a perfect diamond Self within, waiting the chance to form. We are gifted then with an inner vision of the possible human which has the clarity, radiance, and perfection of a jewel.

N O T E S

Complete bibliographical information on works cited in these
notes will be found in the Bibliography that follows.

CHAPTER 1: GENDER IDENTITY,
GENDER ASYMMETRY, AND
THE SEXUAL IMBALANCE OF POWER

1. By "radical androgyny" we refer to the claims made by some
feminists, whether male or female, that there are no differences between the sexes (except what they regard as incidental biological diver-
gences). When it comes to assigning blame, however, particularly for
aggressive behavior and fear of intimacy, some feminists draw very

I would acknowledge some of both of these tendencies

clear distinctions between the sexes, always at the expense of the male. One would think from their claims that women have no Shadow. A woman's only weakness seems to be that she "loves men too much." It is impossible to love someone too much. What *is* possible is to become so addicted to another that personal responsibilities are relinquished. However, shadowy business of this kind is common to both sexes. The idealization of androgyny is against nature and scientific evidence; it is also hypocritical. For related discussion, see Robert Ardrey, in toto but especially *African Genesis*, pp. 143 ff. (Bibliography 1); James Ashbrook, *The Human Mind and the Mind of God*, pp. 57–59, 96–97, 105, 322ff., 324–327, 339 (Bibliography 2); Sam Keen, *Fire in the Belly*, pp. 195ff. (Bibliography 9); Anne Moir and David Jessel, *Brain Sex: The Real Difference Between Men and Women* (Bibliography 2); Anthony Stevens, *Archetypes: A Natural History of the Self*, pp. 23ff., 48ff., 81–84, 174ff. (Bibliography 4); Edward O. Wilson, in toto but especially *On Human Nature*, pp. 16, 18–21, 121ff. (Bibliography 1).

2. An example of this phenomenon is Riane Eisler, *The Chalice and the Blade: Our History, Our Future* (Bibliography 1). Although Ms. Eisler purports to demonstrate a "partnership" model of male/female relationships, she provides a stereotypic negative metaphor of the "Blade" to designate male qualities. Her central image of partnership is of a mother Goddess nurturing her child, by implication her son—hardly a relationship between equals. Also see Mary Daley, *Beyond God the Father and Gyn/Ecology*; and Rosemary Ruether, *Sexism and God-Talk: Toward a Feminist Theology*, pp. 104ff. (both in Bibliography 13).

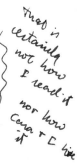

3. Alice Miller, *The Drama of the Gifted Child, For Your Own Good*, and *Thou Shalt Not Be Aware* (Bibliography 9).

4. Research in this area clearly links the development of high civilization (beyond the "high culture" of the late Neolithic) with the advent of sacral kingships and the attendant assemblage of larger nation-states. For an extensive record of sources, see the Bibliography's Kingship listing (5). See there especially Basham; Emery; Frankfort, *The Birth of Civilization in the Near East*; Kwanten; Schele and Freidel; and Wales. See also Julian Jaynes, *The Origin of Consciousness in the Breakdown of the Bicameral Mind* (Bibliography 2); John Weir Perry, *Lord of the Four Quarters* (Bibliography 8); and Wilson, pp. 89–90.

5. Carl Jung, *Aion* in *The Portable Jung*, pp. 148 ff.; Jolande

Jacobi, *The Psychology of C. G. Jung*, pp. 5, 114ff., 120–121; Jung, *Man and His Symbols*, pp. 186ff., and *Mysterium Coniunctionis;* Loren Pedersen, *Dark Hearts;* John Sanford, *The Invisible Partners;* and Stevens, pp. 174ff., 193–194 (all in Bibliography 4).

6. Moir and Jessel, p. 31.

7. Stevens, pp. 79–80; and Wilson, pp. 132–137.

8. See Bibliography 2.

9. David Gilmore, *Man in the Making: Cultural Concepts of Masculinity*, "Work" in the index (Bibliography 1).

10. Don Browning, *Generative Man*, p. 145ff. (Bibliography 9).

11. Niebuhr isn't always as frank about his distrust of power as Lord Acton was when he said, "Power corrupts, absolute power corrupts absolutely." He does frequently, however, cast the desire for power, and its achievement and uses, in an exaggeratedly negative light. He assumes (as liberal Christians have for centuries, and some feminists do today) that the quest for power is inherently mistaken, and that its achievement is invariably destructive for principal and subordinate alike. Writers such as Keen, Ruether, Eisler, and Daley betray an unconscious utopianism in their works—and as Stevens notes in *Archetypes* (p. 139), utopianism will always fail.

12. Gérard Lauzun, *Sigmund Freud: The Man and His Theories*, pp. 64–65 (Bibliography 9); and Reinhold Niebuhr, *The Nature and Destiny of Man*, pp. 44, 192 (Bibliography 13).

13. Anthony Stevens, *The Roots of War*, pp. 36–38 (Bibliography 4); and Anthony Storr, in toto and especially *Human Destructiveness*, pp. 11, 21, 23, 34, 42 (Bibliography 9). Even Gilmore affirms the almost universal necessity for aggressive male behaviors, as channeled into the culturally defined roles of protector, provider, and procreator. Keen finds himself (pp. 112ff.) endorsing "fierce gentlemen" as if they were vital to the survival of the species. This comes after his emphatic rejection of sociobiological claims and the notion of an aggressive instinct, and despite his embrasure of the romantic socialization model of gender definition.

14. Cultures have seldom celebrated initiation ceremonies for their girls. By and large girls have been considered naturally initiated by their first menstruation. Boys have been, in contrast, forcibly taken through initiation rituals designed to awaken in them an awareness of their risk-taking and self-sacrificial responsibilities. This may also reflect a widespread human awareness that innate masculine aggressive

potentials require extremely careful containment and channeling if they are not to become dangerous to the human community in the behavior of irresponsible, immature, "monster boy" males. See the Bibliography under Ritual and Initiation (12); see also Mircea Eliade, *Rites and Symbols of Initiation* (Bibliography 8); Gilmore; Joseph Henderson, *Thresholds of Initiation* (Bibliography 8); Keen, pp. 27–33; Victor Turner, *The Ritual Process: Structure and Anti-Structure* (Bibliography 1); and Hutton Webster, *Primitive Secret Societies* (Bibliography 1).

CHAPTER 2: DECODING THE MALE PSYCHE

1. See Bibliography 4.

2. Carl Jung, "The Relations of the Ego and the Unconscious," in *The Portable Jung*, p. 75; Jolande Jacobi, *The Psychology of C. G. Jung*, p. 1; Aniela Jaffé, *The Myth of Meaning: Jung and the Expansion of Consciousness*, pp. 40–42; Carl Jung, *Psychology and Alchemy*, p. 215; and Anthony Stevens, *Archetypes: A Natural History of the Self*, pp. 43–47 (all in Bibliography 4).

3. Jacobi, p. 1; and Stevens, pp. 43–47.

4. Joseph Campbell, *The Hero with a Thousand Faces*, pp. 3ff. (Bibliography 8); and Jacobi, "Mythology/Myths" in the index.

5. Campbell, p. 258.

6. Mircea Eliade, *Cosmos and History: The Myth of the Eternal Return*, p. 3 (Bibliography 8); Jacobi, pp. 5–10; see the first two chapters on the nature of consciousness in Julian Jaynes, *The Origin of Consciousness in the Breakdown of the Bicameral Mind* (Bibliography 2); and Henri Frankfort, *Kingship and the Gods*, pp. 27–29 (Bibliography 5).

7. Carl Jung, "Aion," in *Psyche and Symbol*, pp. 1–6 (Bibliography 4).

8. John O. Beahrs, *Unity and Multiplicy*, especially chs. 1 and 4 (Bibliography 9).

9. Nearly every school of psychology acknowledges this, in one way or another. The Jungian approach to the Shadow, the work of developmental psychologists with the inner Child (see especially Alice Miller), and the work of hypnotherapists like Dr. John Beahrs with multiple-personality disorders, all are particularly relevant.

10. Carl Jung, "The Structure and Dynamics of the Psyche," in *The Portable Jung*, especially p. 52; and Stevens, especially pp. 26, 40, 51ff.

11. Carl Jung, "The Concept of the Collective Unconscious," in *The Portable Jung*, pp. 59–69.

12. Bruno Bettelheim, *Freud and Man's Soul*, pp. 53–64; and Gérard Lauzun, *Sigmund Freud: The Man and His Theories*, "Id" in the index (both in Bibliography 9).

13. Don Browning, *Generative Man: Psychoanalytic Perspectives*, p. 158 (Bibliography 9).

14. Ibid.

15. Ibid., p. 159.

16. Ibid., pp. 145–147, 158, 159; Jacobi, "Libido" in the index; and Lauzun, "Libido" in the index.

17. See Bibliography. Although Jean Bolen does not do this, she tends to identify the Gods and Goddesses with human personality types. Bolen's Gods and Goddesses do parallel cognition, feeling, and behavioral styles observable in men and women. *But no human being is an archetype, and neither is any God or Goddess.* Bolen's work describes complex configurations of archetypes (our foundational four from the psyches of men and women, as well as countless others that determine our modes of perception) as expressed through different Ego identities, personal complexes, cultural and Superego conditioning, etc. Her Gods and Goddesses are simpler than human personalities, and so on this level they approach the archetypes more nearly than all but the most dysfunctional human personalities. But we believe the Libido takes form at the most basic levels of drive as either a King (or Queen), Warrior, Magician, or Lover, and then after progressive explication and diversification presents itself in complex manifestations. These foundational four are the node around which collect the culture-specific ideals, parental introjects, and other family myths that provide so many layers of archetypal functioning.

18. Jacobi, pp. 1–9ff.

19. Marie Louise von Franz, *Projection and Reflection in Jungian Psychology* (Bibliography 4). See Index under Shadow, Projection of.

20. Individuation is a matter, for Jungians, of bringing into Ego consciousness (1) what has been otherwise split off and repressed, as well as (2) awakening insights that have never been conscious. For the

260

distinction between complexes and archetypes, and their relation to the two categories above, see Jolande Jacobi's *Complex, Archetype, Symbol in the Psychology of C. G. Jung.*

21. See Theodore Millon's excellent work with the concept of bipolarity in *Modern Psychopathology* (Bibliography 9).

22. Theodore Millon, *Disorders of Personality: DSM-III: Axis II*, in toto but especially p. 58 (Bibliography 9).

23. James Hillman et al., *Puer Papers*, especially Hillman's chapter "Senex and Puer: An Aspect of the Historical and Psychological Present" (Bibliography 4).

24. Paul Tillich, *Systematic Theology*, vol. 3, especially ch. 1 and "The Kingdom of God as the End of History" (Bibliography 13).

25. Ibid., "Hegel" in the index; also see Sean Kelly, *Individuation and the Absolute: Hegel, Jung, and the Path Toward Wholeness*, in press.

26. See Bibliography 13; see also Alfred North Whitehead, *Process and Reality* (Bibliography 13).

27. Jung, *Psychology and Alchemy*, "Coniunctio" in the index.

28. In Greek mythology and legend, the Symplegades were two great rocks in the middle of the ocean. When a ship tried to pass between them, they would rush together and destroy the ship.

29. Stevens, pp. 259–275.

30. Ibid., pp. 260, 264. For the relevance of the limbic system to the four foundational archetypes, see Appendix B.

31. Rudolf Otto, *The Idea of the Holy*, in toto but especially pp. 12ff., 25 (Bibliography 8).

32. Eliade, *Cosmos and History*, pp. 12ff., and *Patterns in Comparative Religion*, "Temple," "Tree, Cosmic," "Palace," "Mountain, Cosmic" in the index.

33. Ibid., "Kings," "Rulers," in the index. The literature on sacral kingship, and the king's mediation of the sacred and profane worlds, is vast. See also Bibliography 5.

34. See Bibliography 5. Also see James Frazer, *The Golden Bough*, "King," "Queen," in the index (Bibliography 8); and John Weir Perry, *Lord of the Four Quarters*, p. 32 (Bibliography 8).

35. Jane Goodall, *In the Shadow of Man*, p. 284 (Bibliography 11).

36. Jane Goodall, *Through a Window*, p. 13 (Bibliography 11).

37. See Bibliography 11. Also see Frans de Waal, *Chimpanzee*

Politics (Bibliography 11); Goodall, *Through a Window and In the Shadow of Man;* and Michael MacKinnon, *The Ape Within Us* (Bibliography 1).

38. Geoffrey Bourne, *Primate Odyssey*, pp. 321ff. (Bibliography 11).

39. de Waal: See Index under Alpha Male; Goodall, *In the Shadow of Man*, pp. 112ff.

40. de Waal, pp. 109–110, 200, 204–205.

CHAPTER 3: THE SHAMANIC TRADITION

1. For a discussion of shamanic androgyny, see Joan Halifax's *Shamanic Voices: A Survey of Visionary Narratives* (Bibliography 7), pp. 22–28. Also see works by Joseph Campbell and Mircea Eliade (indexes under Shamanism) as well as Bibliography 7.

2. See Moore and Gillette's *King, Warrior, Magician, Lover: Rediscovering the Archetypes of the Mature Masculine* (Bibliography 4), pp. 27–33.

3. See Appendix B for a further discussion of the structural bases of the archetypes in the brain.

CHAPTER 4: IMAGES OF THE MAGICIAN IN MYTH AND HISTORY

1. Robert Ardrey, *The Social Contract* (Bibliography 1), pp. 121–29; Geoffrey Bourne, *Primate Odyssey* (Bibliography 11), pp. 137–139.

2. Jane Goodall, *In the Shadow of Man*, pp. 35–37 and index under Tool-using for a more general discussion of chimpanzee toolmaking and use. Also see her *Through a Window: My Thirty Years with the Chimpanzees of Gombe*, index under Termites. For a more general discussion of primate tool manufacture and use see Adrian J. Desmond's *The Ape's Reflection*, index under Tool-use. (All in Bibliography 11)

3. A rapidly growing body of literature is available on this subject. For an exceptionally thorough discussion of chimpanzee language use and cognitive capacities see Desmond, *The Ape's Reflection* (Bibliography 11), index under Language.

4. The literature on tribal and traditional religions is extensive, and it overwhelmingly supports the central role of a male Creator God as the primary Deity as well as the important roles of many secondary male Gods. For a brief survey of African religions in this context, see *Africa*, edited by Phyllis M. Martin and Patrick O'Meara (Bibliography 1), pp. 214–218. For a survey of Native American religions in this context, see Krickeberg et al., *Pre-Columbian American Religions* (Bibliography 8), in toto. For an in-depth analysis of Stone Age Native American belief systems which lift up the significance of the male Creator God, see Gerardo Reichel-Dolmatoff's *Amazonian Cosmos: The Sexual and Religious Symbolism of the Tukano Indians* (Bibliography 8) especially Part III, Chapter I. Also see Hutton Webster's *Primitive Secret Societies* (Bibliography 1).

[handwritten margin note: but cf Gimbutas!]

5. Mario Ruspoli, *The Cave of Lascaux: The Final Photographs* (Bibliography 1), pp. 25, 80–89.

6. Ibid., pp. 80–89.

7. See Bibliography 5 and 7, and works by Eliade and Campbell, indexes under Kingship and Shamanism.

8. I.E.S. Edwards, *The Pyramids of Egypt*, pp. 53, 61, 292. See Säve-Söderbergh, *Pharoahs and Mortals*, pp. 201, 258; and Wilson, *The Culture of Ancient Egypt*, pp. 109, 263. (All in Bibliography 3).

9. The literature in this area is vast. For a representative sampling see Franz Cumont, *The Mysteries of Mithra*, in toto; Mircea Eliade, *Patterns in Comparative Religion*, index under Mithra, Mitra, and Zarathustra; Robert M. Grant, *Gnosticism and Early Christianity*, index under Mithraism and Zoroastrianism; Joscelyn Godwin, *Mystery Religions in the Ancient World*, Chapter IX; William W. Malandra, *An Introduction to Ancient Iranian Religion*, index under Mithra and Zoroastrianism; Elaine Pagels, *The Gnostic Gospels*, p. xxxii; Huston Smith, *Forgotten Truth: The Primordial Tradition*, p. 46. (All in Bibliography 8).

10. Kurt Seligmann, *Magic and the Occult*, p. 59.

11. The scholarly work in the area of Gnosticism is enormous. For example, see Robert M. Grant, *Gnosticism and Early Christianity;* Elaine Pagels, *The Gnostic Gospels;* and James M. Robinson, *The Nag Hammadi Library*. (All in Bibliography 8) Also see C. G. Jung's works, indexes under Gnosticism.

12. See, for example, *Mysteries of the Past*, edited by Joseph J. Thorndike, Jr., Chapter 2.

13. Seligmann, *op. cit.*, p. 119.

14. See Gershom G. Scholem, *Major Trends in Jewish Mysticism*, index under Kabbalah, Kabbalism, Kabbalistic Neoplatonists, Kabbalists as outstanding rabbis, and Magic; Gershom G. Scholem, *Origins of the Kaballah*, in toto. (Both in Bibliography 8).

15. See John G. Neihardt's *Black Elk Speaks* (Bibliography 7).

16. Ibid., p. 22.

17. Ibid., p. 36.

18. See Bibliography 10.

19. See Don Browning, *Generative Man: Psychoanalytic Perspectives* (Bibliography 9), Chapters 6 and 7, and Epilogue.

CHAPTER 5: UNDERSTANDING SACRED SPACE AND TIME

1. See Moore and Gillette, *The King Within* (Bibliography 5), index under Sacred Cities and Chapter 3, Note 16.

2. See works by Mircea Eliade listed in Bibliography, indexes under Cosmogony, Initiation.

3. See Joseph Campbell's *The Hero with a Thousand Faces* (Bibliography 8), especially Chapters I through III.

4. Victor Turner, *The Ritual Process: Structure and Anti-Structure* (Bibliography 12), especially Chapters 3–5.

5. Moore and Gillette, *The King Within*, index under Self. Also see Bibliography 4, indexes under Self in references.

CHAPTER 6: THE WAY OF THE MAGICIAN

1. See Moore and Gillette, *The King Within* (Bibliography 5), index under *axis mundi*; and works by Mircea Eliade in Bibliography, indexes under *axis mundi*.

2. Rainer Maria Rilke, *Duino Elegies*, p. 126.

3. See John O. Beahrs, *Unity and Multiplicity: Multilevel Consciousness of Self in Hypnosis, Psychiatric Disorder and Mental Health* (Bibliography 9), in toto.

CHAPTER 7: THE MASTER OF DENIAL

1. See Moore and Gillette, *The Warrior Within* (Bibliography 4), Chapter 10, for a detailed discussion of this process.
2. Theodore Millon, *Disorders of Personality: DSM-III: Axis II* (Bibliography 9), Chapters 4 and 9.

CHAPTER 8: THE TRICKSTER

1. Theodore Millon, *Disorders of Personality: DSM-III: Axis II* (Bibliography 9), Chapters 6 and 10.

CHAPTER 10: THE SORCERER'S APPRENTICE

1. C. G. Jung, *Psychology and Alchemy*, paragraph 325. See Bibliography 4.
2. Moore and Gillette, *The King Within* (Bibliography 5), Chapter 9.
3. Moore and Gillette, *The Warrior Within* (Bibliography 4), Chapter 10.
4. David Feinstein's essay, "A Five-Stage Model for Fostering a Revitalized Personal Mythology," in *Shamanism*, edited by Shirley Nicholson (Bibliography 7), Chapter 18.
5. William Blake, *The Four Zoas* (Bibliography 6).

CHAPTER 11: BECOMING AN EARTHSHAMAN

1. Paraphrase of John 14:2.
2. From the musical *Camelot*, "Follow Me."

APPENDIX B: ARCHETYPES AND THE LIMBIC SYSTEM

The argument of this appendix owes a great debt to George S. Everly, Jr.'s synthesis of the most recent work of a number of brain researchers in his paper "The Biological Bases of Personality: The Contribution of Paleocortical Anatomy and Physiology to Personality and Personality Disorders." He presented this paper at the First International Congress on Disorders of Personality, in Copenhagen, Denmark, in August 1988.

1. Paul D. MacLean, *The Triune Brain in Evolution: Role in Paleocerebral Functions*, p. 257 (Bibliography 2).
2. Ibid., p. 264.
3. Ibid., in toto.
4. Everly, p. 5.
5. Ibid., p. 5.
6. Ibid., p. 5.
7. Ibid., p. 5.
8. Ibid., p. 6.
9. MacLean, ch. 21.
10. Everly, p. 7.
11. Everly, p. 8; and MacLean, ch. 19.
12. MacLean, pp. 322ff.
13. Everly, p. 9; and MacLean, chs. 18–27.
14. MacLean, pp. 497, 498, ch. 27.

APPENDIX C: ARCHETYPES AND THE ANIMA

1. See Alice Miller's discussion of "poisonous pedagogy" and the role of the mother in destroying her children's sense of Self (Bibliography 9).

2. An example of this can be found in the Canaanite Ba'al cycle of myths. In them Ba'al, king of the created world, has two enemies to defeat—chaos (Yamm) and death (Mot). He succeeds against Yamm, but is slain by Mot. His sister and his queen, Anath, kills Mot and resurrects Ba'al. Anath further proves herself to be Ba'al's comrade-in-arms when she summons his enemies to a banquet, locks the doors, and kills them all.

BIBLIOGRAPHY

1. ANTHROPOLOGY

Ardrey, Robert. *African Genesis: A Personal Investigation into the* √
 Animal Origins and Nature of Man. New York: Dell, 1963.
———. *The Social Contract: A Personal Inquiry into the Evolution-* √
 ary Sources of Order and Disorder. New York: Dell, 1971.
Clemente, C. D., and Donald B. Lindsley, eds. *Aggression and De-
 fense: Neural Mechanisms and Social Patterns.* Vol. 5. Berke-
 ley: University of California Press, 1967.
Dart, Raymond A. "The Predatory Transition from Ape to Man."
 International Anthropological and Linguistic Review 1 (1953):
 201–219.

√ Eisler, Riane. *The Chalice and the Blade: Our History, Our Future.* San Francisco: Harper & Row, 1988.

Feilds, Rick. *The Code of the Warrior in History, Myth, and Everyday Life.* New York: HarperCollins, 1991.

Fisher, Helen E. *The Sex Contract: The Evolution of Human Behavior.* New York: Quill, 1983.

Gillette, Douglas. "Men and Intimacy." *Wingspan: A Journal of the Male Spirit* (September 1990).

————. Review of *Manhood in the Making* by David Gilmore. In *Wingspan: A Journal of the Male Spirit* (Spring 1991).

Gilmore, David. *Manhood in the Making: Cultural Concepts of Masculinity.* New Haven: Yale University Press, 1990.

Herdt, Gilbert H., ed. *Rituals of Manhood: Male Initiation in Papua New Guinea.* Berkeley: University of California Press, 1982.

Johnson, Roger N. *Aggression in Man and Animals.* Philadelphia: W. B. Saunders, 1972.

Klein, Richard G. *The Human Career: Human Biological and Cultural Origins.* Chicago: University of Chicago Press, 1989.

√ Laughlin, William S. "Hunting: An Integrating Biobehavior System and Its Evolutionary Importance." In *Man the Hunter,* edited by Richard B. Lee and Irven DeVore. Symposium on Man the Hunter, University of Chicago, 1966. Chicago: Aldine, 1968.

Leakey, Louis S. B. "Development of Aggression as a Factor in Early Human and Pre-Human Evolution." In *Aggression and Defense,* edited by C. D. Clemente and D. B. Lindsley. Berkeley: University of California Press, 1967.

Life Editors. *The Epic of Man.* New York: Time, 1961.

Lopez, Barry Holstrum. *Of Wolves and Men.* New York: Charles Scribner's Sons, 1978.

MacKinnon, Michael. *The Ape Within Us.* New York: Holt, Rinehart and Winston, 1978.

Mahdi, Louise Carus, Steven Foster, and Meredith Little, eds., *Betwixt and Between: Patterns of Masculine and Feminine Initiation.* LaSalle, Ill.: Open Court, 1987.

Martin, Phyllis M., and Patrick O'Meara, eds. *Africa.* Bloomington, Ind.: Indiana University Press, 1977.

Montagu, Ashley, ed. *Man and Aggression.* 2nd ed. New York: Oxford University Press, 1973.

Morgan, Elaine. *The Descent of Woman.* New York: Stein and Day, 1972.

Morris, Desmond. *Intimate Behavior.* New York: Random House, 1971.

———. *The Naked Ape: A Zoologist's Study of the Human Animal.* New York: McGraw-Hill, 1967.

Rappaport, Roy A. "The Sacred in Human Evolution." *Annual Review of Ecology and Systematics* 2 (1971): 23–44.

Roper, M. K. "A Survey of the Evidence for Intrahuman Killing in the Pleistocene." *Current Anthropology* 10 (1989): 427–459.

Ruspoli, Mario. *The Cave of Lascaux: The Final Photographs.* New York: Harry N. Abrams, 1987.

Scott, John Paul. "Biological Basis of Human Warfare: An Interdisciplinary Problem." In *Interdisciplinary Relationships in the Social Sciences,* edited by Muzafer Sherif and Carolyn W. Sherif. Chicago: Aldine, 1969.

Smithsonian Editors. *Man and Beast: Comparative Social Behavior.* Edited by J. F. Eisenberg and Witton S. Dillon. Smithsonian Annual III. Washington, D.C.: Smithsonian Institution Press, 1971.

Tierney, Patrick. *The Highest Altar: Unveiling the Mystery of Human Sacrifice.* New York: Penguin Books, 1989.

Turner, Victor. *The Ritual Process: Structure and Anti-Structure.* Ithaca: Cornell University Press, 1969.

Wallace, Robert A. *The Genesis Factor.* New York: William Morrow, 1979.

Webster, Hutton. *Primitive Secret Societies.* New York: Macmillan, 1932.

Wilson, Edward O. *On Human Nature.* Cambridge: Harvard University Press, 1978.

———. *Sociobiology: The Abridged Edition.* Cambridge: Harvard University Press, 1980.

———. *Sociobiology: The New Synthesis.* Cambridge: Harvard University Press, 1975.

Zillman, Dolf. *Hostility and Aggression.* Hillsdale, N.J.: L. Erlbaum Associates, 1979.

2. BRAIN RESEARCH

Ashbrook, James B. *The Human Mind and the Mind of God: Theological Promise in Brain Research.* Lanham, Md.: University Press of America, 1984.

Harth, Erich. *Windows on the Mind: Reflections on the Physical Basis of Consciousness.* New York: Quill, 1983.

√ Jaynes, Julian. *The Origin of Consciousness in the Breakdown of the Bicameral Mind.* Boston: Houghton Mifflin, 1976.

MacLean, Paul D. *The Triune Brain in Evolution: Role in Paleocerebral Functions.* New York: Plenum Press, 1990.

Moir, Anne, and David Jessel. *Brain Sex: The Real Difference Between Men and Women.* New York: Carol Publishing Group, 1991.

√ Restak, Richard M. *The Brain.* New York: Bantam Books, 1984.

3. *HISTORY*

Albright, William F. *The Archeology of Palestine.* Harmondsworth, Middlesex, England: Penguin Books, 1949.

Aldred, Cyril. *Akhenaten, Pharaoh of Egypt: A New Study.* London: Thames and Hudson, 1968; London: Sphere Books, Abacus, 1972.

√ "Andean Civilization." *Encyclopedia Britannica.* Chicago: Encyclopedia Britannica, 1967. Vol. 1, pp. 889–891.

Barnett, R. D., and Werner Forman. *Assyrian Palace Reliefs and Their Influence on the Sculptures of Babylon and Persia.* London: Batchworth Press.

Barr, Stringfellow. *The Will of Zeus: A History of Greece.* New York: Dell, 1965.

Berger, Peter L. *Facing Up to Modernity: Excursions in Society, Politics, and Religion.* New York: Basic Books, 1977.

Blacker, Irwin R., and *Horizon* Magazine Editors. *Cortés and the Aztec Conquest.* New York: American Heritage, 1965.

Browning, Robert. *The Emperor Julian.* Berkeley: University of California Press, 1976.

Casson, Lionel, et al. *Mysteries of the Past.* New York: American Heritage, 1977.

Cristofani, Mauro. *The Etruscans: A New Investigation.* Translated from Italian by Brian Phillips. New York: Orbis Books, 1979.

Edwards, I.E.S. *The Pyramids of Egypt.* Harmondsworth, Middlesex, England: Penguin Books, 1947.

√ Gernet, Jacques. *A History of Chinese Civilization.* New York: Cambridge University Press, 1982. Originally published in French as *Le Monde chinois*. Paris: Librairie Armand Colin, 1972.

Gimbutas, Marija. *The Goddesses and Gods of Old Europe: Myths and Cult Images*. Berkeley: University of California Press, 1982.

Gurney, O. R. *The Hittites*. Harmondsworth, Middlesex, England: Penguin Books, 1952.

Morley, Sylvanus G., and George W. Brainerd. *The Ancient Maya*. 4th ed. Revised by Robert J. Sharer. Stanford, Calif.: Stanford University Press, 1983.

National Geographic Editors. *The Age of Chivalry*. Washington, D.C.: National Geographic Society, 1969.

Peterson, Frederick. *Ancient Mexico: An Introduction to the Pre-Hispanic Cultures*. Toms River, N.J.: Capricorn Books, 1962. Originally published 1959.

Säve-Söderbergh, Torgny. *Pharaohs and Mortals*. New York: Bobbs-Merrill, 1961.

Steindorff, George, and Keith C. Seele. *When Egypt Ruled the East*. Chicago: University of Chicago Press, 1942.

Thompson, John Eric S. *The Rise and Fall of Maya Civilization*. Norman: University of Oklahoma Press, 1954. Especially Chapter 2.

Time Editors. *The Epic of Man*. New York: Time, 1961. Especially Chapter 7.

Time-Life Books Editors. *The Age of the God-Kings, 3000–1500 B.C.* New York: Time-Life Books, 1990.

Turnbull, Stephen R. *The Book of the Samurai: The Warrior Class of Japan*. New York: W. H. Smith Publishers, 1982.

Wilson, John A. *The Culture of Ancient Egypt*. Chicago: University of Chicago Press, 1951. Originally published as *The Burden of Egypt*.

4. *JUNGIAN THOUGHT*

Andrews, Valerie, Robert Bosnak, and Karen Walter Goodwin, eds. *Facing Apocalypse*. Dallas: Spring Publications, 1987.

Corneau, Guy. *Absent Fathers, Lost Sons: The Search for Masculine Identity*. Boston: Shambhala, 1991.

de Castillejo, Irene Claremont Day. *Knowing Woman: A Feminine*

Psychology. New York: G. P. Putnam's Sons, 1973; New York: Harper & Row, 1974.

De Vries, Ad. *Dictionary of Symbols and Imagery*. Amsterdam: North-Holland Publishing Co., 1984.

Edinger, Edward F. *The Creation of Consciousness: Jung's Myth for Modern Man*. Inner City Books, 1984.

———. *Ego and Archetype: Individuation and the Religious Function of the Psyche*. New York: G. P. Putnam's Sons (for the C. G. Jung Foundation for Analytical Psychology), 1972; New York: Penguin Books, 1974.

Evans, Richard I. *Jung on Elementary Psychology: A Discussion Between C. G. Jung and Richard I. Evans*. New York: E. P. Dutton, 1976.

Garrison, Jim. *The Darkness of God: Theology After Hiroshima*. Grand Rapids, Mich.: William B. Eerdmans, 1982.

Hannah, Barbara. *Encounters with the Soul: Active Imagination as Developed by C. G. Jung*. Boston: Sigo Press, 1981.

Hillman, James, et al. *Puer Papers*. Dallas: Spring Publications, 1979. Especially the chapter by James Hillman, "Senex and Puer: An Aspect of the Historical and Psychological Present."

Jacobi, Jolande. *Complex, Archetype, Symbol in the Psychology of C. G. Jung*. Princeton: Princeton University Press, 1959. Originally published in German as *Komplex/Archetypus/Symbol in der Psychologie C. G. Jungs*. Zurich and Stuttgart: Rascher Verlag, 1957.

———. *The Psychology of C. G. Jung*. London: Routledge & Kegan Paul, 1942; New Haven: Yale University Press, 1973.

Jaffé, Aniela. *The Myth of Meaning: Jung and the Expansion of Consciousness*. New York: Penguin Books, 1975.

Johnson, Robert. *We: Understanding the Psychology of Romantic Love*. San Francisco: Harper & Row, 1983.

Jung, Carl G. *Aion: Researches into the Phenomenology of the Self*. Vol. 9 of *The Collected Works of C. G. Jung*. Princeton: Princeton University Press, 1959.

———. *Civilization in Transition*. Vol. 10 of *The Collected Works of C. G. Jung*. Princeton: Princeton University Press, 1970.

———. *Man and His Symbols*. New York: Dell, 1964; London: Aldus Books, 1964.

———. *Modern Man in Search of a Soul*. New York: Harcourt, Brace, 1933.

————. *Mysterium Coniunctionis: An Inquiry into the Separation and Synthesis of Psychic Opposites in Alchemy*. 2nd ed. Princeton: Princeton University Press, 1970.

————. *The Portable Jung*. Edited by Joseph Campbell. New York: Penguin Books, 1971. Reprint of Jung's work in *Aion*, pp. 148ff.

————. *Psyche and Symbol: A Selection from the Writings of C. G. Jung*. Edited by Violet deLaszlo. Garden City, N.Y.: Doubleday, 1958.

————. *Psychology and Alchemy*. 2nd ed. New York: Bollingen Foundation, 1953; Princeton: Princeton University Press, 1980.

————. *Psychology and Religion: West and East*. 2nd ed. Vol. 11 of *The Collected Works of C. G. Jung*. Princeton: Princeton University Press, 1958.

Layard, John. *A Celtic Quest: Sexuality and Soul in Individuation*. Dallas: Spring Publications, 1975.

Monick, Eugene. *Phallos: Sacred Image of the Masculine*. Toronto: Inner City Books, 1987.

Moore, Robert. *The Magician and the Analyst: Ritual, Sacred Space, and Psychotherapy*. Chicago: Center for the Scientific Study of Religion, 1992.

————, ed. *Carl Jung and Christian Spirituality*. Mahwah, N.J.: Paulist Press, 1988.

————, and Doug Gillette. *King, Warrior, Magician, Lover: Rediscovering the Archetypes of Mature Masculinity*. San Francisco: HarperCollins, 1990.

————, and Daniel Meckel, eds. *Jung and Christianity in Dialogue: Faith, Feminism, and Hermeneutics*. Mahwah, N.J.: Paulist Press, 1991.

Neumann, Erich. *Art and the Creative Unconscious*. Princeton: Princeton University Press, 1959.

Pedersen, Loren E. *Dark Hearts: The Unconscious Forces That Shape Men's Lives*. Boston: Shambhala, 1991.

Perry, John Weir. *Roots of Renewal in Myth and Madness: The Meaning of Psychotic Episodes*. San Francisco: Jossey-Bass, 1976.

Sanford, John A. *Dreams: God's Forgotten Language*. New York: J. B. Lippincott, 1968.

————. *Evil: The Shadow Side of Reality*. New York: Crossroad, 1981.

————. *The Invisible Partners: How the Male and Female in Each of Us Affects Our Relationships*. New York: Paulist Press, 1980.

273

Stein, Murray, ed. *Jungian Analysis*. Boulder, Colo.: Shambhala, 1984.

Stevens, Anthony. *Archetypes: A Natural History of the Self*. New York: Quill, 1983. Originally published as *Archetype: A Natural History of the Self*. London: Routledge & Kegan, 1982.

———. *The Roots of War: A Jungian Perspective*. New York: Paragon House, 1989.

Von Franz, Marie-Louise. *Projection and Recollection in Jungian Psychology*. LaSalle, Ill.: Open Court, 1980. Originally published in German as *Spiegelungen der Seele: Projektion und innere Sammlung*. Stuttgart: Kreuz Verlag, 1978.

———. *Shadow and Evil in Fairytales*. Dallas: Spring Publications, 1974.

Wolff, Toni. "Structural Forms of the Feminine Psyche." Privately printed for the Students Association, C. G. Jung Institute, Zurich, July 1956.

5. *KINGSHIP*

Basham, Arthur L. *The Wonder That Was India: A Survey of the Culture of the Indian Sub-Continent Before the Coming of the Muslims*. London: Sidgwick & Jackson, 1954; New York: Grove Press, 1959. Revised edition, Hawthorne Books, 1963.

Bricker, Victoria Reifler. *The Indian Christ, the Indian King: The Historical Substrate of Maya Myth and Ritual*. Austin: University of Texas Press, 1981.

Chaney, William A. *The Cult of Kingship in Anglo-Saxon England: The Transition from Paganism to Christianity*. Berkeley: University of California Press, 1970.

Emery, Walter B. *Archaic Egypt*. Harmondsworth, Middlesex, England: Penguin Books, 1961.

Engnell, Ivan. *Studies in Divine Kingship in the Ancient Near East*. 2nd ed. Oxford: Basil Blackwell, 1967.

Evans-Pritchard, Edward E. *The Divine Kingship of the Shilluk of the Nilotic Sudan*. Cambridge, England: Cambridge University Press, 1948.

Frankfort, Henri. *The Birth of Civilization in the Near East*. Garden City, N.Y.: Doubleday, 1956; Bloomington, Ind.: Indiana University Press, 1959.

————. *Kingship and the Gods: A Study of Ancient Near Eastern Religion as the Integration of Society and Nature*. Chicago: University of Chicago Press, 1948.

Gadd, Cyril J. *Ideas of Divine Rule in the Ancient East*. Schweich Lectures on Biblical Archeology. London: British Academy, 1948.

Gonda, Jan. "Ancient Indian Kingship from the Religious Point of View." *Numen* 3 (1955): 36–71, 122–155; *Numen* 4 (1956): 4, 24–58, 127–164.

Grottanelli, Christiano. "Kingship in the Ancient Mediterranean World." *Encyclopedia of Religion*, edited by Mircea Eliade, Vol. 8, pp. 317–322. New York: Macmillan, 1987.

Hadfield, Percival. *Traits of Divine Kingship in Africa*. Westport, Conn.: Greenwood Press, 1979.

Hocart, Arthur Maurice. *Kingship*. London: Oxford University Press, 1927.

Hooke, Samuel H. *Myth, Ritual, and Kingship: Essays on the Theory and Practice of Kingship in the Ancient Near East and in Israel*. 2nd ed. Oxford: Clarendon Press, 1967.

Johnson, Aubrey R. *Sacral Kingship in Ancient Israel*. Cardiff: University of Wales Press, 1955.

Kantorowicz, Ernest H. *The King's Two Bodies: A Study in Mediaeval Political Theology*. Princeton: Princeton University Press, 1957.

Keightley, David N. "The Religious Commitment: Shang Theology and the Genesis of Chinese Political Culture." *History of Religions* 17, no. 2 (November 1977 or February–May 1978): 211–225.

Kenik, Helen A. "Code of Conduct for a King: Psalm 101." *Journal of Biblical Literature* 95, no. 3 (1976): 391–403.

Kwanten, Luc. *Imperial Nomads: A History of Central Asia, 500–1500*. Philadelphia: University of Pennsylvania Press, 1979.

Malandra, William W. *An Introduction to Ancient Iranian Religion: Readings from the "Avesta" and "Achaemenid" Inscriptions*. Minneapolis: University of Minnesota Press, 1983.

Meyerowitz, Eva L. R. *The Divine Kingship in Ghana and Ancient Egypt*. London: Faber & Faber, 1940.

Moore, Robert, and Douglas Gillette. *The King Within: Accessing the King in the Male Psyche*. New York: William Morrow, 1992.

Mumford, Lewis. *The City in History: Its Origins, Transformations, and Prospects*. New York: Harcourt, Brace and World, 1968.

Murray, Margaret Alice. "Evidence for the Custom of Killing the King in Ancient Egypt." *Man* 14 (1914): 17–23. London: Royal Anthropological Institute, 1914.

Myers, Henry Allen. *Medieval Kingship.* Chicago: Nelson-Hall, 1982.

Parrinder, Edward G. "Divine Kingship in West Africa." *Numen* 3 (1956): 111–121.

Peters, Edward. *The Shadow King: Rex Inutilis in Medieval Law and Literature, 751–1327.* New Haven: Yale University Press, 1970.

Richards, J. W. "Sacral Kings of Iran." *Mankind Quarterly* 20, nos. 1–2 (Edinburgh, 1979): 143–160.

Ruttan, Karl. "The Evolution of the Kingship Archetype in the Old Testament." Thesis, Chicago Theological Seminary, 1975.

Schele, Linda, and David A. Freidel. *A Forest of Kings: The Untold Story of the Ancient Maya.* New York: William Morrow, 1990.

Seligman, C. G. *Egypt and Negro Africa: A Study in Divine Kingship.* London: G. Routledge and Sons, 1934.

Tucci, Giuseppe. "The Secret Characters of the Kings of Ancient Tibet." *East and West* 6, no. 3 (October 1955): 197–205.

Valeri, Valerio. *Kingship and Sacrifice: Ritual and Society in Ancient Hawaii.* Translated from Hawaiian by Paula Wissing. Chicago: University of Chicago Press, 1985.

Waida, Manabu. "Notes on Sacred Kingship in Central Asia." *Numen* 23 (December 1976): 179–190.

———. "Sacred Kingship in Early Japan." Ph.D. dissertation, University of Chicago, 1974.

———. "Sacred Kingship in Early Japan: A Historical Introduction." *History of Religions* 15, no. 4 (May 1976): 319–342.

———. "Symbolism of 'Descent' in Tibetan Sacred Kingship and Some East Asian Parallels." *Numen* 20 (April 1973): 60–78.

Wales, Horace G. *The Mountain of God: A Study in Early Religion and Kingship.* London: Bernard Quaritch, 1953.

Zuidema, R. Tom. "The Lion in the City: Royal Symbols of Transition in Cuzco." *Journal of Latin American Lore* 9, no. 1 (Summer 1983): 39–100.

6. *LITERATURE*

Aeschylus. *Agamemnon.* In *Greek Literature in Translation,* edited by Whitney J. Oates and Charles T. Murphey. New York: David McKay, 1944.

Blake, William. *The Complete Poetry and Prose*, ed. David Erdman, ✓ rev. ed. Berkeley: University of California Press, 1981.

Bly, Robert. *Iron John: A Book About Men.* New York: Vintage Books, 1992.

Euripides. *The Bachae.* In *Euripides V*, edited by David Grene and ✓ Richmond Lattimore. New York: Washington Square Press, 1968.

Herbert, Frank. *Dune.* New York: Berkeley Publications, 1965; New ✓ York: Putnam, 1984.

Hesse, Hermann. *The Journey to the East.* Translated by Hilda ✓ Rosner. New York: Farrar, Straus & Giroux, 1956.

Lacy, Norris J., ed. *The Arthurian Encyclopedia.* New York: Garland, 1986.

Lewis, C. S. *'Til We Have Faces.* New York: Harcourt, Brace and World, 1956.

Sophocles. *Sophocles I.* Edited by David Grene and Richmond Lattimore. Chicago: University of Chicago Press, 1954. ✓

Tennyson, Alfred. *Idylls of the King.* Edited by J. M. Gray. New Haven: Yale University Press, 1983.

Tolkien, J.R.R. *The Return of the King.* New York: Ballantine Books, ✓ 1965.

White, T. H. *The Book of Merlyn.* Austin: University of Texas Press, 1977.

———. *The Once and Future King.* London: Collins, 1958; New York: Putnam, 1958.

7. *MAGICIANS, MAGIC, AND SHAMANISM*

Castaneda, Carlos. *Journey to Ixtlan: The Lessons of Don Juan.* New ✓ York: Simon & Schuster/Pocket Books, 1972.

———. *A Separate Reality: Further Conversations with Don Juan.* ✓ New York: Simon & Schuster/Pocket Books, 1971.

———. *The Teachings of Don Juan: A Yaqui Way of Knowledge.* ✓ New York: Ballantine Books, 1968.

Doore, Gary, ed. *Shaman's Path: Healing, Personal Growth, and* ⟩ *Empowerment.* Boston: Shambhala, 1988.

Goethe, W. *Goethe's Faust.* Translated by Louis MacNiece. New York: ✓ Oxford University Press, 1951.

Grossinger, Richard, ed. *The Alchemical Tradition in the Late Twentieth Century.* Berkeley: North Atlantic Books, 1979.

Halifax, Joan. *Shamanic Voices: A Survey of Visionary Narratives.* New York: E. P. Dutton, 1979.

Larsen, Stephen. *The Shaman's Doorway: Opening the Mythic Imagination to Contemporary Consciousness.* San Francisco: Harper and Row/Harper Colophon Books, 1976.

Neihardt, John G. *Black Elk Speaks.* New York: Simon & Schuster/Pocket Books, 1972.

Nichols, Sallie. *Jung and Tarot: An Archetypal Journey.* York Beach, Maine: Samuel Weiser, 1980.

Nicholson, Shirley, ed. *Shamanism.* Wheaton, Ill.: Theosophical Publishing House, 1987.

Von Franz, Marie-Louise. *Number and Time.* Evanston, Ill.: Northwestern University Press, 1974.

Wolf, Fred Alan. *The Eagle's Quest: A Physicist's Search for Truth in the Heart of the Shamanic World.* New York: Simon & Schuster/Summit Books, 1991.

8. MYTHOLOGY AND RELIGION

Albright, William F. *Yahweh and the Gods of Canaan: A Historical Analysis of Two Contrasting Faiths.* Garden City, N.Y.: Doubleday, 1968.

Anderson, William. *Green Man: The Archetype of Our Oneness with the Earth.* London: HarperCollins, 1990.

Arberry, A. J. *Sufism: An Account of the Mystics of Islam.* New York: Harper & Row/Harper Torchbooks, 1970.

Baba, Pagal. *Temple of the Phallic King: The Mind of India: Yogis, Swamis, Sufis, and Avatars.* New York: Simon & Schuster, 1973.

Barnstone, Willis, ed. *The Other Bible.* San Francisco: Harper & Row, 1984.

Breasted, James H. *The Dawn of Conscience: The Sources of Our Moral Heritage in the Ancient World.* New York: Charles Scribner's Sons, 1933.

Budge, E. A. Wallis. *The Egyptian Book of the Dead (The Papyrus of Ani): Egyptian Text, Transliteration, and Translation.* New York: Dover, 1976.

Campbell, Joseph. *The Hero with a Thousand Faces.* Rev. ed. Princeton: Princeton University Press, 1968.

————. *Historical Atlas of World Mythology.* Vol. 2. *The Way of the Seeded Earth.* Part 1: *The Sacrifice.* New York: Harper & Row/Perennial Library, 1988.

————. *The Masks of God: Creative Mythology.* New York: Penguin, 1970.

————. *The Masks of God: Occidental Mythology.* New York: Viking Press, 1964; New York: Penguin, 1976.

————. *The Mythic Image.* Princeton, N.J.: Princeton University Press, 1974.

————. *The Power of Myth.* Garden City, N.Y.: Doubleday, 1988.

Carrasco, David. *Quetzalcoatl and the Irony of Empire: Myths and Prophecies in the Aztec Tradition.* Chicago: University of Chicago Press, 1982.

Cohn-Haft, Louis. *Source Readings in Ancient History: The Ancient Near East.* New York: Thomas Y. Crowell, 1965.

Confucius. *The Analects of Confucius.* Translated by Arthur Waley. London: George Allen & Unwin, 1938; New York: Random House/Vintage Books, 1989.

Cumont, Franz. *The Mysteries of Mithra.* Translated from the 2nd revised French edition by Thomas J. McCormack. LaSalle, Ill.: Open Court, 1903; New York: Dover Publications, 1956.

Dodds, E. R. *Pagan and Christian in an Age of Anxiety: Some Aspects of Religious Experience from Marcus Aurelius to Constantine.* New York: W. W. Norton, 1965.

Dupont-Sommer, André. *The Essene Writings from Qumran.* New York: World/Meridian Books, 1961.

Eliade, Mircea. *Cosmos and History: The Myth of the Eternal Return.* Princeton: Bollingen Foundation, 1954; New York: Harper & Row, 1959.

————. *Myth and Reality.* New York: Harper & Row/Harper Torchbooks, 1963.

————. *Patterns in Comparative Religion.* New York: World Publishing, 1963. Originally published in French as *Traité d'histoire des religions.* Paris: Editions Payot.

————. *Rites and Symbols of Initiation: The Mysteries of Birth and Rebirth.* New York: Harper & Row, 1958.

————. *The Sacred and the Profane: The Nature of Religion: The Significance of Religious Myth, Symbolism, and Ritual Within Life and Culture.* New York: Harcourt, Brace and World, 1959.

Originally published in German by Rowohlt Taschenbuch Verlag, 1957.

Evans-Wentz, Walter Y., ed. *The Tibetan Book of the Great Liberation; or the Method of Realizing Nirvana Through Knowing the Mind.* London: Oxford University Press, 1954.

Forsyth, Neil. *The Old Enemy: Satan and the Combat Myth.* Princeton: Princeton University Press, 1987.

Frankfort, Henri. *Ancient Egyptian Religion.* New York: Columbia University Press, 1948; New York: Harper & Row, 1961.

√ Frazer, James G. *The Golden Bough: A Study in Magic and Religion,* 12 vols. 3rd ed. London, 1915. Reprint, paperback edition, 1963.

Gaer, Joseph. *How the Great Religions Began.* New York: Dodd, Mead, 1929. New revised edition, New York: Dodd, Mead, 1938; New York: New American Library/Signet Books, 1954.

Godwin, Joscelyn. *Mystery Religions in the Ancient World.* San Francisco: Harper & Row, 1981; London: Thames & Hudson, 1981.

Grant, Robert M. *Gnosticism and Early Christianity.* New York: Columbia University Press, 1959; New York: Harper & Row/ Harper Torchbooks, 1959.

Graves, Robert. *The Greek Myths.* 2 vols. Harmondsworth, Middlesex, England: Penguin Books, 1955.

Hadas, Moses. *The Apocrypha: An American Translation.* New York: Alfred A. Knopf and Random House, 1959.

√ Hamilton, Edith. *Mythology: Timeless Tales of Gods and Heroes.* New York: New American Library, 1940.

Henderson, Joseph L. *Thresholds of Initiation.* Middletown, Conn.: Wesleyan University Press, 1967.

Hooke, Samuel H. *Middle Eastern Mythology.* New York: Viking Penguin, 1963.

√ James, William. *The Varieties of Religious Experience: A Study in Human Nature.* Gifford Lectures. London: Longmans Green, 1902. Reprint, paperback edition, with foreword by Jacques Barzun, New York: New American Library, 1958.

Jobes, Gertrude. *Dictionary of Mythology, Folklore, and Symbols.* Metuchen, N.J.: Scarecrow Press, 1962.

Kipnis, Aaron R. *Knights Without Armor.* Los Angeles: Jeremy P. Tarcher, 1991.

Kramer, Samuel Noah. *Sumerian Mythology: A Study of Spiritual and Literary Achievement in the Third Millennium B.C.* New York: Harper, 1961.

Krickeberg, Walter, et al. *Pre-Columbian American Religions.* Translated from German by Stanley Davis. New York: Holt, Rinehart and Winston, 1968; London: Weidenfeld & Nicolson, 1968.

Lind, Millard C. *Yahweh Is a Warrior: The Theology of Warfare in Ancient Israel.* Scottdale, Pa.: Herald Press, 1980.

MacCana, Proinsias. *Celtic Mythology.* New revised edition. London: Bedrick Books, 1985.

Malandra, William W. *An Introduction to Ancient Iranian Religion: Readings from the "Avesta" and "Achaemenid" Inscriptions.* Minneapolis: University of Minnesota Press, 1983.

Mansoor, Menachem. *The Dead Sea Scrolls.* Leiden, Netherlands: E. J. Brill, 1964; Grand Rapids, Mich.: Wm. B. Eerdmans, 1964.

Matthews, John, ed. *Choirs of the God: Revisioning Masculinity.* London: Mandala, 1991; San Francisco: HarperCollins, 1991.

May, Herbert G., and Bruce M. Metzger. *The New Oxford Annotated Bible with the Apocrypha.* Revised Standard Version. Expanded Edition. New York: Oxford University Press, 1977.

Miller, Patrick D. *The Divine Warrior in Early Israel.* Cambridge, Mass.: Harvard University Press, 1973.

Moody, Raymond A. *Life After Life: The Investigation of a Phenomenon—Survival of Bodily Death.* With Introduction by Elisabeth Kübler-Ross. Saint Simons Island, Ga.: Mockingbird Books, 1975; New York: Bantam Books, 1975.

Mylonas, George E. *Eleusis and the Eleusinian Mysteries.* Princeton: Princeton University Press, 1961.

Oikonomides, A. N. *Mithraic Art: A Search for Unpublished and Unidentified Monuments.* Chicago: Ares, 1975.

Otto, Rudolf. *The Idea of the Holy.* New York: Oxford University Press, 1923.

Pagels, Elaine. *The Gnostic Gospels.* New York: Random House, 1979.

Perowne, Stewart. *Roman Mythology.* London: Hamlyn, 1969.

Perry, John Weir. *Lord of the Four Quarters: Myths of the Royal Father.* New York: G. Braziller, 1966; New York: Macmillan/Collier Books, 1970.

———. *Lord of the Four Quarters: The Mythology of Kingship.* Mahwah, N.J.: Paulist Press, 1991.

Pritchard, James B., ed. *The Ancient Near East: An Anthology of Texts and Pictures*. Princeton: Princeton University Press, 1958.

Reichel-Dolmatoff, Gerardo. *Amazonian Cosmos: The Sexual and Religious Symbolism of the Tukano Indians*. Translated from Spanish. Chicago: University of Chicago Press, 1971.

Robinson, James M., ed. *The Nag Hammadi Library*. San Francisco: Harper & Row, 1977.

Scholem, Gershom. *Major Trends in Jewish Mysticism*. New York: Schocken Books, 1946.

———. *Origins of the Kaballah*. Edited by R. J. Werblowsky. Translated by Allan Arkush. Princeton: Princeton University Press (for the Jewish Publication Society), 1987. Originally published as *Ursprung und Anfänge der Kabbala*. Berlin: Walter de Gruyter, 1962.

The Secret of the Golden Flower: A Chinese Book of Life. Translated by Richard Wilhelm. New York: Harcourt Brace Jovanovich, 1962.

Seltman, Charles T. *The Twelve Olympians*. New York: Thomas Y. Crowell, 1960.

Shah, Idries. *The Sufis*. Garden City, N.Y.: Doubleday/Anchor Books, 1964.

Smith, Huston. *Forgotten Truth: The Primordial Tradition*. New York: Harper & Row/Harper Colophon Books, 1976.

———. *The Religions of Man*. New York: Harper & Row, 1965.

Smith, Morton. *Jesus the Magician*. San Francisco: Harper & Row, 1978.

Sullivan, Lawrence, ed. *Healing and Restoring: Health and Medicine in the World's Religious Traditions*. New York: Macmillan, 1988.

Thomas, D. Winton, ed. *Documents from Old Testament Times*. Translated with introduction and notes by members of the Society for Old Testament Study. New York: Harper, 1961.

Thompson, Brian. *The Story of Prince Rama*. Harmondsworth, Middlesex, England: Penguin Books, 1980.

Underhill, Evelyn. *Mysticism*. New York: E. P. Dutton, 1911.

Vermes, Geza. *The Dead Sea Scrolls in English*. Baltimore: Penguin Books, 1962.

Walker, J.B.R. *The Comprehensive Concordance to the Holy Scriptures*. S. A. Weston, 1929; New York: Macmillan, 1948.

Watts, Alan, and Eliot Elisofan. *Erotic Spirituality: The Vision of*

Konarak. Photographs by Eliot Elisofan. Commentary by Alan Watts. New York: Macmillan/Collier Books, 1971.

Weston, Jesse L. *From Ritual to Romance: An Account of the Holy Grail from Ancient Ritual to Christian Symbol*. Cambridge: Cambridge University Press, 1920; Garden City, N.Y.: Doubleday, 1957.

Wheatley, Paul. *The Pivot of the Four Quarters: A Preliminary Inquiry into the Origins and Character of the Ancient Chinese City*. Chicago: Aldine Publishing, 1971.

9. *OTHER PSYCHOLOGIES*

Ansbacher, Heinz L., and Rowena R. Ansbacher. *The Individual Psychology of Alfred Adler*. New York: Harper & Row, 1964.

Beahrs, John O. *Unity and Multiplicity: Multilevel Consciousness of Self in Hypnosis, Psychiatric Disorder and Mental Health*. New York: Brunner/Mazel, 1981.

Bettelheim, Bruno. *Freud and Man's Soul*. New York: Alfred A. Knopf, 1983.

Bowlby, John. *Separation: Anxiety and Anger*. New York: Basic Books, 1973.

Bradshaw, John. *Homecoming: Reclaiming and Championing Your Inner Child*. New York: Bantam Books, 1990.

Browning, Don S. *Generative Man: Psychoanalytic Perspectives*. Philadelphia: Westminster Press, 1973; New York: Dell, 1975.

Freud, Sigmund. *Moses and Monotheism*. Translated by Katherine Jones. New York: Alfred A. Knopf, 1939.

———. *Totem and Taboo: Some Points of Agreement Between the Mental Lives of Savages and Neurotics*. Translated by James Strachey. New York: W. W. Norton, 1950; London: Routledge & Kegan Paul, 1950.

Hendrix, Harville. *Getting the Love You Want*. New York: Henry Holt, 1988.

Keen, Sam. *Fire in the Belly: On Being a Man*. New York: Bantam, 1991.

Lauzun, Gérard. *Sigmund Freud: The Man and His Theories*. Translated by Patrick Evans. Greenwich, Conn.: Fawcett, 1962; Paris: Pierre Seghers, 1962.

Lee, Ronald R., and J. Colby Martin. *Psychotheraphy After Kohut: A*

Textbook of Self Psychology. Hillsdale, N.J.: Analytic Press, 1991.

Marcuse, Herbert. *Eros and Civilization: A Philosophical Inquiry into Freud.* Boston: Beacon Press, 1955.

Miller, Alice. *The Drama of the Gifted Child: How Narcissistic Parents Form and Deform the Emotional Lives of Their Talented Children.* New York: Basic Books, 1981. Originally published in German as *Das Drama des begabten Kindes.* Frankfurt am Main: Suhrkamp, 1979.

———. *For Your Own Good: Hidden Cruelty in Child-Rearing and the Roots of Violence.* New York: Farrar Straus Giroux, 1984. Originally published in German as *Am Anfang war Erziehung.* Frankfurt am Main: Suhrkamp, 1980.

———. *Thou Shalt Not Be Aware: Society's Betrayal of the Child.* New York: Farrar Straus Giroux, 1984. Originally published in German as *Du sollst nicht merken.* Frankfurt am Main: Suhrkamp, 1981.

Millon, Theodore. *Disorders of Personality: DSM-III: Axis II.* New York: John Wiley and Sons, 1981.

———. *Modern Psychopathology: A Biosocial Approach to Maladaptive Learning and Functioning.* Prospect Heights, Ill.: Waveland Press, 1983.

Peck, M. Scott. *People of the Lie: The Hope for Healing Human Evil.* New York: Simon & Schuster, 1983.

———. *The Road Less Traveled: A New Psychology of Love, Traditional Values and Spiritual Growth.* New York: Simon & Schuster, 1978.

Rizzuto, Ana-Maria. *The Birth of the Living God: A Psychoanalytic Study.* Chicago: University of Chicago Press, 1979.

Rogers, David J. *Fighting to Win: Samurai Techniques for Your Work and Life.* Garden City, N.Y.: Doubleday, 1984.

Schmookler, Andrew Bard. *Out of Weakness: Healing the Wounds That Lead Us to War.* Toronto: Bantam Books, 1988.

Shapiro, David. *Neurotic Styles.* New York: Basic Books, 1965.

Spencer, Laura J. *Winning Through Participation.* Dubuque, Iowa: Kendall Hunt (under auspices of the Institute for Cultural Affairs), 1989.

Storr, Anthony. *Human Aggression.* New York: Atheneum, 1968; New York: Bantam Books, 1970.

————. *Human Destructiveness*. New York: Basic Books, 1972; New ✓
York: Grove Weidenfeld, 1991.

————. *The Integrity of the Personality*. New York: Atheneum,
1960; New York: Random House, 1992.

Ulanov, Ann, and Barry Ulanov. *Cinderella and Her Sisters: The
Envied and the Envying*. Philadelphia: Westminster Press, 1983.

Winnicott, Donald W. *Home Is Where We Start From: Essays by a
Psychoanalyst*. Compiled and edited by Clare Winnicott, Ray
Shepherd, and Madeline Davis. New York: W. W. Norton, 1986;
New York: Penguin Books, 1986.

Wolf, Ernest S. *Treating the Self: Elements of Clinical Self Psychology*. New York: Guilford Press, 1988.

10. *PHYSICS AND COSMOLOGY*

Ferris, Timothy. *The Red Limit: The Search for the Edge of the
Universe*. New York: William Morrow, 1977; New York: Bantam
Books, 1977.

Morris, Richard. *Time's Arrows: Scientific Attitudes Toward Time*.
New York: Simon & Schuster, 1984.

Time-Life Books Editors. *Voyage Through the Universe: The Cosmos*.
Alexandria, Va.: Time-Life Books, 1988.

11. *PRIMATE ETHOLOGY*

Barnett, Samuel A. "Attack and Defense in Animal Societies." In
Aggression and Defense, edited by C. D. Clemente and D. B.
Lindsley. Berkeley: University of California Press, 1967.

Bourne, Geoffrey H. *Primate Odyssey*. New York: G. P. Putnam's
Sons, 1974.

Davis, D. E. "The Physiological Analysis of Aggressive Behavior." In
Social Behavior and Organization Among Vertebrates, edited by
William Etkin. New York, 1964.

Desmond, Adrian J. *The Ape's Reflection*. New York: Dial Press/
James Wade, 1979.

de Waal, Frans. *Chimpanzee Politics: Power and Sex Among Apes*.
New York: Harper & Row, 1982.

―――. *Peacemaking Among Primates*. Cambridge: Harvard University Press, 1989.

Eibl-Eibesfeldt, Irenaus. *Biology of Peace and War: Men, Animals, and Aggression*. Translated from German by Eric Mosbacher. New York: Viking Press, 1979.

―――. "The Fighting Behavior of Animals." *Scientific American* 205 (1961): 112–122.

Fossy, Dian. *Gorillas in the Mist*. Boston: Houghton Mifflin, 1983.

Goodall, Jane. *In the Shadow of Man*. Boston: Houghton Mifflin, 1971.

―――. *Through a Window: My Thirty Years with the Chimpanzees of Gombe*. Boston: Houghton Mifflin, 1990.

Hall, K.R.C. "Aggression in Monkey and Ape Societies." In *The Natural History of Aggression*, edited by John D. Carthy and Francis J. Ebling, pp. 50–64. London: Academic Press (for the Institute of Biology), 1964.

Heltne, Paul G., and Linda A. Marquardt. *Understanding Chimpanzees*. Cambridge: Harvard University Press, 1989.

Matthews, L. Harrison. "Overt Fighting in Mammals." In *The Natural History of Aggression*, edited by John D. Carthy and Francis J. Ebling. London: Academic Press (for the Institute of Biology), 1964.

Shaw, C. E. "The Male Combat Dance of Crotalid Snakes." *Herpetologia* 4 (1948): 137–145.

Tinbergen, Niko. "Fighting and Threat in Animals." *New Biology* 14 (1953): 9–24.

12. *R I T U A L   A N D   I N I T I A T I O N*

Almond, Richard. *The Healing Community: Dynamics of the Therapeutic Milieu*. Stanford: Stanford University Press, 1974.

Bellack, L., M. Hurvich, and H. Gediman. *Ego Functions in Schizophrenics, Neurotics, and Normals*. New York: John Wiley, 1973.

Benedict, Ruth. "Ritual." *Encyclopaedia of the Social Sciences* 13 (1934): 396–398.

Bossard, James A. S., and Eleanor S. Bell. "Ritual in Family Living." *American Sociological Review* 14 (1949): 463–469.

Davis, Madeleine, and David Wallbridge. *Boundary and Space: An*

Introduction to the Work of D. W. Winnicott. New York: Brunner/Mazel, 1981.

Eliade, Mircea. *Rites and Symbols of Initiation: The Mysteries of Birth and Rebirth.* New York: Harper & Row, 1958.

Erikson, Erik. "The Ontogeny of Ritualization." In *Psychoanalysis: A General Psychology*, edited by Loewenstein et al. New York: International Universities Press, 1966.

Frank, Jerome D. *Persuasion and Healing: A Comparative Study of Psychotherapy.* New York: Schocken Books, 1963.

Gay, Volney P. "Psychopathology and Ritual: Freud's Essay 'Obsessive Actions and Religious Practises.' " *Psychoanalytic Review* 62 (1975): 493–507.

————. "Ritual and Self-Esteem in Victor Turner and Heinz Kohut." *Zygon* 18 (September 1983): 271–282.

Goodheart, William B. "Theory of Analytical Interaction." *San Francisco Jung Institute Library Journal* 1, no. 4 (1980): 2–39.

Grimes, Ronald. "Ritual Studies: Two Models." *Religious Studies Review* 2 (1976): 13–25.

Groesbeck, C. Jess. "The Archetypal Image of the Wounded Healer." *The Journal of Analytical Psychology* 20 (1975): 122–145.

Grolnick, Simon A., and Leonard Barkin, eds. *Between Reality and Fantasy: Transitional Objects and Phenomena.* New York: Jason Aronson, 1978.

Guggenbuhl-Craig, Adolf. *Power in the Helping Professions.* Irving, Texas: Spring Publications, 1971.

Harrison, Jane. *Ancient Art and Ritual.* London: Williams & Norgate, 1913.

————. *Themis: A Study of the Social Origins of Greek Religion.* Cambridge: Cambridge University Press, 1912.

Hart, Onno van der. *Rituals in Psychotherapy: Transition and Continuity.* New York: Irvington Publishers, 1983.

Langs, Robert. *The Bipersonal Field.* New York: Jason Aronson, 1976.

————. *Interactions.* New York: Jason Aronson, 1980.

————. *Technique in Transition.* New York: Jason Aronson, 1978.

————. *The Therapeutic Environment.* New York: Jason Aronson, 1979.

Leach, E. R. "Ritual." *International Encyclopaedia of the Social Sciences* 13: 520–526.

McCurdy, Alexander, III. "Establishing and Maintaining the Analytical Structure." In *Jungian Analysis*, edited by Murray Stein. LaSalle, Ill.: Open Court, 1982.

Moore, Robert L. "Contemporary Psychotherapy as Ritual Process: An Initial Reconnaissance." *Zygon* 18 (September 1983): 283–294.

———. "Ritual Process, Initiation, and Contemporary Religion." In *Jung's Challenge to Contemporary Religion*, edited by Murray Stein and Robert L. Moore. Wilmette, Ill.: Chiron Press, 1987.

———, Ralph W. Burhoe, and Philip J. Hefner, eds. "Ritual in Human Adaptation." Symposium reported in *Zygon* 18 (September 1983): 209–325.

Perry, John Weir. *Roots of Renewal in Myth and Madness*. San Francisco: Jossey-Bass, 1976.

Posinsky, S. H. "Ritual, Neurotic and Social." *American Imago* 19 (1962): 375–390.

Reik, Theodor. *Ritual: Psychoanalytic Studies*. London: Hogarth Press, 1931.

Turner, Victor. *The Drums of Affliction*. Oxford: Clarendon Press, 1968.

———. *From Ritual to Theatre*. New York: Performing Arts Journal Publications, 1982.

———. *Process, Performance and Pilgrimage: A Study in Comparative Symbology*. New Delhi: Concept Publishing, 1979.

———. *The Ritual Process: Structure and Anti-Structure*. Chicago: Aldine, 1969; Ithaca: Cornell University Press, 1969.

———, and Edith Turner. *Image and Pilgrimage in Christian Culture*. New York: Columbia University Press, 1978.

van Gennep, Arnold. *The Rites of Passage*. Chicago: University of Chicago Press, 1960. Originally published in 1908.

13. *THEOLOGY AND PHILOSOPHY*

Daley, Mary. *Beyond God the Father: Toward a Philosophy of Women's Liberation*. Boston: Beacon Press, 1973.

———. *Gyn/Ecology: The Metaethics of Radical Feminism*. Boston: Beacon Press, 1979.

Evans-Wentz, Walter Y., ed. *The Tibetan Book of the Dead*. 3rd ed. New York: Oxford University Press, 1960.

Goldin, Judah. *The Living Talmud.* New Haven: Yale University Press, 1955; New York: New American Library, 1957.

Greenleaf, Robert K. *Servant Leadership: A Journey into the Nature of Legitimate Power and Greatness.* New York: Paulist Press, 1977.

Keen, Sam. *To a Dancing God: Notes of a Spiritual Traveler.* San Francisco: Harper, 1970.

Kelly, J.N.D. *Early Christian Doctrines.* 2nd ed. New York: Harper & Row, 1960.

Kelly, Sean. *Individuation and the Absolute: Hegel, Jung, and the Path Toward Wholeness.* New York: Paulist Press, forthcoming.

Kirk, G. S., and J. E. Raven. *The Presocratic Philosophers: A Critical History with a Selection of Texts.* Cambridge: Cambridge University Press, 1957.

Loye, David. *The Sphynx and the Rainbow: Brain, Mind, and Future Vision.* Boston: Shambhala, 1983.

Nicholas of Cusa. *The Vision of God.* Translated by O. R. Gurney. Edited by Evelyn Underhill. New York: Ungar, 1960.

Niebuhr, Reinhold. *The Nature and Destiny of Man: A Christian Interpretation.* Vol. 1. New York: Charles Scribner's Sons, 1941, 1964.

Nikhilananda, Swami. *The Upanishads.* New York: Ramakrishna-Vivekananda Center, 1949.

Nilsson, Martin P. *Greek Piety.* Translated from Swedish by Herbert J. Rose. Oxford: Clarendon Press, 1948; New York: W. W. Norton, 1969.

Norris, Richard A., Jr., and William G. Rusch, eds. *The Christological Controversy.* Translated by Richard A. Norris. Philadelphia: Fortress Press, 1980.

Pickthall, Marmaduke. *The Meaning of the Glorious Koran.* New York: New American Library, 1953.

Pirsig, Robert M. *Zen and the Art of Motorcycle Maintenance.* Toronto: Bantam Books, 1975.

Plato. *Apology, Crito, Phaedo, Symposium, Republic.* Translated by Benjamin Jowett. Edited with introduction by Louise R. Loomis. Roslyn, N.Y.: Walter J. Black, 1942.

Prabhupada, A. C. Bhaktivedanta Swami. *Bhagavad-Gita As It Is.* Bhaktivedanta Book Trust, 1968; New York: Macmillan/Collier Books, 1972.

BIBLIOGRAPHY

Ruether, Rosemary R. *Sexism and God-Talk: Toward a Feminist Theology*. Boston: Beacon Press, 1973.

Teilhard de Chardin, Pierre. *The Phenomenon of Man*. New York: Harper & Row, 1959.

Tillich, Paul. *The Courage to Be*. New Haven: Yale University Press, 1952.

————. *The Eternal Now*. New York: Charles Scribner's Sons, 1963.

————. *Systematic Theology*. Vol. 3. Part 4: *Life and the Spirit* and Part 5: *History and the Kingdom of God*. Chicago: University of Chicago Press, 1963. See especially Chapter 1 of Part 4: "Life, Its Ambiguities, and the Quest for Unambiguous Life"; and Chapter 3 of Part 5: "The Kingdom of God as the End of History."

Watts, Alan. *The Supreme Identity: An Essay on Oriental Metaphysic and the Christian Religion*. New York: Random House/Vintage Books, 1972.

Wei, Henry. *The Guiding Light of Lao Tze*. Wheaton, Ill.: Theosophical Publishing House, 1982.

Whitehead, Alfred North. *Adventures of Ideas*. New York: Macmillan, 1933; New York: Free Press, 1967.

14. *AUDIOTAPES*

Order the following audiotapes from the C. G. Jung Institute of Chicago, 1567 Maple, Evanston, IL 60201, (708) 475-4848, fax number (708) 475-4970.

Moore, Robert
    Archetypal Images of the King and Warrior
    Archetypal Images of the Magician and Lover
    Cosmos as Myth and Human Possibility
    Creation Mythology and the Search for a Centered Self
    David the King: A Study in Psychology and Myth
    The Ego and Its Relations with the Unconscious, 2 tapes
    The Four Couples Within: The Structure of the Self and the Dynamics of Relationship, 3 tapes
    Healing the Masculine
    Jihad: The Archetype of Spiritual Warfare
    Jungian Psychology and Human Spirituality: Liberation from Tribalism in Religious Life, 5 tapes

The King Within: A Study in Masculine Psychology, 7 tapes

The Liminoid and the Liminal

The Lover Within: A Study in Masculine Psychology, 8 tapes

The Magician Within: A Study in Masculine Psychology, 4 tapes

Masculine Power: Archetypal Potential and Planetary Challenge

The Meaning of Sacred Space in Transformation

Narcissism and Human Evil

The Nature of Sacred Space

Portraits of Crisis: Experience and Theory, 2 tapes

The Psychology of Satan: Encountering the Dark Side of the Self,
    8 tapes

Rediscovering Masculine Potentials, 4 tapes

Rediscovering the Mature Masculine: Resources from Archetypal
    Psychology, 3 tapes

Ritual, Initiation, and Contemporary Religion

The Trickster Archetype: Potential and Pathology, 3 tapes

The Vessel of Analysis

The Warrior Within: A Study in Masculine Psychology, 5 tapes

Robert Moore and Forrest Craver

    Dancing the Four Quarters: Visions of Grassroots Masculine Leader-
        ship in the 1990s

Robert Moore and Douglas Gillette

    King, Warrior, Magician, Lover: Rediscovering the Archetypes of
        the Mature Masculine

Robert Moore and Michael Meade

    The Great Self Within: Men and the Quest for Significance

Robert Moore and Caroline Stevens

    The One and the Two: Gender: Identity and Relationship, 8 tapes

I N D E X

INDEX

integrity, personal, 194–195
intellectual achievement, 204–205, 207–209
American anti-intellectualism vs., 204, 208
study in, 187–188, 208–209, 222, 225
Intensive Journal Workshops, 224
"In the Garden," 107
isolation, self-imposed, 159, 170, 205
Israel, kibbutzim of, 25–26

Jacob, 137
Japan, 252
monkeys of, 81–83
Jaynes, Julian, 77–78
Jerusalem, 136
Jesuits, 66
Jesus Christ, 75, 123, 144, 195
as Christ Pantocrator, 73
early images of, 10
Hebrew name of, 95
as Magician, 11, 87, 192
mythic life stages of, 67–68, 87
power spot located by, 138
sacred kingship of, 72–73
self-sacrifice of, 87, 192
Jews, 207
Holy of Holies of, 136, 139
Kabbalah of, 94–96
John of the Cross, Saint, 125
Johnson, Robert, 223
journals, personal, 224
Jung, Carl Gustav, 31, 79, 89, 101, 120, 145, 153, 185, 200, 207, 248
on centered Self, 211–213
coniunctio oppositorum concept of, 46, 75
contemporary relevance of, 226
Diamond Body in work of, 233–234, 235, 238, 240, 241
on modern technology, 172
on number symbolism, 216
personality typology of, 52, 167, 233, 234, 240, 260
Shadow integration emphasized by, 240, 247
Jungian depth psychology, 31–52, 89, 98, 144, 147–148, 153, 224
current bias against, 225–226

Kabbalah, 94–96
Kauth, Bill, 224
Kazantzakis, Nikos, 138
kibbutzim, Israeli, 25–26
King, 41, 55–56, 65, 71–72, 110, 149, 163, 182, 206, 249, 250
bipolar Shadow of, 43, 48, 156, 254
characteristics of, 56, 73, 171, 196, 238
in Diamond Body, 238, 239
limbic system and, 245, 246
Magician vs., 73
triangular structure of, 43, 45, 47, 48
kings, 56, 58, 72–73, 257, 261
ancient Egyptian, 85–86
King Within, The (Moore and Gillette), 58, 214
knowledge, 83, 103, 183–190, 198, 215
esoteric, 70
misused, 207–208, 227–231
overspecialized, 186, 190
self-understanding in, 206–207, 223
wider perspective gained through, 186, 187, 189–190
see also intellectual achievement; reflection
Kohut, Heinz, 31, 101, 147–148, 207

language, 33
in chimpanzees, 56–57, 83, 262
Lascaux caves, 9–10, 83–84, 96
Mother Goddess figurines in, 84
Last Temptation of Christ, The (Kazantzakis), 138
Layard, John, 234, 236
learning disabilities, 204
legal profession, 65
Trickster in, 165, 230
Libido, 37–38, 39, 108, 260
life crises, 79, 109, 115, 117, 119–122, 129, 213, 219
life-cycle changes, 107, 116, 117–119
limbic system (paleomammalian brain), 54, 55, 242–246
structures in, 242, 244, 245
subsystems of, 243–244, 245, 246
liminality, 108, 111, 125, 127, 133, 139, 173, 208, 216
see also reality, sacred
liminoid reality, 108, 141–144, 173, 208
Lord of the Flies (Golding), 22